HANNAH

781.66 616.9 942

BOTH WAYS

914.5 577.34JOH 781

Hannah Both Ways
Copyright (c) 2015 by Rosie Greenway
All rights reserved.
Published by Rebelight Publishing Inc.

No part of this book may be used or reproduced in any manner whatsoever without the prior written permission of Rebelight Publishing Inc., except in the case of brief quotations embodied in reviews.

Design by Melanie Matheson, Rebelight Publishing Inc., Winnipeg, MB

Rebelight Publishing Inc.
23-845 Dakota St., Suite 314
Winnipeg, Manitoba, Canada R2M 5M3

www.rebelight.com

This book is a work of fiction. Names, characters, places and incidents are products of the author's imagination or are used fictitiously. Any resemblance to actual events or locales or persons, living or dead, is entirely coincidental.

Printed and bound in Canada
10 9 8 7 6 5 4 3 2 1

Library and Archives Canada Cataloguing in Publication

Greenway, Rosie, author
        Hannah both ways / Rosie Greenway.

Issued in print and electronic formats.
ISBN 978-0-9948399-4-7 (paperback).--ISBN 978-0-9948399-5-4 (ebook)

        I. Title.

PS8613.R4435H35 2015   jC813'.6   C2015-906105-9
                                                C2015-906106-7

HANNAH BOTH WAYS

781.66 616.9 942
914.5 577.34JOH 781

ROSIE GREENWAY

2015 rebel!ght PUBLISHING INC.

For C, with love.

Chapter 1

My Corner

I GRAB THE YELLOW Post-it note with the number scribbled across it and stuff it in the front pocket of my jeans. 914.5. That's all it says.

Running late, I gallop down the stairs. "I'm leaving!" I shout to no one in particular.

No one in particular doesn't answer. No one in particular must still be in bed.

And she's not alone.

I realize this fact as I trip over yet another unfamiliar pair of men's shoes in the front hall by the door.

I sit alone on the bus as I've done every day for the last three months. At first, I was the centre of all gossip. Now, I'm invisible. Old news. Nobody cares enough to give me a second glance. This is a relief.

At school, I go straight to my locker to stow my coat and grab my books. I close my eyes for a few seconds and breathe, remembering that 914.5 is safely stashed in the front pocket of my jeans.

After being off for the Easter long weekend, my attention span has dwindled, and I can't get back into the groove. Math isn't my favourite, so I play with words while Mr. Murray discusses our weekend assignment on asymptotes. "Awesome tokes," I scribble. I'm a huge fan of words.

English Lit class perks me up. We're each reading poetry, looking through anthologies for a poem to analyze. I can't write poetry worth a damn, but I love reading it. Within five minutes, I find "You fit into me" by Margaret Atwood. It only has sixteen words, but it's deeply disturbing and considering the poem's length, it's amazingly dense. The idea of a fish hook slipping into a human eye freaks me out. Margaret Atwood does it to me every time.

I take the poem to the front of the room for approval. Mrs. Shore looks at me over her glasses, which sit crookedly on the end of her nose. "It's a little short, Hannah." She sighs.

"I like it."

She seems exasperated, but she's been told to go easy on me. They all have. It's getting a little old, and some of them are probably fed up with me by now, but I smile at her hopefully anyway.

I'm such a phony.

She sighs again, probably not fooled. "Okay, it's your choice. You're the one who has to put together a 250-word analysis."

Oh, ye of little faith. "It has an opening simile, a closing analogy, a paradoxical juxtaposition of images and shock value. No problem," I say.

She rewards my brilliance with a reluctant half-smile.

I drag my butt back to my seat and lose myself in the poem. Writing 250 words will be simple. I could easily churn out four times as much. I'm not saying I'm any good at writing, it's just that it's what I *like* to do. That's why Writer's Craft is my favourite class. It's last period. Something to look forward to during Study Hall after lunch.

I need it to be lunchtime, but the clock moves too slowly. I click the end of my pen in time with the passing seconds. Click . . . click . . . click. The clicking is a nervous habit. Sometimes I don't even realize I'm doing it. A few people sitting near me glare, so I stop clicking and glare right back.

I have awesome eyebrows for glaring. They furrow so beautifully. Not that I've ever been what you'd call smiley, but a few months of glaring and frowning has etched a permanent ridge between my eyebrows. To hell with Botox. Why would anyone sabotage their ability to frown like that?

Two minutes pass while I contemplate the beauty of my furrowed brow. The bell will ring in mere seconds. I slide the Post-it note out of my pocket and curl my fingers around it.

914.5.

The bell rings. I jump up and vault for the door before the echo of the bell has died away. At my locker, I swap morning books for afternoon ones, squash what passes for lunch into my knapsack and slam the metal door shut. With a cursory look around to make sure the coast is clear, I hurry down the hall with my head lowered, eyes on the floor ahead of me. The crowds open and close around me.

Girl on a mission, coming through! Nothing to see here. Move aside.

I trust my feet to take me where I need to go. If my feet forget, the Post-it note stuck to my palm will remind me.

914.5 . . . 914.5 . . . 914.5 . . . .

All that matters right now is 914.5 and getting out of the damn hall.

The moment when I heft open the library door is always one of the best parts of my day. Sweet relief. I'm always among the first to arrive at lunch time, so for now, the library is quiet. Soon the panicky study groups and chronic procrastinators will arrive to descend on the computers and fill the table area. Those people are not my concern.

I head straight for the last set of stacks, silently chanting *please, please, please* as I make my way down the shelves, trailing my finger across the spines of the books, row upon row of books. Some are old and decaying, some are brand new, but each one is ripe for the picking—assuming the numbers are right, of course. I keep walking, past the 800s into the 900s . . . *please let there be something . . . .*

And there is. Or should I say, there are. On the middle shelf, eight books have the 914.5 call number. Victory. Abundant victory. What will I choose? It's the first day back to school after Easter Monday, so I decide on the first of the eight books. Excellent logic on my part.

914.5 ADA. *Rome.* Succinct title, just like the poem I picked in English class. I'm having a succinct day. Maybe "succinct" is the word of the day. In Writer's Craft, I'll try to incorporate the word into my writing without sounding contrived. This will be challenging, but I think it's important to set myself a challenge every day.

I take the book and head to the corner of the library.

My corner.

Everyone knows this is where I sit. Since no one wants to be anywhere near me, it's an oasis. There's not much to it, just three decrepit chairs, the springs long gone, clustered around a small end table. But this is my haven—a quiet nook near a shelf of dusty teacher resources in a forgotten corner of the library. I face the wall and sneak celery dipped in peanut butter into my mouth.

I'm sneaking for two reasons. First, I'm not supposed to eat in the library. Second, no one is supposed to eat any peanut products outside the cafeteria. Some unsuspecting soul could have a severe allergic reaction and go into anaphylactic shock. Not that anyone would willingly get close enough to me to even get a whiff of the peanut butter, but if they did, I'd have a field day with an EpiPen. I'd take great enjoyment in ramming that sucker into someone's leg. I'd save the ever-loving hell out of their life, and I'd be a hero.

Except not.

How can I be a hero when I shouldn't be eating peanut butter in the first place? Still, I've been carrying a tub of it around the school for months, eating some in the library almost every day, and no one has died yet, despite my efforts.

I turn my attention to the book on my lap. Instead of reading from the beginning, I always flip through to see what grabs me. Sometimes the book decides for me, and that's what happens this time. The spine is well broken-in, and the book falls open in the middle. On one side, there's a picture of some street in Rome with a canal running along the side. I read the opposite page, licking the peanut butter off the celery and then methodically crunching the stalks.

"We've all heard that old cliché, 'Rome wasn't built in a day,'" page 138 says. "In fact, Rome has been evolving since the eighth century BC."

Huh. That's a damned old city. I scan the page for new and interesting words, listening to the crunching sound in my ears and tuning out the rest of the world. Tuning out the rest of the world is what I do best now. If I don't look at people—if I stay hidden behind the brown curtain of my hair—they can't see me either. This infantile way of viewing my existence pleases me.

Of course, it's worth mentioning that the world is tuning me out too. I'm not worried. It's a win–win situation. This is called "symbiosis." Great word. Snagged that one in Grade Ten biology.

"Succinct" and "symbiosis." Two kick-ass words in a day. I'm on a roll.

My life is predictable. I'm okay with that. Unpredictability is scary. Knowing every day will be the same isn't as bad as it sounds. I've done it for ages.

For example, the next morning, I wake up knowing that my mother probably won't be waiting to see me off at the door. But I'm almost guaranteed to trip over a pair of unfamiliar men's shoes. Sure enough, there they are. Brown loafers. Bending to pull on my own shoes, I get a noseful of loafer stench. Yuck. Granted, they're not as bad as the shoes I found in the hall a few times in the weeks before Christmas. *They* were revolting. I named that guy Mr. Funky Feet. You'd think someone who wears black Italian leather shoes with a shiny gold buckle would have better foot hygiene. Sadly, this is not true.

I rush out the door, pulling a swath of hair across my face. The scent of mango-citrus shampoo wipes out the reek of man-foot fungus. I sit alone on the bus, alternately staring out the window and glancing at today's Post-it note in my hand.

577.34

The bus is loud. Now that Easter has come and gone, everyone is talking prom.

"Let's get our hair and nails done together."

"I'm telling you man, limo sex."

"I've already got a forty of vodka."

"Hey, Brett booked the campsite for the after party, right?"

"Did you see Sarah's promposal on Instagram? So cute!"

The thought of the promposal I won't receive makes my stomach lurch. I return to that safe place in my head.

577.34 . . . 577.34 . . . .

At school, the Post-it note goes safely into my pocket. I follow my usual route to my locker and then take the remaining 240 or so footsteps to math class. Mr. Murray is always available for extra help first thing in the morning. Sometimes I have to wait outside the door for him to arrive, but usually he's at his desk, the door wide open, inviting me in.

Most people don't find math classrooms inviting. I do. I don't ask for help. I don't ask for anything, except a quiet place to park my butt until class starts. Sometimes, Mr. Murray dashes off for a few minutes to do whatever teachers do before class. This thing he does probably involves a boatload of coffee. Teachers always have the worst coffee breath.

Not that I blame them. Faced with the mind-numbing task of trying to educate a bunch of pinheads, I'd need a massive caffeine buzz to make it through the day too. I'd probably slip something stronger into my coffee, just to take the edge off.

Math class is boring. English is worse. We have a substitute teacher with large dark eyes and a wild mass of curly black hair. She wears a chunky silver ring on every finger. Too bad we're not studying *Macbeth*. She'd be a shoo-in for Lady Macbeth.

After listening to her drone on about poetic devices, we fill in a worksheet. It's easy and should probably only take about twelve minutes to complete, but there's an unwritten rule among students about substitute teachers. Everyone has to take as long as possible to fill out a worksheet because if even one person hands it in, another boring handout will appear, and everyone will be forced to do that one, too. No one wants that. Not even me. This is one of the few times I'm on the same page as everyone else in the class.

Lady Macbeth thumbs through a magazine while the class pretends to be hard at work. In reality, people pass notes or text each other on phones hidden under desks or behind the backs of the people in front of them. In the row beside mine, a couple of boys are even playing games on their handheld devices. It's pathetic, really.

Like I said. Pinheads.

As the class nears its end, I slip my Post-it note into my palm and watch the clock. I'm out the door with the bell, the substitute teacher's voice ringing out behind me—something about a poetry quiz on Friday. The quiz goes on the to-do list for later. Right now, there's somewhere else I need to be.

Locker, library, 577.34. In that order.

Usually, my feet are programmed to follow the route from my locker to the library without incident. Today, I'm not so lucky. Just around the corner, mere metres away from my final destination, a sharp object jabs my right boob.

"Ouch, you moron, what the hell are you doing?" I back up, rubbing my chest and glaring at this guy standing stupidly in the middle of the hall with a pencil—a very sharp pencil—jutting from his left hand.

"Oh, sorry. I'm sorry. I'm, ah, I'm lost. I was just trying to figure out . . . ." He brushes hair out of his eyes, frowning and scanning a sheet of paper. He spins the page around in circles and looks up and down the hall.

"Yeah, that was a rhetorical question." I push past him, which doesn't go as well as I'd hoped because he's tall, and I'm not strong enough to shove him out of my way.

Oh well. It's the effort that counts.

The fact is, people who are sorry or lost slow me down. The longer it takes to get to the library, the greater the chance of crossing paths with someone I'd rather not see. The only thing I have time for right now is 577.34.

As usual, before venturing into the stacks in search of my book, I send up a quiet prayer to the Dewey Decimal deity—kick-ass alliteration, right?—and my prayers are answered. Today, there's only one matching book. 577.34 JOH. It's thin and hard-covered. I pull it from the shelf and look at the title. *The Amazon Rainforest.* Hmmm. I've never read about rainforests before.

In my corner, I haul the contraband out of my backpack and start to eat, spooning peanut butter into my mouth with celery sticks.

Dip, bite and chew. Dip, bite and chew.

I repeat the motion over and over again and flip through the book. I'm disappointed with my pick until I spot an unfamiliar word in a subheading: "Agroforestry." A new word—and one with five syllables!

A thud directly behind me interrupts this moment of bliss. I cringe and turn my head ever so slightly to look at the floor. It's a backpack. The chair beside mine slides closer, scraping noisily over the floor, and then two long legs stretch out in front of it. Someone is sitting in my personal oasis.

My corner.

I glare over my shoulder. It's him. It's sorry-lost-boy. He tosses a wayward lock of sandy-brown hair out of his eyes. Brown eyes. Or are they hazel? They don't seem dark enough to be brown. I remind myself not to care what colour they are and focus on my scowl, because sorry-lost-boy is trespassing. "Hey, sorry-lost-boy," I snap. "You're in my corner."

"I'm sorry?" he says.

"Stop saying you're sorry. While you're at it, stop doing crap that'll make you have to say you're sorry."

I try to stare him down.

He doesn't move. He doesn't even blink. "I wasn't apologizing," he says. "When someone says 'I'm sorry' in an interrogative tone like I just did, it means 'Pardon me.'"

"What the fuck did you say?" I try not to raise my voice. It's not easy. He's too calm. Too pleasant. He's rattling me.

"That works too. You could say 'Pardon me,' or 'What the fuck did you say?'" He looks at me blandly. "If that's what you prefer."

Ha. That's clever. It's bordering on funny—but I don't want to find him funny.

"What I'd prefer is not talking to you right now." I retreat behind my hair and return to my book, discovering, much to my amazement, that rubber trees used to flourish in the Amazon rainforests. Who knew?

"Look, you dropped this in the hall. Don't you need it to find a book?"

He stretches his hand out, invading my space. He's holding my Post-it note—the one with "577.34" written on it. I must have dropped it when we crashed into each other.

I don't make a move to retrieve the slip of paper. "Nope. Don't need it." Truth be told, I haven't needed it since writing the numbers down last night. As always, repeating the numbers like a mantra has made the Post-it redundant.

"Come on. Cut the new kid a break, would ya? Maybe we could chill for a few minutes, and you could help me get the lay of the land?"

New kid? He's new? Who switches schools in April? Every time I've transferred, it's been in September, or at least at the start of a term. Anyway, he's a newbie, which explains why he's not running screaming in the opposite direction. No one has gotten to him yet. He doesn't know that Hannah Forde is radioactive.

"Listen, new kid," I snap. "I don't do 'chill.' I definitely don't do 'help.'"

Apparently I do "lay," but you'll find that out soon enough on your own.

I turn my chair, square my shoulders and present him with my back. I smile when I'm rewarded with the sound of a scraping chair and receding footsteps.

Sit in my corner? I don't think so.

It's one o'clock. Twenty-five minutes left to kill in Study Hall period. Writer's Craft is next, and then I can go home. The rainforests book is closed on the small table beside my chair. I've given up on it. Sometimes the random page I pick sparks a sudden interest in the topic, and I keep reading. But not today. Today I feel like writing. I'm in the mood to vent. To rant. Writer's Craft is going to be good.

Sneakers squeak on the tile floor. Then there's a tap on my shoulder. Jesus. It's him—not Jesus—but sorry-lost-boy. The new kid.

I turn and give him the full effect of my eyebrows.

"So what's your problem, anyway?" he asks.

"Right now? You are. Didn't they teach you anything about taking hints where you came from? 'Cause around here, when someone says they don't want to talk to you, it usually means go away. And not just for an hour."

"'Usually' doesn't mean 'always.'" He blinks at me. His brownish-hazelish-whatever-the-hell-colour-you'd-call-it eyes are unreadable.

"Well, let me clarify. In this case, it definitely means 'go away.'"

"I don't think it does," he insists.

I'm amazed at his persistence. No. "Amazed" is not a strong enough word. I need others. I am nonplussed. I'm agog. Flummoxed. Gobsmacked. Yes, I am absolutely gobsmacked. "Okay, you said you want to know the lay of the land, newbie? Fine. Stay away from me if you know what's good for you. You're bugging the hell out of me, but you seem like a decent enough guy. Trust me. Just. Go. Away." I turn around and pick up my abandoned book, hoping for a better pick tomorrow. I'd much rather be reading about coral reefs or foolproof ways to repel sorry-lost-boys.

The rustle of his bag behind me interrupts my thoughts. Then, he leans over and slowly slides my Post-it note into my hand.

"You don't fool me. I know you," he says.

What the—?

I turn to watch him lope out of the library. He knows me? How does he know me? I've never met him before. I would remember him. Or maybe he *has* already heard about me, and that's what he means. I'm dying to know what he's talking about.

But now he's gone, and I can't ask him.

In Writer's Craft, I close my eyes and listen to the hiss of the heating vent, the hum of computers and the tapping of keyboards around the room. Someone should make a relaxation CD capturing this chorus of sounds. I'd snap up every copy. Mr. Vesters makes the rounds, his voice a soft murmur as he checks in with students. When he reaches my station, he pulls up one of the chairs beside mine and sits. Mr. Vesters always sits down when he chats with me, perhaps because there's always an available seat. I have one of the best seats in the class, right in the middle of a row of computer tables that runs the length of the room facing the windows. Even so, the computers on either side of me have been vacant since the first day of the term. It's as if no one wants to inhale the air I exhale.

Fine with me.

"Sorry to interrupt," Mr. Vesters whispers. "You look like you're in the zone. Everything going okay?"

He leans forward, his elbows on his knees and his hands clasped. His eyes search mine. This is not an idle question, and it might not even be entirely about my writing. Mr. Vesters is one of those teachers who cares about what's happening with kids—and not just in his classroom. He could be ridiculed mercilessly for his seemingly never-ending supply of argyle sweater vests or the saucer-sized raspberry coloured birthmark that stains his right cheek, but most kids would defend him before mocking him.

"I'm just warming up," I say, cracking a few knuckles for effect.

"And your portfolio is coming along?"

"Getting there." This is a lie. I've been struggling with my monthly portfolio, but panic hasn't set in yet. There are still a few days to pull things together.

"Well, you know where I am if you need help."

After my nod of confirmation, he moves on to another student. I close my eyes again, waiting for inspiration to strike, but I can't seem to focus.

Excited shrieking erupts outside. I crane my neck to look out the window. A bunch of kids from the elementary school next door are rolling down the hill that descends to our track. It must be recess. I miss recess. No—scratch that, I don't miss recess—I miss snack time.

What I don't miss is being the serial new kid, the burning desire to be accepted into the other kids' games. Wandering around alone for fifteen minutes, trying to break into the long-established cliques.

No one would miss that.

A vague lingering feeling scratches at the back of my mind. I recognize the feeling. It's guilt.

Come on. Cut the new kid a break, would ya?

I didn't cut the new kid a break, but surely he's persistent enough to manage just fine without any assistance from me. Besides, guys blend in better than girls do. He'll be high-fiving and fist-bumping new buddies in the hall before the ink is dry on his timetable.

Comforted by this convenient line of reasoning, I turn my attention to my computer screen and finally settle in. I forget everything when I'm writing. It's the best place to be—lost in a twisted maze of ideas. Words chasing thoughts until they catch them, overtake them and mercifully erase them.

I don't watch the clock in Writer's Craft. More often than not, the bell startles me, rousing me from the deep tangle of my words. Because I'm not sitting close enough to the door to bolt out at the first hint of the bell, I wait for everyone else to leave to avoid the potential fallout of getting whisked up by the crowd.

I don't actually need to worry anymore—because people pretend I don't exist—but waiting for the room to empty is an ingrained habit now. After long weeks of being tripped, or "accidentally" jabbed with a compass, or hearing hissed whispers about how I'm so dead after school, I'm afraid my luck will run out. Bottom line: invisibility is a good thing. Invisible people don't get threatened.

Clearly, they were empty threats because I'm still very much alive.

On the outside.

Chapter 2

Going Through the Motions

DESPITE WHAT PEOPLE might say, I'm not a bad person. I'm a victim of circumstances that are beyond my control. You can't control what other people say and do. You definitely can't control your parents. My mother's actions, in particular, are completely out of my control.

Allow me to clarify: my mother is out of control. Period.

I'm not trying to be dramatic. I'm simply stating the facts.

My mother doesn't hurt me. She's not physically abusive, and she's not a druggie or an alcoholic. She keeps a roof over our heads and buys groceries, makes dinner and pays bills, like most mothers do. But unlike most mothers, my mom is a cocktail waitress in a club. A nightclub. The kind of place where waitresses wear plunging necklines and short skirts and get huge tips.

Most of the time, Mom leaves for work before I get home from school, and she doesn't roll in until midnight. Sometimes even later.

I don't wait up.

We don't see each other much, except on weekends and her occasional night off. Once in a while, I see her in the morning, but mostly, I see the shoes. Then I know she's otherwise occupied. Emerging from her room to pat me on the head and say, "Have a good day, dear," isn't a top priority.

When I get home from school on Wednesday, Mom doesn't hear me come in. Music blasts in the kitchen, and she's dancing between the sink, the fridge and the stove. I lean against the kitchen doorway, watching. One thing about my mom, she's got moves. Even when she's not dancing, there's something fascinating about the way she carries herself. It's no wonder the guys who frequent the club are drawn to her. There's nothing motherly about her appearance, nothing about her that says, "I have a seventeen-year-old daughter." The fact that she had me when she was seventeen might have something to do with that. The plunging necklines and short skirts help.

I make my way across the kitchen to turn the music down, and she jumps, clutching her hand to her heart.

"Jeez, Hannah, I didn't hear you."

"No wonder. It's party central in here." I scan the collection of bowls lined up on the counter. "Are you making lasagne?"

"Yep. Completely from scratch."

"Huh. Didn't someone stay over last night? I wouldn't think you'd have the energy for this."

"Don't be sassy."

Don't be sassy. That's what she always says. Or *don't be cynical.* That's a favourite too. I can't help being cynical. After years of rising hopes and subsequent disappointment, cynicism comes naturally. Sadly, it's usually Mom's fault when my hopes get squashed.

I know it's not easy being a single-mom. My dad bailed when I was five, so she's been alone for a long time. That's why I try to go easy on her. She's lonely. It's how she deals with the loneliness that gets us into hot water—like accidentally hooking up with a married man at the club, or having simultaneous flings with several of the regulars and causing fistfights among these guys who all think they have exclusive booty call rights. This is what I dread—things getting dicey and my mom being forced to quit her job, or worse still, being fired. That's when she hauls out the boxes, and I know another new school is on the horizon. This has happened more times than I care to count.

I need a fresh start. She says that line a lot.

The last time she said that, I told her she really needed fresh meat. She told me not to be cynical. I thought I was being honest. Since when did telling someone the truth mean you're cynical?

She interrupts my thoughts with a jab of a wooden spoon.

"Was your day okay?"

"It was a day."

I open the fridge and scan the shelves, and then close it without taking anything out. I open a cupboard and close it. I want something, but

I don't know what. This pointless opening and closing is enjoyable. It's a daily routine. Routine is my saviour.

"You keeping your marks up?"

"Yep. It's all good."

As usual, I'm suitably vague so Mom won't worry. There are probably case studies about kids like me—typical children of divorced parents who don't want to rock the boat more than necessary. Some kids blame themselves for their parents' divorce, but I was five, how could it have been my fault? Still, that doesn't mean I want to be a source of misery for my mother.

"Can you get the mozzarella out of the fridge?" Mom hands me the cheese grater, and I become her sous chef.

"Grate the cheese."

"Stir the sauce."

"Layer those noodles."

"Measure some parmesan."

We work together without talking, the music filling the spaces between her instructions. I wonder sometimes if she has a million questions she wants to ask but is afraid to go there because she doesn't want to know the answers. She can't ask me about friends—I don't have any. Which means questions about parties, dances or other afterschool activities are irrelevant.

I sound like a total loser. I'm really not. I know what it's like to have friends, but I also know what it's like to leave friends behind. Over and over again. There's nothing worse than having to start over every year or two, trying to meet new people all the time. It got harder the older I got. With each move, Mom promised that this time, things would be different. This time, we'd put down roots. She'd find a great guy to settle down with.

How many times have I heard those words? Eventually, I had to stop believing them. It was a waste of time. Instead of trying to find a place in the social fabric of the school, I went about my business, going to class, studying and focusing inward instead of worrying about what was going on around me.

I probably would have carried on doing that and had a completely uneventful twelfth grade year at yet another new school if not for my Sociology teacher. She picked groups for an assignment in the middle of October and forced an unfortunate alliance between me and the

Dipsy Duo—Allison Dawson and Marla Stevens. They were both total dingbats, but I was stuck with them for two weeks in class, trying to scrape together an assignment worth ten percent of my sociology grade. There was nothing I could do but try to get along with them.

Co-operating with airheads has never been my strong point, but I made an effort to smile and be friendly, which isn't easy when you're out of practice and, frankly, socially lazy.

What I'm *not* is academically lazy. It didn't take me long to figure out that Allison and Marla were bottom feeders. Not wanting my mark to suffer because of their idiocy, I ended up doing more than my fair share of the work. Ironically, it was my academic prowess rather than my social graces which opened the doors to social acceptance and made me an asset to Allison Dawson.

She started messaging me. We became Facebook friends. We connected on Twitter. Marla followed suit. I tried not to notice most of their messages to me involved questions about schoolwork, but let's face it, my mother is right. I am cynical. I was sure they were using me, so I took their attention with a grain of salt. Okay, maybe it was more than a grain. Maybe it was enough salt to do serious damage to my blood pressure.

The social fringe benefits made the salt go down a little easier.

Mom and I eat dinner in front of the TV. That's another classic avoidance technique. If we're engrossed in whatever show is on the idiot box, we can't talk to each other. I'm actually not that interested in the shows my mom likes to watch. She's addicted to reality TV. I'd much rather watch *Jeopardy!*

Her phone chimes. She sits up and scans the room. "Is that your phone or mine?" she says.

I want to laugh. There isn't a single person who'd be contacting me. I pretend to think. "Um, no, I'm pretty sure that was your text alert. Your phone's on the kitchen table."

Mom breezes off to the kitchen, plate in hand. She lets out a sharp, high-pitched laugh. Probably one of her "gentleman friends." He must be a real joker. If the guy were here, she'd drape herself all over him while she laughed, making him feel like the king of the world.

I can't help envying how easily she interacts with guys. I've always bumbled my way through social situations. I've never been much of a laugher—never the type to bat my eyelashes at boys and giggle at their dumbass antics. I pretended to be that girl for a while. It didn't go so well.

I guess it was October when that fateful announcement blared across the school PA system.

"Tryouts for the cheerleading team this Friday! Five girls needed! All new members welcome!"

Allison and Marla, not surprisingly, were cheer squad veterans. They joined in ninth grade. I've always watched cheerleaders from afar. They're like a different species, the way they behave when they're together, flipping their hair and rolling their eyes, hanging off the arms of the cute boys, flirting and giggling.

Someone like me could never win the attention of those kinds of boys. I would never be flirtatious and extroverted enough to fit in entirely, but I allowed Allison to convince me to try out for squad. How hard could it be? I took dance classes for years as a kid and have rhythm, just like Mom. Before writing, venting my frustrations through dancing kept me sane. Sadly, dancing didn't work out for me. For one thing, my inability to smile drove my dance instructors crazy. Surly ballerinas tend to have short careers. Then there's the money factor. Mom simply couldn't afford it.

Anyway, somewhere in one of the dark recesses of my brain, I decided I might actually be a pretty good cheerleader because of the dancing, and at the very least, joining the squad would help me fit in. I'd finally found a way to break in to that impenetrable group: the cool kids. Maybe I would never be naturally playful and outgoing like Allison and Marla, but I could certainly go through the motions, at least the physical ones requiring co-ordination and agility.

Allison coached me. She taught me an audition routine. I tried in vain to figure out her motivation. In retrospect, I'm convinced it had to do with the very fact that I didn't flirt with other girls' boyfriends or giggle whenever a hot guy walked by.

"It's so great that you're not an attention whore, Hannah." That's what Allison used to say. I wasn't a threat. If you want to stand out in a crowd, it's best to surround yourself with mediocrity.

I earned one of the five coveted spots on the cheerleading squad. Turns out, I was pretty good. I underestimated myself.

So did Allison.

Chapter 3

Invasions

MY SCHOOL DAYS are planned precisely. Mrs. Palmer, a guidance counsellor, helped me work out a manageable schedule. It's all part of the conflict mediation plan that's been in place since January, so I don't get hassled after all the crap that went down. My timetable changed too, so I wouldn't have to worry about being harassed during class.

As for non-class time, I go straight to the math room in the morning. I spend lunch hour in the library to avoid the washroom and cafeteria, because that's where *they* will be. I stay in the library for Study Hall and then go to Writer's Craft. At the end of the day, I get on the bus and go home.

It's all very straightforward and usually goes according to plan. But sometimes, shit happens. Anyone doubting this should check out the T-shirt vendors in the mall. They'll find many shirts exposing this truth in bold, white letters across a black cotton background.

Shit happens.

Does it ever.

It's Friday and I'm in the library during Study Hall reading *Fast Food Nation*. At first, I catch myself peering over my shoulder from time to time, wondering if the new kid is watching from somewhere in the stacks. Knowing he could be lurking around and invading the sanctity of my quiet corner aggravates me. Acknowledging that he's invading the sanctity of my mind more than aggravates me.

It horrifies me.

How dare he?

Every time someone pulls a book from a shelf or shuffles through the stacks behind me, I spin around, certain I'll see him, but no. He's not here. Paranoia, that's all it is. I eventually relax and become engrossed in today's book. *Food Nation* was a great pick. There's a chapter all about why fries taste so freaking awesome. It's kind of fascinating. When I finally glance at the clock, there's only a little over ten minutes until last period.

I reluctantly abandon the book early and leave for the washroom before classes change to avoid running into any unsavoury characters. At lunch hour and during class changes, the girls' washroom is a minefield of catty bitches—human landmines. You can't escape without detonating one of them. I know this because I've had a limb or two blown off in the main floor girls' washroom.

Figuratively, of course.

With everyone still in class, I can safely pee without fear of flying shrapnel.

At first, I'm alone, as I anticipated. I'm going about my business in the stall, about to flush, when the outer door crashes open, and two girls' voices invade the quiet of the washroom.

"Substitute teachers are so clueless," says one of the voices. "She didn't even notice us sneak out."

"I know. They're the best," the other replies.

I know both voices. Marla and Allison. Marla is relatively harmless—although "relatively" is a relative term. She's basically a sheep. Allison is the real problem. She single-handedly ruined any chance I had of enjoying my last semester of high school. Well, not single-handedly. Her boyfriend, Dallyn, was essential to my ruination. But she was the mastermind.

I don't know a lot about landmines, but I figure when one goes off, it will detonate others. That's what it's like with Allison. She goes off and triggers everyone else. Like domino land mines.

If either of them happens to look down the long row of stalls and sees my feet, my shoes might give me away. It would be just like Allison to wait for me to emerge and then ambush me, stealing my shoes and flushing them down the toilet or something. Worse still, they could wrestle my shirt off and push me into the hall in my bra. I may be overreacting a smidge, but I've learned the hard way that where Allison Dawson is concerned, I should listen to my gut.

Survival instinct kicks in. I carefully step onto the toilet seat and crouch down, hovering with my feet planted on either side of the toilet seat, waiting for them to get out.

"I heard Brett's going to prom with Kelly. That sucks," Allison says to Marla.

"Yeah. I knew he'd never ask me. I'm gonna end up going with a total loser."

"We'll get you a date," Allison says. "Dallyn . . . is . . . working . . . on . . . it."

From the way she smacks her lips together between words, she's obviously putting on lip-gloss. She's always reapplying lip-gloss. The perils of sucking face with your boyfriend non-stop until he's wearing most of it.

"Those jeans are great by the way," she adds.

"Hey, thanks." The pride in Marla's voice is unmistakeable. You don't take a compliment like this from the high priestess of fashion lightly.

"So we're still meeting at the spray tanning place at noon tomorrow, right?" Allison says. "Then we can hit the mall. I'm totally thinking of getting that strapless dress for prom. You know, the hot pink one?"

"Oh, you have to. It looks so awesome on you."

"I know. It was practically made for me."

On and on it goes.

Like I was saying, these two are the pinhead poster girls. How I hung out with them for three months without suffering brain damage is a mystery. I tune them out, trying not to focus on how uncomfortable I am, but then Allison says, "Hey, I forgot. I have an awesome Hannah story to tell you!"

Good old Allison. She's full of awesome stories. Her stories about me lean toward fiction for the most part. I shift my weight from side to side, trying to relieve the pressure on my knees.

"You know how her mom works at that club, right?" she says.

"Yeah."

"Well, Dallyn's brother, Dean, is home from college and he took Dall to the club last night—he had a fake ID and stuff—and Hannah's mom totally hit on Dean."

I close my eyes and hold my breath. I can almost hear the grenade rolling across the bathroom floor.

"Get out," Marla says, her voice a shocked whisper.

"I'm serious. Dean said she told him to wait till the end of her shift—"

"No!"

"Totally."

"Oh my God!"

Oh my God is right. The grenade rolls closer. I cringe, my face burning with shame for my mother, dreading the rest of the story, but desperate to know what happened.

Did I see shoes in the front hall this morning?

"What did he do?" Marla asks.

No doubt she's bouncing with excitement. Marla always bounces when she's excited, her boobs jumping grotesquely in their less than supportive bra.

I clench my jaw, waiting for Allison's answer.

"Nothing. Dall had to be home by eleven. But Dean said she practically stuck her tongue in his ear. He said he'd totally tap that if he had a chance."

"That's insane!" Marla gasps.

It's not all insane. I'm taken aback by this news, but not exactly bowled over in shock. Just mortified.

"I know!" Allison squeals.

From the sound of her voice, she's enjoying herself. At this point, she might be bouncing right along with Marla.

"Did Dallyn tell his brother who she was?"

"No. He said it was too much fun watching Dean flirt with her."

Far be it for Dallyn to ruin his own fun. Jackass.

"The whole thing is gross," Allison says. I can hear the sneer in her voice. "It's bad enough that she's got a kid, but Hannah's her kid, which makes it super-disgusting. What a skank."

I can't stand that word. Allison loves it. I'm sure there's a correlation between those two facts.

Get the fuck out of here . . . get the fuck out of here . . . get the fuck out of here.

"Although . . . ," Marla says. "Mrs. Forde is kinda hot, I guess. She's only, like, thirty-four or something. How old is Dean?"

"Twenty-three. I'm sorry, but that's freaking rude." The water runs and then Allison spits out one more word. "Pedophile."

She laughs, the sound echoing around the bathroom. Awesome acoustics. Marla joins in, but hers is an uncomfortable laugh. I can imagine her face, her awkward expression. She's not cut out for hard-core bitchery. She's still learning the ropes.

"Don't tell anyone I told you," Allison warns Marla. Her tone is ominous. "I'd get in so much crap if I was caught spreading rumours about Hannah. I can't lose my prom privileges."

"Oh, I won't tell anyone. Don't worry."

Allison's suggestion that they go shopping for prom shoes once she's secured her dress is the last thing I hear as the door swings shut behind them.

I unfold myself, make my way out of the stall and stare at my reflection in the mirror. There's a red spot in the middle of each cheek. Lunch gurgles unpleasantly in my stomach. Can I waltz into Writer's Craft and carry on as if I didn't hear anything? I'm not up for it. I can't stay in the bathroom, though.

I emerge into an empty hallway, look left and right and then bolt toward the guidance office. Mrs. Croft, the secretary, looks surprised to see me. I haven't visited in a while.

"Hey, Hannah, what's up?" she says, sunny disposition in full force.

"I'm not sure." I hesitate. "I think I need to sit for a sec."

I perch on the nasty vinyl couch in front of the windows.

"Do you want me to see if Mrs. Palmer is available for a chat?" She picks up the phone to call the head counsellor before I've even had a chance to answer her.

"No." I shake my head. "I'm okay. A little lightheaded. That's all. Maybe I didn't eat enough lunch." I already regret coming in and sitting down. I have no intention of telling anyone what happened in the bathroom. "You know what? I think I'm fine."

As I retrace my steps toward the door, I half expect Mrs. Croft to leap out of her seat and throw her arms around me. Mrs. Croft is the most sympathetic person I know. I could clock her in the nose, and she'd probably look concerned, wondering if I hurt my hand.

All weekend, I debate talking to my mother about what I heard in the bathroom. I'm so angry at her for making a fool of herself and dragging me down with her. Not that it's possible to be dragged much lower, but she's given Allison extra ammunition. What's worse, I'm sure Allison's not making any of this up. The more I think about it, the more convinced I am that there weren't any guy's shoes in the front hall Friday morning. And there definitely wasn't a mysterious car in front of the house when I ran for the bus. All of which lines up with Allison's story.

Mom struck out on Thursday night, plain and simple. She unsuccessfully hit on a twenty-three-year-old, who just happened to be Dallyn's big brother. And since my universe is one notch below zombie apocalypse on the screwed up scale, Dallyn also happens to be Allison's hunky boyfriend, the one who, along with his grenade-throwing girlfriend, made the last three months of my life so miserable.

Excellent pick, Mom.

I'm leery of telling her what she's done, though. After all, I survived Friday afternoon. Nothing out of the ordinary happened in Writer's Craft. There was no renewed interest in my existence. No whispers of "I hear your mom's a pedo" following me around the room. Maybe Allison really *is* worried about getting caught spreading rumours. She did tell Marla not to blab.

Besides, if I tell Mom, she'll feel awful. She'll order me to start packing my bags. I can't face another move. The townhouse is starting to feel like home, and breaking the lease would cost money we can't afford. Graduation is a mere two months away.

I can do this.

And so I don't breathe a word of Allison's story to my mother. She remains blissfully ignorant, while I, unfortunately, don't.

Mom leaves for work at four on Sunday afternoon. With the house to myself at last, I lose myself in ritual. I eat dinner. I shower. I make lunch for the next day. All this requires is to wash, slice and wrap several celery sticks and to make sure there's plenty of peanut butter left for dipping. Not much to it, but it's comforting because I can see myself the next day, sitting with a book in my corner, safely dipping and crunching.

The next part of my ritual is the best part—discovering a new library call number. It's what allows me to fall asleep at night. It keeps me safe in the knowledge that I'll have a goal the next day at school—a book to find in the library, one that will allow me to escape from this world and enter a new one or, at the very least, teach me a new word.

In my room, I turn on some music and grab the dice shaker—the one that used to belong with the ancient backgammon set which now sits abandoned on the top of my bookshelf. Dice in hand, pen and a Post-it note ready, I begin.

On Friday, I took a book from the first row of stacks. I want a higher number this time, so I'll roll two dice the first time. I shake and roll. A seven. I write the number down and use two dice for the second roll. Two fours. Using a single die for the third roll, I wind up with a one.

781.

That's in the arts area. There are tons of books there. I can safely extend the call number by two more digits. Both times I roll a six.

781.66

I feel a familiar flutter of excitement for the thrill of the chase, which isn't a chase at all, I guess. The books just sit there waiting to be found. Even so, it's exciting. But fear settles in when I wonder what'll happen if there aren't any books matching that call number. The odds of that happening are slim to none, though. Our library is huge. There's always a corresponding book for my call number, even if the book is sometimes covered in dust with a faint musty basement smell. I squash the fear and stare at that Post-it note like it's my salvation.

I imagine sitting there alone, reading, munching celery and minding my own business. It's comforting. Then the new kid intrudes. He shows up and ruins everything with his mysterious one-liners, not to mention his long legs and hazelish eyes.

I know you.

What did he mean? And how did he weasel his way into my daydream?

No. The chances of him showing up again are minimal. We didn't cross paths on Thursday or Friday. Maybe he went back to where he came from.

This is probably for the best.

For both of us.

Chapter 4

Troubled

IT'S MONDAY. I'VE eaten my lunch and I'm enjoying 781.66. It's about the evolution of punk music. Interesting stuff. No, really. Sid Vicious might have been a maniac, but he was fascinating. I'm staring at this crazy picture of Sid with razor cuts all over his chest when the new kid emerges from the stacks and saunters over, leaning against the wall across from my chair.

In my corner.

My stomach does a weird flip-flop. So he hasn't gone back to wherever he came from. Exactly how long has he been creeping around behind the bookshelves watching me? Maybe he was back there spying on me last week after all.

I stand and toss the book on the table, pulling my backpack over my shoulder to let him know I'm leaving. I have no destination in mind, but staying here is not an option. I'm not interested in any more of his weird, cryptic comments.

"You read a lot," he says, pointing at the book. "And you read about different stuff every day. You're eclectic, eh?"

"Yep, you know me," I say, crossing my arms and tapping my foot. I regret my words instantly. Why didn't I tell him to get lost instead of so specifically referencing the last thing he said to me? What if he jumps to the conclusion that I've been thinking about him—pondering our conversation from the week before?

"Hey, I'm sorry about last week. I didn't mean to offend you."

I narrow my eyes. "You apologize a lot, you know that?"

"Actually, I don't. Only to you, I guess. I don't know what else to say to you. You seem annoyed by pretty much everything."

I give him my shock and awe face. "Wow, you really do know me."

"Look, about that," he says, holding his hands out, palms up, "I obviously don't know you, but I do think I know where you're coming from. That's all I meant."

"So that's what the creepy 'I know you' bit was all about?"

He frowns, drawing his head back. "Creepy? I wasn't trying to be creepy." He scans the dusty shelves against the wall and waves his hand at the three droopy chairs. "I just get your deal. You like hanging out alone over here. That's cool. But I thought maybe we could . . . ."

He jiggles his leg and twists his mouth as if there's a word he can't quite come up with, but he doesn't leave. It's like he's glued to the spot.

Why is he so intent on getting in my face? His persistence makes me suspicious. "Look, sorry-lost-boy, I'm not sure what you think you know about me or what you understand, but wherever you disappeared to last week, you should probably go back there. Look somewhere else for a new BFF."

"I'm not going back there. And are you gonna call me 'sorry-lost-boy' for the rest of the semester? 'Cause I do have a name."

"Yeah. I don't do names."

He scrunches up his face. "See, what's that even supposed to mean?"

"I don't care about your name. I don't care. Period."

"You're so full of it." He shakes his head and smiles.

"Oh, am I?" I tighten my crossed arms and jut out my chin. "Well, if that's what you think, why don't you leave me alone?"

"I'm not exactly sure," he admits. Suddenly he looks so defenceless . . . vulnerable even.

Wow. I'd been this close to storming off, but the look on his face stops me. Part of me wants to get a closer look at his vulnerability. But what the hell am I thinking? Why is he still talking to me? It's all an act. Someone must have put him up to this. Dallyn and Allison want to torment me with the new information they have on me, but to cover their own asses, they've drawn the new kid in. Now the three of them are in cahoots.

Using the word "cahoots" gives me untold pleasure, even if I have used it in the privacy of my own mind.

"What?" he says. He's looking at my mouth.

Oops. I'm celebrating the word *cahoots*, and my smile has given me away. I frown quickly, my eyebrows doing what they do so well. I should make a dash for it before he messes with my head any more, but before I can bolt, an educational assistant appears from around the corner with one of the Special Ed kids.

"But I don't want to go to the Resource Room," the kid complains, his voice echoing through the stacks. He doesn't seem to understand the concept of *library voice*.

"We have to," the educational assistant says, guiding him towards the exit. "We need to plug in your laptop."

"Mr. Wilding should have plugged it in last night!" The kid is wailing now, flapping his hands around his head. "He should have remembered. He always forgets. Why does he always forget everything?"

The educational assistant keeps the boy moving while dodging his helicoptering arms. The new kid watches them make their roundabout way past the circulation desk and out the door.

"Don't mind him." I bob my head at the door. "He's not quite all there. Takes the short bus, you know?" I'm posturing. Kids like that freak me out. How do you interact with someone who can't be reasoned with?

A muscle in sorry-lost-boy's jaw jumps a little as he frowns at me. "You shouldn't make fun. He can't help it."

My spine stiffens. "I'm not making fun. I'm stating a fact. The Special Ed bus *is* shorter than the regular bus. It's not like I called him a retard or something."

He scowls. "Don't use that word."

"I wasn't." I scowl back. "I said at least I didn't call him that. Jesus."

I roll my eyes at him but he's not looking at me. He's staring at a point about two feet above my shoulder.

"I know how it feels, that's all. To be made fun of. For something you can't help."

There's that vulnerability again. Or is it a weakness? Now I'm intrigued. "Why? What's your deal?" I ask. I tilt my head, pretending I'm only vaguely interested.

He perches on the arm of the chair across from the one I've just vacated. "Dyslexia. Totally screwed me up when I was learning how to read. Had to develop 'strategies.'" He makes air quotation marks with his fingers. "Kept getting pulled out of class to go to the Spec Ed room. Grade One sucked. Kids called me 'retarded.' Teachers called me 'troubled.'"

Again with the air quotation marks.

"And were you? 'Troubled,' I mean." I mimic his gesture.

He snorts, but he's not smiling. "Yeah, I was troubled all right. With a capital *D*."

I don't get it. For a second, I don't get it. Then I realize what he means. People with dyslexia sometimes see letters or words backward.

"That's funny," I say, wishing I hadn't found that funny, and already regretting the compliment.

"Thanks."

Now he smiles. His chest puffs up slightly, as if he's patting himself on the back. "So you noticed I was gone last week, huh?" he says, tapping the small table between the two tub chairs with his shoe.

I don't want him to think I've been looking for him or thinking about him, though he has popped into my head several times over the past few days, much to my continuing horror. "I noticed you not being in here breathing down my neck, that's all. Anyway, it was a good idea for you to find somewhere else to hang out."

"I didn't find somewhere else to hang out. I wasn't here."

"A little soon to start ditching class isn't it, newbie?"

"I wasn't ditching," he says. His eyebrows scrunch and his lips pinch together. "I had . . . things to do." His jaw jumps again.

"Things to do? Sounds like a fancy code for ditching if you ask me."

"Nope. It's a fancy code for 'mind your own business.'" He stands and takes a few steps backward. "I've gotta hit the guidance office. My timetable's screwed. I'll see ya."

During the course of our conversation, I forgot I was supposed to be suspicious of him and his motives. Five minutes ago, I was the one looking to escape, and he beat me to it.

Great.

Chapter 5

Judgment

IN WRITER'S CRAFT, we work on our portfolios. I'm still not happy with the way mine is going. For our next assignment, we're supposed to take a pivotal event from our life and tell the story using three different writing modes. I'm avoiding the event I really want to write about, even though it would be so easy, because at the time it seemed like I was watching it all unfold from somewhere outside of my body. Like watching a movie.

I'd had a few drinks and the memories are a little blurry, but I'm sure if I were to write about it, my imagination would fill in the gaps. Then, of course, there are the pictures. They always help me to remember the fuzzy details.

I'll stay after class to ask Mr. Vesters for an extension, or at least for some advice about how to move forward. He always helps bring everything into focus.

For now, I stare at the computer screen, clicking my pen and wondering where to start. An out-of-place conversation at the front of the room distracts me. I try not to look up, not wanting to break my concentration, but I know that voice—the relaxed undertone and easy playfulness. It's the new kid.

What's he doing here?

I sneak a look around my hair, and he catches me. He smiles and bobs his head as if to say "Hey, it's you."

Mr. Vesters points in my direction, and they walk toward me. I groan. The empty seats on either side of me are the only available spots in the room. I drop my pen and begin to type mindlessly.

What I type looks something like this:

jijvjcedmvoed'/kmvoledmvk;mvikbv.vnl/cm/cmlcm

With the new kid hovering behind him, Mr. Vesters leans over my shoulder and speaks to me quietly. "This is Lucas Owens. He's a new student." He taps the chair to my right. "Would you be okay with him sitting here?"

Lucas. His name's Lucas. Lucas Owens.

Mr. Vesters looks pained. His face is so red that the purple birthmark on his cheek has almost disappeared. I'm sure he hadn't intended to single me out and make me uncomfortable, but right now he doesn't have a choice.

I look around the room. Several of my classmates stare at us, their mouths open. Perhaps they want to intervene and explain to Lucas the unfortunate consequences of sitting so close to me. Well, to hell with them. "Of course that's okay," I say.

"Great." Mr. Vesters lets out a breath as he straightens up, the colour around his birthmark slowly draining away. "Stick around after class, Lucas. We'll talk a little more about modifying your program."

"Sure thing," Lucas says.

Mr. Vesters gives me a small smile. I'm glad I was co-operative. If he weren't such a good guy, I'd have made him sweat it out longer.

Lucas makes a big deal of messing around with the mouse, feeding the cord around the back of the monitor and moving the mouse pad to the other side of the keyboard.

"I'm left-handed," he whispers.

"I'm sorry to hear that," I say.

He shakes his head and gives me a baffled look. "Meaning?"

Since when does everything I say have to mean something? That's just the first thing that came out of my mouth. "Meaning nothing. Forget it." I fix my eyes on my screen.

"If I'm going to sit here for the rest of the semester, it would be nice to know your name," he says.

I hold my fingers to my lips and frown. "Shh. I'm writing."

He sighs. He must be exasperated. I'm really good at exasperating people. How satisfying to see he's not immune to my powers. I angle my screen a little to the left and set my shoulders, trying to refocus. I can't concentrate though because Lucas is so freaking distracting. He flips through some sheets Mr. Vesters gave him, and then logs onto the computer and jiggles his leg under the desk until his desktop appears.

Is he spying on my screen? His presence makes me self-conscious. I quickly delete the line of gibberish I'd typed a few moments before. Out of the corner of my eye, I watch him stare at his screen for a few seconds before he starts typing.

He's the slowest typist on the planet. This must have something to do with his dyslexia. I gaze at my hands, trying to ignore the deliberate tap-tap-tapping of Lucas's fingers and waiting for inspiration. It's not happening, but I write anyway, my fingers flying across the keys. Random ideas tumble out. I'll worry about making sense of them later.

"Do you think he wears those on purpose?"

I jump, my hands skidding across the keyboard. "Huh?" Once I get going, regardless of what I'm writing or how good it is, I tend to get lost in my words. I have no clue what Lucas's question is about.

"The sweater vests," he says. "Do you think he wears them on purpose? Because of his name. *Vesters*. Get it?"

Yeah. I get it, but I don't want it. He won't win brownie points with me by treating Mr. V. as the enemy. "Don't be rude." Even as I say the words, I'm overwhelmed by their irony.

Lucas snorts quietly. He may have a learning disability, but he's not stupid. You don't have to know how to spell hypocrisy to recognize it. He doesn't speak again.

Left to my own devices, I spend the next forty minutes typing, bolding the awesome stuff, highlighting the weak stuff, and striking through words and phrases I'll probably get rid of entirely. I don't delete the strike outs. Most of the time they're completely inappropriate, but they're usually damn inspired. Reading them later will amuse me to no end.

This is my process.

When the bell rings at the end of class, everyone else gets up to leave, but I continue tapping away. I want to talk to Mr. Vesters about my portfolio, but I'll wait until everyone's gone.

Lucas vacates his seat with a clipped, "See ya." I don't look up, but Mr. Vesters calls him over, and I catch bits and pieces of their conversation.

There's a lot of jargon I don't understand—stuff about modifications and identifications, learning plans and locally developed expectations. It all goes over my head, but when I take a quick peek over my shoulder, Lucas is nodding. He says, "Cool, that's cool," a bunch of times before claiming he has to head out because someone's catching a ride home with him.

He's giving someone a lift home.

He already has friends at the school.

I close my eyes and let the implications of this tidbit settle in. That explains everything. He knows exactly who I am, and he's been screwing with me. I'm not sure what makes me more mad—the realization that he tricked me into thinking he knew no one and was desperate for a friend, or the fact that I was starting to think he was a decent guy, and that he might kind of like me.

I fume quietly as I pack up my knapsack, but Lucas is gone, and there's no point taking my wrath out on Mr. Vesters. It isn't his fault if the new kid is a jerk who likes to play mind games.

"How are things going with you?" Mr. Vesters asks, leaning back in his chair as I approach his desk.

I shrug. I'm not interested in talking about my issues. I'm certainly not going to tell him about my mother's recent cringe-worthy life choices.

"Things are okay."

He points to his desktop computer. "I got an email from Mrs. Croft at the end of the day on Friday. She said you stopped by the guidance office, but then you didn't stay to talk to anyone. Are you sure everything's okay?"

Good ol' Mrs. Croft. I knew it was a mistake to go to the guidance office. "Everything's fine. Really."

"Well, that's good. Listen, thanks for being so gracious about Lucas." He leafs through a small pile of papers. "This is a strange situation. I'm not quite sure how best to deal with it. School changes can be challenging at the best of times, but so tricky in the middle of a semester. I feel bad for Lucas. He seems like a nice enough kid."

Don't let him fool you. I don't need to say this. Mr. Vesters is a good judge of character. He'll figure things out soon enough.

"Anyway, that's neither here nor there." Mr. Vesters abandons the pile of papers and turns his attention back to me. "Did you want to discuss your writing?"

"Well, yeah. I'm kind of having trouble with my portfolio. I was wondering if I might be able to have an extension. It's just not flowing."

"That's not like you."

"I know. I don't think I've picked the right event. I don't feel . . . I don't know . . . ."

"Inspired?" Mr. Vesters prompts.

"I guess. It's like you were saying at the beginning of the semester, some words want to flow, and you shouldn't push them back to make room for the ones you think you should write instead. I might be doing that."

Mr. Vesters looks up at me quizzically. "So why not write the ones that want to flow?"

I shrug and gaze at the poster behind him on the whiteboard.

Remember your audience.

He continues to look at me. He knows full well what I'm staring at.

"Do you remember me also mentioning that I'm here to assess your writing skills, not to stand in judgment of the content?" he asks.

I nod.

"Among its many other purposes, writing can be cathartic," he points out. "If you've got something that needs to be purged, I say go for it."

"Okay. I'll try."

"If things don't go well this week, take the weekend as an extension. Maybe a few extra days will take some of the pressure off. Hand in your portfolio next Monday."

"Thanks."

"No problem."

See what I mean? Mr. Vesters is an awesome guy. If he's not going to judge me on what I write, why on earth would I judge him for his geeky wardrobe?

Chapter 6

The Centre of the Universe

THE NEXT MORNING when I arrive at school, I slide my hand into my pocket to make sure my Post-it note is safely tucked inside. Not that it matters. 522.1 is already seared into my brain. I maneuver through the crowd clogging up the lobby and make my way down the hall to my locker. Up ahead, Lucas leans against the wall outside the art room. I scowl and rush past, but he jogs lightly to catch up and falls in step beside me.

"Hey, it's Hannah Forde."

He knows my name. He's probably known my name all along, playing stupid and pretending he doesn't know precisely who I am. He caught me off-guard, but I won't give him the satisfaction of seeing me rattled. I pick up my pace.

"What's going on?" he asks, in a way that seems to mean *hey, wait up brand new BFF. Let's compare notes on what we did last night.*

I don't want to wait up. I don't want to compare notes, either. Let's be honest, I have no notes.

"Aren't you surprised that I found out your name? Not that it's a state secret," he says, shrugging in a self-satisfied way.

Exactly.

I keep walking, eyes fixed on my destination—my locker—about two hundred yards away. That's about six hundred feet. If I cover two feet with each step, that means my locker is three hundred steps away. Counting footsteps often distracts me from the aggravating things happening around me. Right now, Lucas is the aggravating thing.

I wrap my arms around myself and keep walking. Dallyn and

Allison must be somewhere in the crowd, watching Lucas bait me. I can't let them see that he's getting to me.

"Huh. Guess I was wrong," Lucas says, still striding purposefully beside me.

Wrong about what? He's good at this. Masterful, even. I don't answer. *Thirty-four, thirty-five, thirty-six....*

"You see, I figured out pretty quickly you're not a midday person," he says. "And you were cranky yesterday afternoon too, so I thought maybe you're a morning person. I guess not though, huh?"

"Nope."

I speed ahead, disappearing into the crowd before he can make some snide comment about how I must save up all my good will for late-night basement parties, or something along those lines. At my locker, I glance around quickly, relieved to see he hasn't followed me.

It's probably a strategic move. Retreat and reload.

When I arrive at math class, Mr. Vesters and Mr. Murray are chatting at the front of the room. I hang around outside the door, not wanting to intrude, but Mr. Murray waves me in, claiming Mr. V. is there to speak to me. Mr. Murray says he's on his way out to grab a coffee, and I make my way to my desk and unpack my books.

"Chess at lunch?" Mr. Vesters says, following Mr. Murray with his eyes. Before leaving the room, Mr. Murray turns and gives him two thumbs up.

"Math teachers and English teachers aren't supposed to get along, are they?" I ask, as Mr. Vesters perches on the desk beside mine.

He grins and shrugs. "Mr. Murray and I have known each other for twenty years. I put up with his incomprehensible fascination with numbers and he tolerates my penchant for words. So listen. I want to ask a favour, Hannah. I know you're having a stressful semester, and I don't mean to put more pressure on you, but I think I might need help with the new boy, Lucas."

"What do you mean help? Is he in trouble?" Part of me hopes he's in a whole mess of trouble.

"No. Of course not," Mr. Vesters says.

Too bad. "Okay, that's good," I say.

"I guess I hoped you could help him along a little. I'm not suggesting formal tutoring, but between one thing and another, I'm afraid he might struggle a bit . . . ."

"Are you talking about his dyslexia?"

Mr. Vesters draws his head back. "He told you about that?"

"We've talked a couple of times. In the library and stuff."

"Oh. Okay. Good." Mr. Vesters nods. "I didn't want to speak out of turn, but if he's told you himself, it would be quite natural for you to help him out from time to time. The tricky part is, he's working toward a mainstream English credit, not a Writer's Craft credit. You're always ahead of everyone else, though, and since he's sitting beside you, it makes sense."

I try to imagine myself being all buddy-buddy with Lucas, after he's been messing with my head. My imagination falls short.

"I don't know, Mr. V."

"Well, give it some thought. It might be nice if he had someone in the class who'd help him without making a big deal about it. I'm sure he's had his fair share of teasing."

Wow. Mr. Vesters is truly brilliant. He's used the old "treat others as you'd want to be treated" routine on me without saying those actual words. I admire his wiliness. "I'll think about it," I say, but my fingers are crossed under the desk.

"Excellent." He rubs his hands together like this is the most exciting development ever. "I hope we can keep this between us. I don't want to embarrass him."

I wonder who Mr. Vesters thinks I'll tell.

Lucas leaves me alone for the rest of the day. He doesn't materialize from the stacks while I'm in the library at lunch, and he keeps to himself during Writer's Craft. Either he's finally taken the hint, or he's stopped harassing me so that he and whoever he's plotting with can lull me into a false sense of security.

While the rest of us work on our portfolios, Mr. Vesters has given Lucas an alternate assignment to complete. I don't know exactly what it is, but he spends a few minutes flipping through a multi-page handout. Ten minutes into the period, he takes his phone out of his bag and starts fiddling with his headphones.

"We're not allowed to listen to our music in class," I whisper, in case he doesn't know the school rules. The least I can do is get him up to speed. Besides, I don't relish the idea of having to listen to music buzzing out of his earbuds for the rest of the class.

"You should probably get some work done," he says, without looking at me.

My spine stiffens, and I have to clamp my teeth to bite back a retort. Fine. I'll just mind my own business and leave Mr. Vesters to deal with him. Lucas plugs his headphones into the computer. If he's planning to log onto YouTube, he'll quickly learn that YouTube is blocked.

I continue to sneak glances at his computer, but he doesn't log on to the Internet. He opens a document of some sort. Then a pop-up window appears on his screen, highlighting the words as he scrolls through the document. When Mr. Vesters checks on him to ask how the reading software is working, Lucas assures him everything's fine and retreats to his own world again.

Reading software? So that's why Lucas is using his headphones. There's a computer program reading to him. I feel a flicker of sympathy and squash it. I can't allow sympathy to cloud my judgment.

I assume I'll make it through the whole class without having to talk to him, but two minutes before the bell, everyone starts to pack up, and Lucas takes off his headphones and turns to look at me. I don't invite conversation, continuing to stare at my computer screen, but he speaks anyway.

"Did you read a good book at lunch?" he asks me.

"Yep."

I say this with a note of finality, not once looking away from my screen to let him know that the conversation is over before it's even begun. Again, he fails to properly interpret my body language and seems oblivious to the clipped tone of my voice.

"What was it about?"

I huff out a breath and once again provide a one-word answer. "Astronomy."

"Hey, I used to love astronomy. I had one of those high-powered telescopes and everything."

I don't reply. I'm kind of interested in what he's saying, but he must be baiting me. I won't be drawn in.

"You must like astronomy too, right?" he persists.

He's jumping to the conclusion that because I was reading a book about astronomy, I must be interested in the topic. He doesn't understand my book selection system. I'm not about to correct him. He forges ahead anyway.

"What I mean is, you seem to enjoy the heliocentric model of existence," he says. "You being the Helios part, of course."

I have no idea what a heliocentric model is, so as everyone floods out of the room with the bell, carrying Lucas along with them, I hit up Google and discover that heliocentrism refers to the sun as the centre of the universe. "Helios" means sun.

If I was mad at him before, now I'm steaming. Sure, it's another new word, but there's no new word fabulous enough to lessen the sting of an accusation of self-centredness.

My spirits lift a bit when I get home and discover my mother made a tuna casserole, leaving a large dish of it in the fridge for me to heat up. I eat while watching *Jeopardy!*, pushing the peas to the edge of my plate and shouting answers at the TV. I know a ton of useless information, a lot of it gathered over the last three months at lunch hour in the nonfiction section of the library.

Sometimes, I fantasize about going on *Jeopardy!* and winning a ton of money. I'd likely get massive stage fright and clam up if I were a competitor on the show, though. Being so rarely the focus of anyone's attention, I've never had a chance to get comfortable in the centre of it.

That's why Lucas's accusation pissed me off so much. How can he say I'm self-centred when all my life I've lived on the margins? Even as a cheerleader last fall, when everyone thought I was so great—such a performer—they didn't know that my performance went beyond the time on the field. Hanging out with Allison and Marla, going to the mall and to parties, chilling with Dallyn and the guys? The whole thing was a performance.

Once *Jeopardy!* is over, I toss my plate in the dishwasher and head to my room, settling in at my desk to rework my portfolio. I'm going to take Mr. Vesters' advice and write the words that want to flow.

The instruction sheet says, "Choose a pivotal life event and select three modes of writing to tell the reader your story. Remember, you are the star of your own story."

I am the star of my own story.

What if I don't want to be the star of my own story? Maybe Mr. Vesters and Lucas have been comparing notes. No. I mustn't think about Lucas. Thinking about him will mess with my writing mojo. Instead, I get out my highlighter and pen, brainstorming the best way to narrate the event I've chosen.

Mr. Vesters would be proud. Usually, I start writing furiously without thinking first, which drives him crazy. Beside the poster that says, "Remember Your Audience," there's another one: "Take Time to Think Before Spilling Your Ink."

According to Mr. V., being a good writer is twenty percent planning and editing, thirty percent talent, and fifty percent successfully avoiding the distractions of the Internet—social media in particular.

Social media doesn't distract me. I have no social media connections.

I turn on my laptop. An old clunker, it takes forever to power up. It's painful. It's almost as painful as watching Lucas type.

Damn it! Why can't I banish him from my brain?

I refocus, reading over the list of suggested writing modes, quickly cancelling a few options. I suck at writing poetry and song lyrics, I don't want to write a personal essay, and a comic strip would call for drawings. I've never been able to draw. My Grade Nine art teacher brought an abrupt end to my artistic aspirations by "strongly suggesting" I take drama in Grade Ten to get my second arts credit.

Awkward turtle that I am, my drama mark sucked even worse than my art mark.

Despite my lack of acting skills, the idea of writing a one-act play intrigues me. One of my favourite parts of writing fiction is the dialogue. Isn't a script essentially all dialogue? I review an old handout reminding us of the conventions used in writing plays and then open a blank word processing document.

Once I start to write, the words come out in a steady stream—with lots of embellishment.

I write like I'm possessed. Normally, my imagination ignites my ideas, but this time, I'm fuelled by memories of New Year's Eve when my spot at the cool kids' table was swiftly and irrevocably snatched away.

Portfolio #6: Selected Mode #1—One-Act Play—Rough draft
Title: Nominated

CHARACTERS
Hannah
Allison
Marla
Dallyn
The girls from the cheerleading squad
Boys from various athletic teams

Scene 1: A teen girl's bedroom. New Year's Eve.
Music blasts from wireless speakers perched on the four-drawer dresser. Allison, Marla and Hannah get ready for a party. Allison and Marla compete for access to makeup, hair accessories and the mirror.

  MARLA: (Applying mascara.) What time is everyone coming over?

  ALLISON: Eight o'clock. Dallyn's brother is dropping him off and bringing some beer. They'll be here soon. (She examines her face in the mirror.) I gotta finish up.

  MARLA: You already look awesome.

  ALLISON: (Puckering her lips at her reflection, she uses her phone to take a selfie in the mirror.) You think?

  MARLA: (Nodding ~~stupidly.~~) I love your shirt.

  ALLISON: Dall really likes it too. Says he wants to motorboat my cleavage the whole time I'm wearing it.

  ~~**HANNAH:** And that's a good thing? God, you're such a pinhead.~~

MARLA: So, are you guys okay after that fight you had yesterday?

ALLISON: I made him promise to stop hanging out with that loser druggie guy and now we're totally fine. He gave me these. (Allison pulls her hair back, showing the girls her sparkly earrings.)

MARLA: Those are gorgeous. Are they real?

ALLISON: Of course they're real.

HANNAH: They look expensive. Where'd he get that kind of coin?

ALLISON: (Shrugs.) Does it matter? I'm totally worth it.

~~**HANNAH:** That's debatable.~~

ALLISON: Look, don't tell anyone about our fight, okay? There are so many skanks waiting for us to break up. I don't want anyone getting ideas.

MARLA: I won't tell anyone. Don't worry.

HANNAH: I can't imagine you two breaking up. You're meant to be together. ~~Dallyn may be dumb as a post, but he's really hot. Just like you, I guess.~~

ALLISON: (Adding another coat of lip-gloss and puckering her full lips at her reflection.) Yeah. We are sorta made for each other.

~~**HANNAH:** Dude, stop reading my mind.~~

Marla drops onto the bed and watches Allison finish doing her hair. Hannah joins her, already tired of pretending she cares about makeup and flat irons.

MARLA: So who's coming tonight?

ALLISON: (Rolling her eyes.) Everyone. You know, the whole cheer squad, Dall's team, some other guys. I hope it doesn't get out of control. My parents said I could have a few friends over since it's New Year's, but I don't think they meant forty people.

MARLA: You're so lucky. My parents would never go away for New Year's and let me have people over. Your mom's cool too, Hannah. My mom and dad are such tight-asses.

HANNAH: I wouldn't say my mom's cool. ~~Just oblivious.~~ Just busy.

MARLA: Whatever, you're still lucky.

Allison leans over to turn up the volume on the wireless speakers. She dances around the room, gyrating and posing.

ALLISON: God, I love this song. (She grinds against the bedpost.)

MARLA: (Cheering Allison on) Work it, girl!

ALLISON: (Allison abandons the dance, licking her lips seductively.) Better save some moves for later. Nothing's better than having sex when you've got the whole house to yourself.

HANNAH: (Deadpans.) I'll have to take your word for it.

MARLA: I wouldn't know, either. (She flops onto the pillows theatrically.) Why is it so hard to get a decent guy? They're all either taken or gay.

HANNAH: Or slimebags.

MARLA: I'd settle for a guy who's a slimebag right now.

ALLISON: Trust me, Mar, you don't want to hook up with a slimebag. I bet you'll both get some action tonight. Especially you, Hannah. (She smiles slyly at Marla.)

HANNAH: Why especially me?

ALLISON: Are you kidding me? Lisa's quit the squad, and you've been nominated for head cheerleader. That's huge.

HANNAH: Being nominated and getting the most votes are two different things, Allison. Since you're the other nominee ~~and all the girls are terrified of crossing you,~~ I'd say my chances are slim to none.

ALLISON: You're right. I mean, no offense, but I've been on the squad since ninth grade. I've got way more experience . . . .

MARLA: I don't know, Ali. Hannah's got the moves. I'd say she's got a good chance.

ALLISON: (Gazing at Hannah ~~snottily~~ challengingly.) Better bring your A-game when we do our routines next week before the vote, that's all I'm saying.
(Allison turns back to the mirror, applying yet another coat of lip-gloss before smiling at her reflection.) Perfect.

Scene 2: Two hours later. Main floor of the house. The party is in full swing. Loud music plays. Teenagers dance and drink throughout the main floor of the house. Pot smokers spill out into the back yard. In the kitchen, girls gossip and boys play drinking games.

Dallyn enters the kitchen alone. He stops to cheer on the drinking game participants. Then he sees Hannah and Marla leaning against the kitchen counter watching the boys trying to knock each other's beer caps off the tops of bottles. ~~They're both bored. Hannah looks like she wants to claw her own eyes out.~~ He squeezes between the two of them and throws one arm around Marla and the other around Hannah.

    DALLYN: (Bobs his chin at the empty bottles sitting beside them on the counter.) Ladies, that cooler of beer ain't gonna drink itself, you know. ~~Besides, if you don't drink a whole lot more, Hannah, it's gonna be way harder to screw you over later.~~

    MARLA: (Holding up her hand.) I'm good.

    DALLYN: How about you, Hannah?

    HANNAH: Yeah, I've had three. I'm okay right now.

    MARLA: Where's Allison? I haven't seen her for half an hour.

Dallyn ignores the question and lines up three small glasses on the counter. He sneaks a bottle of tequila from an overhead cupboard, pours three shots and then hands the girls a glass each.

    DALLYN: Come on. You gotta celebrate with me.

    MARLA: (Giggling and bouncing on her heels.) What are we celebrating?

    DALLYN: New Year's, of course. (He smiles at Hannah. ~~Lecherously.~~) Plus, Hannah's been nominated as cheer captain. That's reason enough, right there.

HANNAH: Thanks, Dall, but I don't like tequila. And it's just a nomination. I'm sure I won't win.

DALLYN: That's not what I've heard. Anyway, don't be a buzz-kill. (Dallyn taps the girls' glasses.) Drink up.

Marla and Hannah exchange a look. Marla brings the glass to her lips, and Hannah does the same, bending to Dallyn's coercion. ~~They don't call it peer pressure for nothing.~~ All three down the shot. The girls shudder, but Dallyn takes their glasses and refills them anyway.

HANNAH: (Grimacing as she watches him pour.) I can't. It's so nasty.

DALLYN: One more. We have something else to celebrate. (He hands the girls their glasses again.)

MARLA: Okay, what are we drinking to this time?

DALLYN: (Once more, clinking his glass against theirs and leaning in so only they can hear him.)
My freedom.

Dallyn downs his drink, slamming the glass on the counter afterwards. Hannah and Marla struggle to get their shots down, both looking at Dallyn in confusion. Marla splutters and coughs.

MARLA: Did you and Ali fight again? Is she ticked off because you brought some weed? What's going on?

DALLYN: (Grabbing Hannah's hand and hushing Marla.) What's going on is Hannah's coming downstairs with me.

HANNAH: (Panicking.) I don't want to go downstairs.

MARLA: Wait, what'll I tell Allison?

DALLYN: (Steering Hannah across the room.) Tell her whatever you want.

HANNAH: I shouldn't leave Marla by herself, Dall—

DALLYN: She'll be fine. Come on. (He tugs on Hannah's hands and looks at her plaintively. ~~His performance is Oscar worthy.~~) I need someone to talk to. I need a friend ... Please ....

Scene 3: A room in the basement. Dallyn turns on a lamp, flicks on the stereo and leads Hannah to the couch. He pulls her down to sit with him and then twirls a lock of her hair around his finger.

HANNAH: (Trying to move away from him.) I really don't think—

DALLYN: (He scoots along the couch to join her. Whispers.) I really like you, Hannah. You like me, too, right?

HANNAH: Well, yeah, ~~as long as you don't talk~~ but—

DALLYN: Then what's the problem?

HANNAH: I don't know. Allison will kill me.

DALLYN: (Dallyn leans in to kiss Hannah's neck. Whispers again.) Allison won't know.

HANNAH: We're in her basement. She could come down any second. Anyone could.

DALLYN: She hates it down here. She says it gives her the spooks when—

My hands freeze above the keyboard. I thought I'd be able to do it—to write everything down clinically—but I can't. I can't detach myself. Dallyn told me how much he loved a girl who took control, suggesting I straddle his lap and unbutton my top. He smiled luridly when I undid the top three buttons of my shirt, revealing my hot pink lace bra. He asked me to hold his wrists in place on the back of the couch and kiss his neck.

I complied.

Willingly.

My face burns as the memories flicker through my mind. Especially horrifying is imagining Mr. V. reading my words. I can't write about that night! What was I thinking?

"Remember Your Audience."

Oh, I'm remembering all right.

How can I possibly share how much I enjoyed Dallyn's advances and how I gladly did what he told me to do, because for once in my life, I felt wanted? I remember the sensation of my heart thrumming and the sound of my own breathing, but most of all, I remember that through the haze of tequila and desire, I knew what I was doing was wrong.

That's why I clambered off Dallyn's lap, re-buttoned my top, and told him I couldn't do it. I told him we were making a mistake. He and Ali would work out their argument. Betraying Allison was wrong.

Turns out my mistake had nothing to do with betraying Allison. My mistake was thinking Dallyn was really interested in me. How could I have believed he chose me over her? Why couldn't I see that the two of them were playing me? While I sat on Dallyn's lap and wrestled with my conscience, Allison was hidden behind the furnace no more than six feet away, documenting the entire scene with her camera.

I always thought she was stupid, but Allison, like many of history's greatest bullies, proved to be a genius. All that effort to eliminate the one obstacle standing in the way of captaining the cheerleading squad. Ironically, if she'd asked me nicely, I probably would've stepped aside. I didn't really want to be captain. Somewhere along the way, I'd forgotten that.

I slam my laptop closed. Writing about that night in January is one of the dumbest things I've ever done. I know what Mr. Vesters meant when he said writing is cathartic, but it can also be masochistic. Why stir up memories of an event I'd be much better off forgetting?

I push my laptop aside, grab my Post-its and work my way through my nightly ritual. Then, I fall into bed.

616.9 . . . 616.9 . . . 616.9 . . . .

Nope. My mantra isn't working. Even after thousands of repetitions, my eyes remain open, fixed on the ceiling. Mom comes home just after two in the morning, somewhere around the millionth "616.9." She whisper-giggles her way up the stairs with her catch of the day. Her door clicks shut, and there's a loud thud and a shriek of laughter.

Jesus, did they even make it to the bed?

Instead of lying there listening to her extra-curricular activities, I get out of bed, turn my laptop back on and plug my headphones in to drown out the sounds coming from across the hall.

I reread the half-written one-act play. Then I torture myself further by opening a document of comments copied and pasted from the Twitter timeline that erupted in January, the day after the pictures of me and Dallyn were leaked.

Mr. V. would be annoyed by my use of the passive voice in that last sentence. "The pictures 'were leaked?'" he'd say. Then he'd ask, "What's more effective, Hannah? 'The dog wagged its tail or the tail was wagged by the dog?' Identify the doer! The pictures 'were leaked?' Who's the subject of your sentence? WHO leaked the pictures?"

I would then be forced to explain to him that someone named @Bitch_Please leaked them.

A fascinating conversation would follow, during which I'd educate him on the ins and outs of trolls with fake Twitter accounts and the fine art of retweets and subtweets, DMs, mentions and hashtags, after which I'd tell him all about those fabulous little gems known as Twitpics.

Maybe at the end of the conversation he'd say, "So, wait a minute . . . who's @Bitch_Please?"

I'd respond, "Well, Mr. Vesters, @Bitch_Please is the subject of my sentence. Duh."

Chapter 7

A Sign

THE NEXT DAY at lunch, I make a beeline to the library stacks, where I scour the 616 section, looking for a book with the right call number. I check the shelf twice but can't find one.

Oh my God, there's no 616.9. How is this possible?

Breathe, Hannah, just breathe.

My eyes burn from lack of sleep. Am I just confused? Again, I scan the shelf, mumbling numbers, my fingers tracing the book spines.

Nope. There are tons of 616 books, but no 616.9.

Damn it.

This is a first. Three months of Dewey Decimal therapy, and this is the first time I've come up empty-handed. I'm a failure. I actually might cry. This is irrational, but I'm tired, and being rational is well beyond my scope. I need a plan B, but that seems more than I can pull together.

Finally, I grit my teeth. Starting at the first book in the 616 section, I count nine books down the shelf, landing on *The Family Genetic Sourcebook*. It's not 616.9, but it is the ninth 616 book on the shelf. This compromise will have to do.

I shuffle off to my corner, completely dispirited but determined to salvage my routine. I turn my chair to face the corner and sit, trying to summon some excitement about the new words I'm learning. To be honest, I couldn't care less. This is so unlike me. My universe is out of alignment. To put it in genetic terms, my chromosomes are malfunctioning.

As I make the short journey from the library to Writer's Craft before last period, I pay attention to what's happening around me for the first time in weeks. Kelly Sparks and Brett Calder are down the hall leaning against a locker, catching a quick grope between classes. Allison and Marla stand near them with a group of girls, cackling at some shared hilarity. All that's missing is the smoking cauldron. A few months ago, I would have been one of those cackling girls, although usually what they were laughing about wasn't even remotely funny. It's comforting not having to pretend any more.

What isn't comforting is seeing Lucas no more than twenty feet beyond them, having an intense conversation with Dallyn. So I'd been right all along. They do know each other.

Having my suspicions confirmed knocks me back a few steps. I can't possibly go to Writer's Craft and sit beside him for the next hour. Not finding a 616.9 book made my nerves jangle, and now, Lucas is buddying up with Dallyn? What if Lucas says something stupid in Writer's Craft and I snap? I'm usually a master at passive aggression, but I can see myself quickly resorting to aggressive aggression if Lucas pushes my buttons today.

Instead of going to class, I return to the library. Mrs. Fry is in the lab helping a student at a computer. She doesn't notice me duck past and return to my quiet corner. Just a few minutes to pull myself together is all I need. If she sees me and asks what's going on, I'll say I'm not feeling well. She wouldn't report me to the office. Mrs. Fry is cool that way. In fact, Mrs. Fry is so cool, that back in January, she helped the universe give me a sign, a sign that has brought me back to the library every lunch hour for the last couple of months.

Of course, Mrs. Fry has no clue that she helped the universe to give me a sign. I'd tell her, but I don't want her to think I'm a total freak.

The Universe gave me a sign three months ago.

It was a Monday. Monday, January 5th, to be exact—the first day back after Christmas vacation. The pictures from Allison's New Year's Eve party had leaked onto Twitter the day before.

Dallyn quickly claimed innocence. In other words, he lied his stupid face off. He said I'd forced myself on him, so what was he supposed to do?

If people doubted his claims, the pictures backed up his every word.

There I was, sitting on his lap with the top three buttons of my shirt undone, flashing my bra at him while holding his hands down. He and I both knew what had happened—and I knew full well he'd framed me—but history is written by the victors, and I certainly wasn't coming out of this one victoriously.

I spent most of that day exercising my hindsight, playing the "what if" game. What if I hadn't started hanging around with Allison and Marla? What if I'd never allowed myself to get drawn in to their dim-witted and poisonous social circle? Most of all, what if I could undo New Year's Eve? Not go to Allison's party, not have five drinks, not go down to the basement with Dallyn, not believe his stupid lies....

Not, not, not, not....

While playing the "what if" game, I also tried to deal with Allison's vicious phone calls and texts while dodging Twitter attacks. I'd be willing to bet over a hundred people created anonymous Twitter accounts with the sole intention of commenting on what I'd done. My phone chimed all day long with a steady stream of Twitter alerts—"slut-face;" "boyfriend stealing whore;" "nice rack, show me your panties;" "do us all a favour and kill yourself...."

Do us all a favour and kill yourself?

What kind of person says something like that?

It didn't matter who said it. I was screwed. My short-lived social acceptance, along with any hope of continuing my cheerleading career, was over.

The first day back to school after Christmas break, I was frozen out on the bus. School bags slid across seats to fill empty spaces; raised eyebrows dared me to sit. I returned to the front of the bus and sat behind the driver. I slid down in my seat, but hiding was futile. My name, along with words like "whore," "sleaze" and "slut" figured strongly in each gleeful conversation. I could have countered these half-whispered taunts with explanations that calling a virgin a slut is a total oxymoron, but that wouldn't have gotten me far, I'm sure.

When I arrived at school, circles of people purposely closed in as I walked by. Eyes flickered to mine then away. So-called friends—people who were friendly before Christmas—turned their backs and snickered.

I went straight to the Phys Ed office and told the cheer squad teacher-advisor that I was declining the nomination for captain and withdrawing from the squad.

"I'm so sorry to hear that, Hannah. Are you sure?" she asked.

"I need to focus on the exams and buckle down on my second semester courses. My marks are slipping," I told her. An outright lie. My marks were, and always had been, stellar.

"We'll be sorry to see you go. I suppose that means Allison will be named captain by default."

I shrugged. "I guess so."

Allison won, achieving exactly what she'd fought so hard for. But victory didn't last.

That's a whole different story.

After bailing on cheer squad, I headed for my locker. A banner decorated the front of it, the kind that friends tack to your locker when it's your birthday. It didn't say "Happy Birthday." It said one word, in purple and pink curlicue letters: "skank." Allison's favourite word.

My face burned with humiliation, and my pulse thrummed in my ears as I looked around the crowded hallway, sure that everyone who walked by was watching me. Every laugh or snicker felt like it was aimed at me. I ripped the banner down and stashed it in my locker. The rest of the school year stretched out in front of me.

Even the thought of making it through the day was more than I could wrap my head around. Where would I eat lunch?

During physics class I got a lot of knowing looks and heard plenty of whispering about me, but with none of the heavy hitters in the class, it wasn't so bad. History class gave me the first taste of my new reality. I sat there willing myself to be invisible, trying to pretend I wasn't dying of mortification, and that I didn't know why everyone was laughing at me behind their hands and looking apologetically at Allison.

The victim.

My history teacher wrote the date on the white board.

1.05.15

I copied down everything he wrote, pretending Kelly Sparks wasn't behind me kicking my chair over and over again, and Brett Calder wasn't holding up a piece of paper with "I like your pink bra" written across it in large letters. Dallyn stared at me, his tongue sliding back and forth inside his lower lip, and Allison turned around every few minutes to hiss at me, the protracted *s*-sound a not so gentle reminder of the banner she'd stuck to my locker.

Sssssssss for "skank."

I ignored them all. It was just Mr. Napiers, the whiteboard, me and my notes. I focused entirely on Mr. Napiers' mouth as he spoke.

"Make sure you do some extra reading to prepare for the philosophy section on the exam," he said. "Check out the school library at lunch or after school for resources."

Allison rolled her eyes, and Dallyn muttered under his breath. "As if. As if I'm gonna go to the school library at lunch. Whatever. Hang out in the library like a loser after school to look up philosophy? Doubts."

I clicked my pen and allowed the implications of these words to slowly sink in.

My history book clutched against my chest, I went to the library at lunch that day. I dashed unnoticed to the first row of stacks and scanned the space. Between the crowded computer lab and the tables teeming with kids, the place was packed. Where would I sit? I spun in slow circles and stared vacantly at the shelves surrounding me. And how on earth would I find a philosophy book?

I snuck a peek around the end of the stacks. A few heads bobbed up, faces peering curiously over the tops of computer screens—nerdy guys, most likely speculating about the colour of my underwear. Even geeks have Twitter accounts. Let's face it, a couple of geeks probably invented Twitter.

The librarian—Mrs. Fry, according to the plaque on her desk—stood behind her computer, her attention split between the action in the room and the screen in front of her. I tried to ignore the numerous pairs of eyes burning holes in the back of my head and approached the desk warily. She looked up and smiled.

"What can I do for you, sweetie?"

"Um, I'm looking for a book about philosophy. For my history class."

"Anything in particular? We have an extensive philosophy section."

I fumbled my binder onto the counter and flipped to the notes I'd taken that morning.

"Thomas Hobbes," I said. "A book with stuff about him would be good."

"Okay, let me see."

She looked back at the computer, sliding the mouse this way and that as she clicked around the screen, and then she picked up a pencil and reached over, her hand poised above my notebook.

"Try this," she said, jotting a number on my page. "In the stacks, find the book with the call number 105.15. The book is called *One Hundred Philosophers*. You should find something in there."

I thanked her and hid behind my hair as I rushed back to the stacks, away from the curious onlookers and their gleeful whispers.

"Down there," Mrs. Fry coached me from behind the circulation desk. "That's it. Look to your left."

I followed her directions, scanning the shelf and looking down at my binder to confirm the call number. There were so many books. Hundreds of them. The sheer volume of words, millions and millions of words, swirling around me was overwhelming—dizzying almost.

A minute or two later, Mrs. Fry appeared at the end of the stacks.

"Did you find it?"

"I'm not sure." Translation: in case you hadn't noticed, I'm still standing here like a complete moron.

"Right there," she said, reaching in front of me and pulling the book off the shelf without even seeming to look.

"Wow, how'd you do that?" I stared at the book in my hand as if she'd given me the contents of the Ark of the Covenant or something.

"Practice." She laughed. "Let me know if you need any more help."

She walked back to her desk, her shoes clicking with every step. Instead of following her, I exited the stacks at the opposite end and peered around the side, spying what is now my oasis—three dilapidated chairs clustered around a small end table in a quiet corner. Empty.

Salvation.

I claimed a chair facing the wall, rested my open binder on my lap and turned my attention to *One Hundred Philosophers*. The last person who'd read it left sticky flags throughout. I flipped to one of the yellow Post-its and read the words the last reader had left behind:

"Rather than getting caught up in the past, one should examine the present and figure out how to deal with it. (Summary of Han Fei, Chinese philosopher.)"

I knew nothing about Han Fei, but his philosophy made sense. I peeled the Post-it note free and stuck it onto the page in my binder, contemplating the message.

And that's when I noticed it: 105.15.

Mrs. Fry had written the call number for the book at the top of my history note, right beside the date.

The date: 1.05.15.

The only thing separating the book's call number and today's date was a period. A dot. The tiniest speck.

I shivered involuntarily, the creepiness of the coincidence making me conclude that I was supposed to find that book, and I was meant to find it that day. I'd never been more certain of anything in my life. It was a sign—a sign from the universe. The universe told me not to dwell in the past, but instead to examine the present and figure out how to deal with it.

You don't ignore a sign from the universe.

I took the Post-it note, folded it in half and tucked it into my pocket. For the rest of the day, every time someone whispered or sneered at me, I slipped my hand into my pocket.

Examine the present and figure out how to deal with it.

Spending forty hassle-free minutes in the library that day convinced me I should go back the next day. If finding a temporary reprieve in that quiet corner helped me make it through the school day, then I was all for it. But what to read next?

I needed new numbers. I couldn't leave things up to the universe though, hoping another numerical coincidence would occur the next day. What if nothing happened? No. Too risky. In the end, I left my fate to a roll of the dice in the most literal sense.

That evening, I sat at my desk with my backgammon set, using the dice to help me put together a call number. Then I rummaged in my desk for some unused yellow Post-it notes to write the numbers on. I have repeated this routine every weeknight since. It is one of the most soothing parts of my day.

Eventually, I snuck my lunch into the library. Dipping celery sticks in peanut butter became almost as reassuring as the Post-it notes and the books. The universe didn't tell me to sneak peanut butter and celery lunches into the library, potentially causing someone anaphylaxis in the process. That part was my idea. Allison Dawson is allergic to nuts. Enough said.

My lunch hour ritual was comforting and safe. It was also utterly foolproof, or so I'd thought.

Until today. Until I couldn't find a book with the call number 616.9. Is this a new sign from the universe? If it is a new sign, I'm not sure what the universe is saying. But whatever it is, I don't like it.

Chapter 8

Honesty

"DON'T YOU HAVE a class?"

"Huh?"

Mrs. Fry is beside me, her hand on my arm. "Writer's Craft?" she says. "That's where you should be, right?"

I can't tell her I've been having a little stroll down memory lane, thinking about her role in helping the universe give me a sign back in January. I can't tell her I think the universe is giving me a new sign today by denying me a book with a 616.9 call number. She'll think I'm a head case.

I give her a vague story about feeling a little out of sorts. She scoots into her office to call Mr. Vesters for me, to find out if he'll let me spend my Writer's Craft period in the library. A moment later, she pops her head out of her office door. "Mr. Vesters is fine with you staying here. He says you know what you should be working on."

Relieved, I take out my Writer's Craft binder. My mind is as blank as the lined pages staring back at me. It's official. I'm stumped for portfolio ideas. I've never experienced such overwhelming writer's block in my life. Not surprising. My routine has gone out the window. It's Lucas's fault. I had everything down to a fine art until he arrived. I toss my Writer's Craft binder on the table with a frustrated sigh.

Perspective and distance, that's what I need. I should step away from my portfolio for a couple of days and focus on other things. The sad thing is, I can't think of anything else worth focusing on.

My life is completely void of substance.

I didn't think it was possible for the day to get worse, but when I cross the parking lot to get to the school bus loading zone at 3:15, it starts to rain. I mutter curses at the sky and weave between cars in the parking lot. I don't bother to run. Just making it through the day has sapped my energy.

Surely things are as bad as they're going to get. Then I spot Lucas cutting between cars in the parking lot. Unlike me, he's running. He's running hand-in-hand with a girl—a blonde girl. They stop running when they reach a compact red car. She climbs in the passenger side, and he gets in the driver's side.

This is the girl who caught a ride with him the other day. I'm sure of it. He doesn't just have friends at the school. He isn't just buddy-buddy with Dallyn. He also has a girlfriend. I stop at the edge of an enormous puddle to watch them drive away. As they pass, Lucas reaches over and wipes the hair out of the girl's eyes.

My heart seizes. What must it be like to be treated with such tenderness?

I tilt my head back and blink up at the clouds. Rain patters across my face. I close my eyes for a moment. When I open them again, the red car is gone.

I stuff my wet hands into my pockets and briefly consider hopping across the puddle in front of me. Instead, I slosh through it. My shoes get soaked right through. I don't care about my shoes. I definitely don't care about Lucas. He made a point of getting in my face all week, and even if he wasn't purposely antagonizing me, he's totally not my type, and I'm sure he wouldn't give me a second look anyway. So why would I care?

He has a girlfriend and she's cute and blonde and they were holding hands and he's driving her home in a red car and they're warm and dry, and I'm soaked and cold and I shouldn't care, but for some reason I totally care and I despise the whole universe and its stupid signs and non-signs with every fibre of my being.

And yes, I know that was a run-on sentence. So sue me.

At home, my mother lies on the sofa in her silk bathrobe with the curtains closed and her arm flung over her face. As I lock the door, her head moves, but she doesn't open her eyes.

"Hannah?"

"What are you doing home?" I drop my bag and coat in the front hall and kick off my shoes. A puddle forms on the linoleum. "I thought you were on four to midnight all week."

"Worst headache. Had to call in."

"That sucks."

"Sure does. All-you-can-eat wings night. I'm missing great tips."

"I was talking about the headache, not the tips."

She pushes herself up on her elbows and squints across the room at me.

"You're all wet."

No shit, Sherlock. "It's pouring."

"I should've come to pick you up," she groans, dropping back onto the cushion, her arm flopping over her eyes again.

Yes, yes you should have. I don't contradict her. Instead, I say, "I'm gonna grab a shower and change. I'll clean up the mess by the door later."

"How was your day?" she asks.

I'm already halfway up the stairs.

"Fine." Of course my day wasn't fine, but what else would I tell her? The truth? In the shower, I imagine what an honest answer would sound like.

My day was awful. There's this cute new guy who's got these amazing eyes. You can't really tell what colour they are sometimes. He's tall and left-handed and kinda funny. He has a learning disability, but I don't think he's dumb or anything. Actually, he seems smart. Anyway, I thought maybe he liked me, but I was imagining that because he's obviously friends with Dallyn, and he's been antagonizing me all week. Today after school, I saw him holding hands with a girl and giving her a ride home. To top it all off, I've got massive writer's block, got soaked after school, couldn't find a book with a 616.9 call number AND the universe hates me . . . .

Wow. Honesty makes me sound like a crackhead. It also makes my heart hurt. It's so much easier to cope when I lie to myself. I pull on my robe and look in the mirror, watching the water drip from my hair onto my face and down across the pale landscape of my cheeks. The water looks like tears. I'm not crying, though. Crying won't solve anything.

It's so much easier to cope when I lie to myself.

How was my day? It was fine.

A three-digit call number. 942. I'm flying on a wing and a prayer. I didn't risk extending the number further.

There has to be a book today. There *has* to. I repeat the number over and over to myself on the bus, trying to tune out the prom talk, which has reached a hysterical pitch. Prom is still weeks away. Why is everyone freaking out? I'd put it down to spring fever if it weren't so gross and rainy out.

942 . . . 942 . . . 942 . . . 942 . . . .

I'm on my thousandth 942 when a guy somewhere behind me mentions Lucas's name. My ears perk up. I temporarily pause the 942 soundtrack in my brain to listen. Everyone's talking over each other. It's hard to keep up.

An unidentifiable male voice says, "Lucas? Is that the new tall guy? Brown hair—"

"Yeah, he transferred in from Midtown Collegiate."

"I hear he got in major trouble over there with a—"

"Marla's hot for him," a female voice interrupts. It's Kelly Sparks. Since she's a cheerleader friend of Marla's, she would know. I guess.

"He is cute," another girl says. "I heard Marla wants to ask him to prom."

"Marla likes him? I saw him going in the Spec Ed room at lunch. There's no way she'd go to prom with—"

"Wait, he's a sped?"

This last voice belongs to Brett Calder. He's one of Dallyn's buddies and, therefore, an asshole by way of association. He's also an asshole by way of assholiness.

As soon as he says "sped," everyone laughs, and I forget that Lucas has been antagonizing me since the day he arrived. Instead, I remember the conversation we had in the library on Monday, the faraway look in his eyes as he talked about being teased for being a Spec Ed kid when he was younger. "Sped" is an offensive term, only slightly less offensive than "retard".

Instead of telling them all to shut their stupid traps, I clench my teeth and train my eyes on the window, watching rain splash against the glass with increasing intensity. Not sticking up for someone who's being teased is as bad as participating, but I'm no fool. I need to tread carefully. I have to remain invisible.

The jabbering continues behind me, but the topic shifts back to prom crap—tuxes, before parties, after parties, who's buying the weed, and who's bringing the booze, blah . . . blah . . . blah. I tune them out again and sift through what they said about Lucas.

It's all rumours, the stuff about him getting in trouble at his old school and the bit about Marla wanting to go to prom with him. I wouldn't be surprised if Marla already had her eye on Lucas, though. Without a prom date, she's looking to get first dibs on the new guy. I hope she does ask him. Then he'll have to tell her he already has a girlfriend. The thought of Marla's hopes being dashed lessens the pain in my own heart a little.

I scan the school lobby, relieved that Lucas isn't there, ready to follow me down the hall. I wouldn't want to talk to him anyway. I definitely don't want to listen to his persistent chattering and fantastically insightful observations about my nature. The six-hundred-step journey to my locker will be much more enjoyable alone.

I'm definitely not thinking about him while staring into space during math class, and I don't feel seething anger when I see him talking to Marla in the hall on my way from math to English. They're so involved in their discussion, he doesn't even notice me walk by. She's giggling and smiling, bouncing like a buffoon—certainly not the behaviour of someone having her heart ripped out.

In English, we're still studying imagery. We're supposed to think about something beautiful and then use figurative language to communicate the beauty of the object. I picture someone's eyes.

His eyes are a warm hazelnut. Sometimes, depending on the light, his eyes are so beautiful and golden that I have to tear my gaze away because if I don't, I might end up trapped in his eyes forever, like a locust eternally preserved in amber.

I reread the passage and decide this is a fantastically inspired description, even though I have no idea whose eyes have inspired it.

This lie isn't even remotely convincing.

After English class, I compose an argument in my head as I travel from my locker to the library. The argument goes something like this:

Me: The universe better not screw with me again today, I swear to God....
Me: You need to settle down.
Me: What if there's no 942, though?
Me: There will be.
Me: But what if there isn't?
Me: Can you calm down and stop freaking the hell out?
Me: You know what? You'd be freaking out, too, if you were me.

Me: I am you.

At this point, the argument breaks down. I can't win. Or I can't lose. Either way, it's ridiculous. I scowl at the mud-stained floor for the remaining eighty-seven footsteps to the library.

As soon as I pull open the metal doors, it's clear that something's not right. A half-dozen kids cluster around the circulation desk, bitching at Mrs. Fry about the computer network as if a system failure is somehow her fault. I leave the bickering crowd behind, veering between the computer and table area to get to the last row of bookshelves in the nonfiction section. I take a deep breath before venturing down the stacks.

Please . . . please . . . please . . . .

I scan the stacks quickly, mouthing the numbers, fingers jumping from book to book. There, in the last set of shelves, is an entire row of 942s—at least thirty books to choose from. I can't even pretend to be blasé. In all honesty, my knees almost buckle, I'm so relieved.

Natural order has been restored.

Actually, that's not true. If I make it through Writer's Craft without incident, get home from school to find that my mother has gone to work, and then see a pair of funky smelling gold-buckled Italian loafers or high-top sneakers or dusty cowboy boots in the front hall tomorrow morning, that's when I'll know natural order has been restored.

Chapter 9

Questions

For some reason, when I heard the whining in the library, I didn't make the connection between failed computers and Writer's Craft. As soon as I walk through Mr. Vesters' door at the beginning of last period, it's obvious we aren't going to be using the computers. The screens are blank. The system is down.

Lucas is at his station, moving the keyboard out of the way. He pulls his binder out of his back pack and flips through it. I slip into my seat without speaking to him, even though my brain teems with questions.

Did you really get into trouble at your old school?

When you were talking to Marla earlier, was she asking you to prom?

Did you tell her about your blonde girlfriend?

What are Dallyn and Allison cooking up for me, and what's your part in their grand plan?

Would you describe your eyes as light brown or hazel?

From the front of the room, Mr. Vesters interrupts my imaginary inquisition, apologizing for the computer situation. He explains that we can either work on our portfolios by hand and type later, or work ahead on the next module from our writer's handbook.

Around me, panicked whispers begin. It's crunch time. Our portfolios are due tomorrow, but with my extension until Monday already secured, I'm not quite as worried. Surprisingly—actually, not at all surprisingly—I have no plans for the weekend. Plenty of time to churn out a few pieces of writing once I get on a roll.

Though I'm not in the mood to work on grammar exercises, I haul out my writer's handbook anyway. Lucas jiggles his leg under the desk.

He scans a page in his binder and puts his hand up.

Mr. V. makes his way across the room. "Problem, Lucas?"

"Yeah, well, not really, but you said I should read this story today and then do all these activities after reading?"

"Right."

"It's all due tomorrow?"

"If possible, yes."

"Okay, I'll try. It might take me a while to read this without the, uh . . . ."

Lucas points at his blank computer screen.

"Oh, right." Mr. V. lowers his voice. "I don't suppose you have the assistive software programs at home?"

Lucas shakes his head.

"Hmm. I'd give you an extension, but I really need to assess some of your work. I was hoping to look at it over the weekend. I guess . . . do you want to go to the resource room? See if anyone has time to read it over with you?"

I cringe, thinking of what Brett Calder said on the bus. *He's a sped?*

"I could read it to him. We could go to the library." The words are out of my mouth before I've had a chance to think.

Mr. Vesters' eyebrows travel up to the top of his forehead. This is not mere surprise. This is incredulity.

"Well, that's very nice of you, Hannah."

I'm as shocked as you are, Mr. V.

Despite the millions of questions bubbling behind my lips, I don't say anything as Lucas and I make our way down the main hallway. He whistles, checking out the bulletin boards and posters that line the walls. Not talking makes me feel awkward, so I hang back, pretending to look for something in my backpack. I've never been an amazing conversationalist, but with Lucas, I have to keep my guard up. I can't say anything that might give him a loose thread to pull. He's likely to continue pulling until I completely unravel.

As we pass through the lobby and toward the Arts wing, he breaks the silence.

"Hey, thanks for doing this."

"I'm not doing it for you. I'm doing it for Mr. V."

Lucas shakes his head. "Would it kill you to say, 'You're welcome, I'm happy to help'?"

"Yeah, see, that would go against my heliocentric world view."

He expels a gusty breath. "Look, I'm sorry I said that. You seem so . . . I don't know . . . so self-absorbed sometimes—"

"I don't remember forcing you to talk to me. Anyway, you don't know me."

"That's the whole point of talking to someone. To try to get to know them."

"I don't get why you're bothering." Of course I have my suspicions, but I'm not about to share them with him.

"I switched schools in the middle of a semester. I'm trying to make friends." He sighs again and jams his hand in his pocket. "Never mind. I wouldn't expect you to understand how hard it is."

Oh, believe me, I understand. "I'm really not that interesting," I say.

"Can you let me decide that?"

"Suit yourself."

"Does that mean I get to ask you a question without you biting my head off?"

I can only imagine what he wants to ask me. *Are you wearing your hot pink bra? Can I have a lap dance?* "You can ask. I may or may not bite your head off."

We turn the corner, making our way down the library corridor.

"You're a cheerleader, right?" he asks me.

This is his burning question? He's not looking at me, but I narrow my eyes anyway. "Cheerleaders are bitches," I say.

"Yeah, that was my first clue." He chuckles and for some reason, I want to laugh too.

"The hair swingy thing you do when you walk was my second clue, in case you're wondering. All cheerleaders do that. It's like a secret code or something. Dead giveaway."

"Well, sorry to burst your bubble, but you're wrong. I'm not a cheerleader." *Not anymore.*

"Dancer?" he guesses.

"Why would you say that?" Instantly suspicious, I imagine Allison and Dallyn laying out my biography for him.

"It's obvious." He says this defensively. "Look at your feet."

I look down. "What?"

"When you walk, your feet angle out. You walk like a duck. A lot of girls who've taken dance classes walk like ducks."

"What are you talking about?"

"Here, stop for a second."

He draws me to a halt in front of the library doors and points at my feet.

"Now what?"

"Your feet. They're in first position," he explains. "Dancers do that all the time, too."

First position? How in the hell does he know about first position?

"Well, Nancy Drew. You think you're clever, I guess," I say.

"So you are a dancer?"

"Whatever you say, Nancy."

"I'm not Nancy. I'm Nancy's boyfriend. I'm Ned."

I look up at him in amazement. "You know Nancy Drew's boyfriend's name was Ned? Where'd you come from? 1974?"

He smiles and this faraway expression passes across his face. His eyes seem to lose focus as he looks off to the distance over my shoulder. "My cousin used to spend a lot of time at my place in the summer. She was obsessed with my mom's old Nancy Drew books. She'd read them and make me act the stories out with her, like a game." He shrugs. "Lame, I guess."

"Whatever. You were a kid." It is kind of a dumb game, but I'm prepared to be conciliatory if it means he'll keep talking with that dreamy look in his eyes. "So you played the part of Ned?"

"Yeah. At first, my cousin wanted me to play the part of George, the sporty, tomboy chick. Said it wasn't really weird because the sporty one's name is George. I said I'd rather be Ned. She said that was weirder since she's my cousin, and that would make me her boyfriend." He stops talking and frowns. "It was kinda stressful playing the Nancy Drew game. But it helped me hone my craft."

My heart clenches. I don't think my heart can help it. He looks so serious. "Your craft?" I ask, trying to reclaim the thread of the conversation.

"Yeah. Thanks to Nancy Drew, I have excellent powers of deduction." He grins as he leans over to open the library door and motions for me to walk through ahead of him. I hesitate. I'd like to do circuits of the school with him for an hour instead of going into the library. The fact that this three-minute walk down the hall with Lucas was easily one of the highlights of my week is pathetic. Thinking about how pathetic I am makes me angry, and in the blink of an eye, my mood plummets again.

Lucas greets Mrs. Fry by name as we walk past the circulation desk.

"Hi, Lucas," she says. She smiles at me as well. "Hi, Hannah."

"The librarian already knows your name?" I whisper, as we pull out two chairs at a table by the window.

"Yeah, well, you know, I like to make friends with the important people as fast as I can."

I wonder if Dallyn and Allison are included in the group he considers the important people. Not to mention Marla and the petite blonde. "I saw you with a girl in the parking lot after school yesterday. You really do work fast." Damn! What is wrong with my filter?

"And you jump to conclusions," he says. He doesn't look at me as he unpacks his school bag.

What conclusion have I jumped to? Is he suggesting he doesn't work fast? Maybe he knew the blonde girl before he transferred here. Maybe they've been dating for years. I don't ask. I shouldn't have opened my big mouth in the first place. I cross my arms.

"Look, you don't have to do this. I'll be fine." He turns away, dropping the handout on the table. "It'll take me longer, that's all. You can go back to class."

When he takes a ruler out of his bag and places it on the paper, moving it down methodically as he reads each line, I groan and reach over to grab the page. He snatches it back. "I'll be fine," he insists.

"Man, you're stubborn."

"Did you just call me stubborn?"

"Look, do you want to get out of here by three or don't you? I'm sure blondie won't be too happy about having to wait for a lift home."

His jaw twitches and he frowns, glancing out the window and then at the clock. Finally, he sighs and hands me the paper.

I wait for him to stop fidgeting, and then I clear my throat and start to read. It's a story called "Hey, Come on Out." I studied it in eleventh grade. I read slowly, trying to use as much expression as I can. He watches me, his chin resting on his hand. When I get to the end, I pass the booklet back to him.

He stares down at it, his lips pursed. "That's a weird story. It's kind of out there."

"You're not supposed to take it literally. It's a metaphor. A really awesome extended metaphor."

"Yeah, yeah, extended metaphor . . . allegory. I figured that part out."

What the hell? Lucas knows what an allegory is? Sped, my ass. I want to track down Brett Calder and punch him in the throat. Lucas studies my face. I look away. I have to. His eyes . . . .

"You like English, right?" he asks.

"It's my best subject, I guess."

"I'd probably still be on the first page if you hadn't read it for me. It must be nice to be able to read so fast. You're lucky."

I want to tell him we have very different definitions of luck. Instead, I say, "You should probably get started on the questions."

He looks at me through narrowed eyes, but then he picks up his pencil and writes the title at the top of a piece of lined paper. I expect his writing to be messy, but it's not. He prints, the small careful letters escaping from the end of the pencil in a measured pace. I imagine him as a little boy, his tongue sticking out with the effort of not mixing up his *d's* and *b's*.

My heart. I have to get out of here. "I should go back to class." I don't move.

He looks at me again, his lips pressed into a flat line. He could be smiling if the rest of his face joined in. "Yeah, okay. Can you tell Mr. Vesters I'll stay here until the bell?"

"Sure."

"Oh, and thanks for the help."

I shrug. "Like I said, I did it to help Mr. V. I figured I'll get a few brownie points. You know. It's all about me, right?"

Now I move. I had the last word and have to get out quickly before he has a chance to reply.

Back in class, I flip through the writing module from the handbook, but I can't concentrate. I wish the computer system wasn't down. I need some keyboard therapy. For the first time ever, I count the minutes left in Writer's Craft and feel guilty for sneaking glances at the clock. I hope Mr. V. doesn't see me.

I don't just miss my keyboard. I miss Lucas's presence in the seat beside me.

This makes no sense.

It makes perfect sense.

Chapter 10

Uncomfortable

THE BELL RINGS, and I collect my books. Once the crowd at the door has cleared, I start to make my way out. Mr. V. stops me.

"Hannah? Do you have a minute?"

"I have to catch the bus—"

"I won't keep you. I wanted to thank you again for helping Lucas today and not making a big deal of it. Did everything go okay in the library?"

"I think so. I read the story and left when he was starting to work on the assignment. I'm sure he was fine. He seems smart."

"There's a common misconception that having a learning disability correlates to lower intelligence. That couldn't be further from the truth."

"Yeah, I can see that." If only the Brett Calders and Dallyn Wades of the world could see that.

"So how's your portfolio coming along?"

"Rough start," I admit. "I'll have it in by Monday, though." *Please don't ask me what I'm writing about.*

"Sounds good. Well, have a nice night."

"You too."

I emerge from the classroom to find the after school exodus well underway. At my locker, a blur of spandex passes me—four cheerleaders on their way to the field. Then two more green-and-white uniforms come toward me. The other four flew past too quickly for me to identify them, but these two have faces—faces with raccoon eyes.

Gotta love fake tans.

Marla, who is usually content to pretend I don't exist, glares at me and turns to keep looking at me with narrowed eyes as she passes. My heart rate escalates.

Allison loops her arm through Marla's and says, "It's okay, Mar. She's not worth it."

They walk away, ponytails swinging and hips shimmying.

Now what's the problem?

Whatever. Let them get all worked up about some imaginary drama. Instead of allowing them get to me, I grab my coat and slam the locker closed, then walk purposefully down the hall, trying to picture what I look like from behind.

The hair swingy thing you do when you walk was my second clue, in case you're wondering. All cheerleaders do that. It's like a secret code or something.

Do I really swing my hair? And what guy notices that sort of thing? Maybe blondie used to be a cheerleader, and that's why Lucas is so well-versed in their mannerisms. Or maybe she's never been one, and the two of them sit around laughing about how stupid cheerleaders are.

Or maybe they make out for hours and hours and they never talk.

No, I can't. I won't let myself. *One . . . two . . . three . . . four . . . .*

A few hundred footsteps later, I pass the lobby doors. It's still raining, so I jam my hands into my pockets, psyching myself up to get soaked again. Halfway down the hallway to the parking lot, Lucas leans against the wall by the doors with his arms crossed. He's with the blonde. She's putting on her coat. They'll run hand-in-hand toward the little red car . . . .

I consider retracing my steps to go out the front doors instead, but Lucas lifts his head. Our eyes meet for the briefest second. He grimaces and rests his head on the wall. Guess he doesn't want to introduce me to his girlfriend. I don't want to meet her either, but he's seen me, so there's no turning back now. I keep walking, my eyes fixed on the exit doors. Blondie suddenly turns and walks in my direction.

As she gets closer, I recognize her from an assembly before Christmas. She screeched so loudly that I thought someone was murdering her, and a couple of teachers escorted her out of the gym. Since then, I've noticed her in the hall between classes sometimes, pacing and talking to herself.

Is Lucas actually dating her?

She keeps coming as if she's going to crash into me, but then she turns abruptly and walks back toward Lucas. Then she spins around and heads toward me again, pivoting three feet in front of me and turning back to Lucas.

What's up with her?

"Hey." Lucas grabs her arm "We have to go."

"It's raining," she whines, shaking her arm free of his grasp.

"I know it's raining, but we have to go. Remember how we ran to the car yesterday? We'll do that again."

"I got really wet."

"But then we went home, and you dried off and got changed and everything was fine."

We went home?

Lucas turns to look at me. His lips are pinched, and his shoulders are drawn up. He holds up his hand and gives a reluctant wave. "Hey, Hannah."

"Hey."

He tilts his head toward the blonde. "Um, this is my cousin. Nancy."

His cousin. She's his cousin!

"Nance, can you say hi to Hannah?"

Blondie—Nancy—walks away, not even acknowledging my existence. She stops at the doors, looks out the window and rocks back and forth.

"Nancy hates rain," Lucas says. He continues to look at me without speaking, inviting a response. What does he expect me to say?

My brain fires on all cylinders. She's his cousin. "I'm not a big fan of rain myself," I say, watching Nancy rocking.

Lucas scratches the side of his face, glances at Nancy, then back at me. "Do you, uh, want a ride?"

Is he serious?

"I saw you heading for the bus yesterday," he explains. "You were soaked."

"It's okay," I blurt. "I'm used to it."

"She's totally harmless you know," Lucas says, watching Nancy. She's still rocking but now her lips are moving too. Anxious words float down the hall, but I can't hear what she's saying.

"She's giving herself a pep talk," he says. "Sometimes it takes a while." He walks over to her and stoops to meet her eyes. "Nance, we can't stay here all day. You want to get home to finish your homework so you can watch *Law and Order* later, right?"

Nancy stops rocking. Then her head snaps up and she's suddenly on the move, grabbing Lucas's hand, pushing the door open and dragging him through it.

"Are you coming, Hannah?" he calls.

The door slams shut behind them before I can answer. This is like reaching the end of a chapter with the biggest cliff-hanger ever. So many questions! I have to turn the page. I force my feet to a run, following them out the door into the rain.

As Nancy climbs in the passenger side of the red car, Lucas turns and sees me sprinting between cars. He opens the back door for me. I tumble into the back seat and pull the door closed. Lucas reaches over to the floor at Nancy's feet to grab a fistful of tissues. He hands them to her. "For your face," he says, peeling a clump of hair away from her cheek and tucking it behind her ear.

"Yuck, yuck, yuck," Nancy chants as she wipes her face. Then she starts wiggling. "I'm itchy."

Lucas takes her complaints in stride. "You'll be fine," he assures her, reversing out of the spot and then heading for the parking lot exit. He looks back at me between the two seats. "Where to?"

Like driving me home is no big deal. Like his cousin isn't freaking out beside him. Like I didn't infer an hour ago that his cousin was his girlfriend. Like I haven't said a million offensive and ridiculous things to him in the short time I've known him. "Um, left at the lights. I live past the mall."

"Gotcha."

"Right," Nancy says. "Turn right at the lights. Right, then left."

"We're gonna take Hannah home first, Nance."

"Turn right. Turn right! I want to go home. I'm itchy."

She scratches at her thighs, and Lucas casts me a worried look. "Do you need to get home by a certain time?"

I shake my head. My mother wouldn't even know if I didn't get home until midnight.

"If it's okay, I'll take Nance home first. Her legs are uncomfortable."

Dude, my whole freaking existence is uncomfortable. "Yeah, sure, whatever's easier," I say, shrugging. I've never felt less like shrugging in my life. *Whatever's easier?* It would have been way easier if I'd taken the bus, but it's too late for that now.

Nancy finally stops raking her fingernails up and down her jeans and settles into a steady stream of chatter. Her non-stop talk is kind of annoying, but it's less annoying than the scratching sound which was right up there with nails on a chalkboard in the grand scheme of annoyingness.

I have no clue who and what she's talking about, but Lucas nods as she talks, occasionally saying, "Uh-huh." Basically, he's letting her ramble. She's filling what could otherwise be an awkward silence, and both of them seem to have forgotten I'm in the back seat. This suits me fine. I need a chance to think.

What I really need to do is prepare myself for what will happen when Nancy's no longer in the car.

Lucas will drive me home.

There will be no one else in the car.

Lucas will drive me home, and we will be in the car alone.

As mild panic sets in, Lucas turns into one of those neighbourhoods where it's easy to lose track of where you are. Boulevards and crescents, left and right turns. If he pulled over and abandoned me on the side of the road, I'd have no clue how to find my way home.

Serious panic sets in.

After a final left turn onto a street lined with big, old oak trees, we pull into the double driveway of a two-storey house. Lucas presses a remote garage door opener on his sun visor, and as the door glides open, he slowly inches inside.

Nancy pushes open the car door before Lucas has put the car in park. He cuts the engine and hops out with her. "Say goodbye to Hannah, Nance."

Nancy mumbles something that might be, "Bye, Hannah." It might also be, "Bah humbug." But she doesn't look at me. She hasn't looked at me the entire time we've been together. I wave, a gesture she doesn't see. Lucas pokes his head back into the car.

"I'll be two minutes," he says. "You can move into the front if you want."

He follows Nancy, and as the door to the house swings shut behind them, he calls out a greeting. I imagine what he might say to whoever's inside. *I'm giving a friend a ride home. I'll see you later.*

Friend? That seems unlikely.

There's this annoying girl who sits beside me in Writer's Craft. For some reason,

I offered her a ride home. She helped me with an assignment. I guess I owe her one. Be back ASAP.

Or better yet . . . There's this girl at school who I've heard gives free lap dances. She's in the back seat of the car right now. Convenient, huh? I'm driving her home. Don't wait up.

Yes, that's much more realistic.

I suddenly realize the back seat is the last place I should be when he returns, and honestly, why did I get in this car in the first place? I climb out, contemplating my idiocy—wondering if it's too late to make a break for it and trying to remember if there were any city bus stops on the way here—when the door to the house reopens. Lucas appears, whistling, the car keys swinging from his fingers.

He stops when he sees me standing there, my school bag clutched to my chest, looking like the victim of a kidnapping who's ready to bolt at the first whiff of freedom. "You okay?"

He sounds so normal, so collected. He makes me feel like a complete psycho.

"Yeah, I was about to get in the front seat." I'm super calm. Totally normal. Not at all a freak.

He watches me walk around the rear of the car and climb in, and then he slides in beside me. Though he jams the keys back in the ignition, he doesn't start the car. He just sits there with his hands on the steering wheel. His face is flushed. Now, I want to ask him if he's okay, but I can't speak. My tongue is plastered to the roof of my mouth. Finally, he lets out a long breath.

"Asperger's." That's what he says.

"Ass burgers" is what I hear. My tongue unsticks itself from the roof of my mouth.

"What?"

"That's what's wrong with her. That's what you were going to ask me, right? What's wrong with Nancy?" There's an edge of defiance in his voice.

"I wasn't . . . I didn't . . . ." But I was. I totally did.

"When she was two, she was diagnosed with Asperger syndrome. It's a form of autism."

I've never heard of this thing that sounds like "ass burgers syndrome," but I know what autism is. What's the best way to respond? No amount of back pedalling will erase the conversation we had on

Monday in the library when that kid walked past with his educational assistant trying to steer him toward the doors.

He takes the short bus. That's what I told Lucas.

No wonder he got defensive. My face burns at the memory.

"It's okay to feel put off by her," he says. "I know she seems weird. She's really not. She can't help it. She's smart, but she's not good with people. Plus, she's got this thing called tactile sensitivity. It's hard to explain."

"Like when the tag in the back of your shirt itches your neck, and you have to cut it out so it doesn't drive you out of your mind?"

"Exactly!" He looks at me like I'm brilliant. "That's totally it." Then he smiles.

Remember when I said I didn't know why I got in the car in the first place? When he smiles at me like that, I know exactly why I got in the car.

Chapter 11

The Door

I TRY TO take my cue from Lucas.

Be normal, I tell myself. *Stay calm. Think of something inoffensive and pleasant to say.*

Not my forté.

"Hey, is Nancy the cousin who used to read your mom's Nancy Drew books?" I ask. Good. That was good. I give myself an imaginary pat on the back.

"Yeah. The summer she was eight, she came to stay with us for a week. She saw the books on my mom's bookshelf—the name caught her attention. She thought they were written especially for her."

"So that was the summer you started honing your craft—working on your deductive reasoning skills?"

"That's right."

I allow myself to relax. Who knew I was such an amazing conversationalist?

Lucas smiles, glances at me and clears his throat. "So, uh, you didn't accept my apology earlier."

"About what?"

"About the heliocentric thing. You made another smartass comment about it when you left the library this afternoon. You're still ticked off about it."

"I guess it kind of hurt my feelings." Hurt my feelings? What am I? Four?

"Okay, I really am sorry. I said the first thing that came into my head, and it wasn't very nice. It's easy to feel kind of lost at a new school."

"Well, will you look at that? Sorry-lost-boy is back."

"Huh. It's been four days since you called me that. I was kind of hoping you'd forgotten about it."

"All the more reason to remember," I say.

He laughs and shakes his head, and I can't help smiling a little too. "Hey, that must mean I'm forgiven," he says.

"What?"

"You're almost smiling. I figure you don't almost smile for just anything."

He's right. I don't almost smile for just anything. I banish the almost-smile as he backs out of the driveway. "I guess you're forgiven," I say. "I've been known to blurt out whatever comes into my head now and then myself."

"No way," he deadpans. "You?"

I look out the window and steel myself. "Like, I shouldn't have jumped to conclusions earlier. About Nancy being your girlfriend." With my fingers wrapped tightly around the straps of my backpack, I sneak a peek at him, but he's staring straight ahead.

He addresses the dashboard. "Instead of snapping at you, I could have told you that I didn't have a girlfriend—that the girl you saw me with was my cousin."

"So how come you didn't?"

He glances at me briefly before refocusing on the road.

"What would I have said? 'No, you're mistaken. Blondie isn't my girlfriend. She's my autistic cousin who hates to be touched, but who holds my hand when it's raining because she's afraid of getting wet and feels better knowing I'm there protecting her'?"

His cheeks are pink again. I stare out the window, feeling like a supreme moron for a bunch of reasons, not the least of which is the fact that I'd been so certain he was plotting with Allison and Dallyn to make my life miserable. That seems incredibly far-fetched now. I can't think of anyone he'd be less likely to buddy up with. Sure, he talked to Dallyn in the hall, but having a conversation with someone between classes doesn't automatically mean you're best friends forever.

What was I thinking?

We don't talk about Nancy anymore. In fact, we don't talk at all for the longest time. There are so many clichés about silence, and because we're not talking, they all start running through my head.

Silence is golden. I wouldn't call our silence golden. There's something stagnant about it, something murky.

The silence was deafening. No, it's not deafening either. My thoughts are deafening. The questions I want answers to are loud and all-encompassing. I want to know what he was talking to Marla about earlier. I want to know if he really got in big trouble at his old school, and if so, what happened. I should respect his privacy. I shouldn't be nosy. I should and shouldn't be a hundred things.

"Do you and your family live with Nancy's parents?" This might sound like an innocent question to him. It's not. It's an invitation to spill.

He shakes his head. "No. Just me. I'm here until June. Then I'll go back home."

Hmm. Not nearly enough detail. "Because you got in trouble at your old school?" With these nine words I go from innocent conversationalist to nosy interrogator in three seconds flat.

Lucas doesn't answer, but he clenches his jaw the same way he did earlier when we were in the library and he was annoyed with me.

"So, what happened?" I'm digging now and I hate myself, but I can't help it.

His jaw twitches again. "Misunderstanding."

One word. That's it. I could scoff at him and make some flippant comment. *That's what they all say.* I bite my tongue.

I know a thing or two about misunderstandings. I don't say that either. Saying that would invite questions I'm too afraid to give him answers to. So a five-syllable word hangs in the silence between us while a two-syllable word taunts me from the back of my mind: "coward."

During the last few minutes in the car, the only conversation between us consists of me giving Lucas directions to my neighbourhood. When we pull into my driveway, I'm self-conscious. My house is so small compared to his aunt and uncle's house. Plus, now he knows where I live. And how will we act tomorrow?

He parks and turns to look at me. "So, can I add you on Facebook?"

"I don't have Facebook."

"Really? How about Instagram? Twitter?"

My spine stiffens. "I don't have a Twitter account."

"Are you saying that so I'll leave you alone?"

I shake my head. I have a good reason for hating Twitter. *Please don't leave me alone.*

I can't admit either of these things. "Is it a crime not to like Facebook and Twitter?"

"Do you have a phone, at least?"

"Yes, I have a phone." The snark is back in my voice. I'm not stupid. Intellectually, I know my snarkiness is a defensive mechanism. I'm also not stupid enough to offer him my number, as much as I'm dying to. The only thing I want to do in the whole world is give him my number, which is why I clamp my mouth shut and start gathering my things.

He sighs. "You're hard work, you know that?"

"Feel free to quit any time." I pop the car door handle.

"Someone told me today that I should quit," he says. "Quit hanging out with you, that is."

I stare at him. "Someone? Who?"

He frowns. "Dirty-blond hair. Kinda bouncy. Fake tan."

Allison? But Allison's hair is platinum blond, almost white. No one would describe it as dirty blond. *Bouncy?* "Marla?"

He snaps his fingers. "Marla. That's it. I couldn't remember her name."

"She told you to quit hanging around me?"

"In a roundabout way, I think so. Weirdest conversation ever."

"What did she say?" This is called morbid curiosity.

"Something about since I'm new I don't know the scene, but she's noticed me talking to the wrong people, and I should be careful who I hook up with. She said she'd be happy to introduce me to the right people since she's got connections."

Bitch! I want to ram her pompoms down her throat. Maybe force-feed her some cod liver oil to help them slide down. "That sounds like good advice," I say. "You should listen to her."

"I don't think so."

"Is that what you told her?"

"No. I think I said I'd have my people get in touch with her people. She seemed to think that was a riot. Then I split. I had to get to class."

I remember the look on Marla's face as I walked by them earlier between classes. She was giggling like a loon, and I thought he was accepting her invitation to prom. Apparently not. "I guess you'd better get in touch with your people, then." My hand tightens around the strap of my bag.

"My people are busy right now." He frowns. It's that serious face he gets when he's about to say something that'll make my heart clench. "They're trying to get in touch with your people. Your people aren't co-operating."

Yep. My heart. He's got a direct line to my chest cavity. How does he do that? I shake my head. "I don't have people."

"Everyone has people," he insists. His eyes lock onto mine, and my heart cartwheels sideways. I can't do this.

"Um, look, I have to go. Thanks for the ride."

I clamber out of the car, fumbling for my house key. A car door opens and slams shut, and then he's traipsing up the steps and standing beside me on the porch.

"What?" I say, giving him half my attention as I pull open the storm door. "Shouldn't you get home?"

"Yeah, probably. I told my uncle I'd be right back."

"Well, don't let me hold you up."

"It's just—I thought maybe . . . ." He peers intently at the mailbox

"You really don't know how to take a hint, do you?" I ask.

He sighs and jams his hands in his pockets. His narrowed eyes flicker to mine again. "When you knock on a door and no one answers, what do you do?"

"What? What door?"

"Come on, this is a metaphor. You love metaphors, right? You knock on a door and no one answers. What do you do?"

"I have no idea what you're talking about." I'm lying. He's right, I do love metaphors, and I know exactly what he's talking about. I turn my house key, and the deadbolt snaps open.

"The way I see it," he says, ignoring the key in the door and my foot on the step, both signalling my imminent escape, "if no one answers, you could walk away, assuming there's nobody home, or you could knock again, in case the person is home, but didn't hear you."

I jiggle my knee against the storm door. "What if someone's home, but they don't want to answer the door?"

"Then you keep knocking until they change their mind. Or you could try the doorbell. Maybe even tap on a window."

I want to tell him there is no doorbell and although there may be windows, they're all boarded shut. I don't. I thank him again for the ride and quickly duck inside, leaving him alone on the porch. I slam the door and lean against it for the longest time, coat and shoes on, backpack still slung over my shoulder.

He doesn't knock. He doesn't ring the doorbell. There are no taps on the window.

What Lucas had described metaphorically has suddenly taken on wildly literal proportions in my mind.

Five minutes go by before I hear the car start and back out of the driveway.

Once I'm sure he's gone, I turn and bolt the door.

Chapter 12

Protocol

THANK GOD MOM left macaroni and cheese for dinner instead of some meaty casserole. The lump in my throat makes chewing and swallowing soft noodles challenging enough. Even *Jeopardy!* can't bring me out of my misery.

The events of the day—watching Lucas interact with his cousin and seeing what he's really like—have brought me face-to-face with the truth. Lucas isn't in cahoots with Dallyn and Allison. Not one little bit. I'd been an idiot to think so. Concluding this begs the question: why am I so miserable?

Because I overthink things. That's why. I'm alone inside my own head so much that I can't help overthinking. As soon as I've decided once and for all that Lucas isn't Allison's puppet, the next question to ponder is why he's been so intent on getting in my face. Earlier he said he was simply trying to get to know me—to make new friends. But why me? What's he really after?

He may not be buds with Dallyn, but that doesn't mean he hasn't heard the rumours about me. Maybe he's desperate for a quick bump and dump, and I seem to be an easy target. That must be the reason for his attention.

I'd like to believe otherwise—would love to get swept away in amazing door-knocking metaphors and lured in by his amber eyes and heart-wrenching one-liners—but I can't let him in. There's no way Lucas hasn't heard about my infamous New Year's activities. Everyone knows. Even the teachers know. Sure, they were out of the loop at first, but juicy stories like that have a way of spreading.

I wasn't surprised to find out the teaching staff had caught wind of the Twitter fiasco. What surprised me the most was how long it took. Let's face it, bullying is a hot topic. Using social media to do it is incendiary.

A little over a week-and-a-half after the pictures spilled onto Twitter in January, I'd already started my new routine of invisibility. I adapted so quickly to my new normal that when my homeroom teacher handed me an appointment slip from the guidance office, I assumed I was being called in to discuss college applications or something.

In the guidance reception area, the secretary greeted me and ushered me into Mrs. Palmer's private office. Mrs. Palmer invited me to sit down. Then she closed the door and gave me this weird searching look. "How are things going, Hannah?" she asked.

"Fine." I squirmed a little in the seat. "Is this about college apps? I filled everything out and submitted all my forms by the deadline—"

"I'm glad you have all your paperwork in order for college, but no, that's not why I called you down here."

"Oh."

"Are you sure everything's going okay? Nothing you'd like to talk about?"

She reached across her desk, dragging a file folder closer. She tapped on it with her fingernails. The glossy edges of several eight by ten photographs poked out the side of the folder. There was no mistaking the content of the photographs.

She knew. Not only did she know, but she had copies of the pictures. How did she get those? And what did she expect me to say? *Oh, okay, everyone knows I wore a hot pink lacy bra on New Year's Eve and thinks I'm a lap-dancing, boyfriend stealing whore. Guess it wouldn't hurt to talk about it.*

"I gather you've been having some problems for the last couple of weeks, Hannah?"

I stared at a tell-tale sliver of photograph spilling from the folder for a few seconds. When my voice emerged, resigned is the only way to describe it. "Where did you get the pictures?"

"We received an anonymous letter yesterday indicating that you've been bullied on Twitter. Twitter usernames and the identities behind them were revealed and the pictures were attached."

I pointed to the folder and tried to meet her eyes. "Hey, it's really not that big of a deal. Whoever posted them on Twitter deleted the account. The pictures are all gone." My attempts to shrug the incident off were futile.

"Hannah, this is a very big deal. Using social media as a defamation tool is a serious offense. We can't simply pretend it hasn't happened."

I wrapped my arms around myself, squeezed my eyes shut and rocked back and forth, trying to convince myself none of it was happening.

"Well, I guess that answers my question about whether you were the one who wrote the letter," Mrs. Palmer said.

"No way." I shook my head. "There's no way I'd do that. If anyone finds out you know about all this, I'm dead."

"I'm sure that's an extreme way of putting things—"

"No it's not! You don't know what she's capable of."

"I assume you're talking about Allison Dawson?"

"I didn't say that. I didn't mention her name."

"You didn't have to," Mrs. Palmer said, tapping the file folder. "Whoever sent this was very informative."

"You can't say anything. Please don't say anything." I was verging on desperation.

"We have to, Hannah. If people aren't called to account for their actions, they'll continue to think this sort of thing is okay. It's not okay. The school board has strict cyberbullying guidelines. We have a protocol to follow."

"She'll deny everything. She'll say she's being framed. You can't prove she posted those pictures. She used a fake name."

"I don't think that will be an issue. The police have experts who can trace IP addresses."

That's when panic set in. "You're calling the police?"

"That depends."

"On what?"

"On what really happened that night. Were you violated in any way? Did they hurt you?"

I shook my head, trying not to bring the events of that night too clearly into focus. "I left right after the pictures were taken. Please don't call the police."

"We'll have to see how forthcoming Allison is," Mrs. Palmer said.

"I wish you wouldn't make a big deal of this. Okay, it was awful for a couple of days, but it's better now. Really. Everyone's ignoring me. I'm cool with that."

She sat there, immoveable as a brick wall. There would be no reasoning with her. That's when I started crying.

My tears were wasted. Protocol won.

The guidance department started hauling kids in to find out exactly what happened on Twitter. For once in their lives, Allison and Dallyn used their meager brains, choosing to co-operate instead of making things worse for themselves. In the end, the police weren't contacted, but school suspensions were doled out.

Both Allison and Dallyn were hit with five-day "vacations" and Allison was stripped of her cheer squad captainship. The squad's been without a captain ever since. Administration decided that holding another election for the position would stir up more drama.

No kidding.

When Allison returned after her suspension, we had to work out a conflict resolution plan, and then our second semester schedules were rearranged so we wouldn't be in any of the same classes.

Of all the consequences Allison faced, the one that hit home the most was losing her spot as cheer squad captain. She placed the blame squarely on my shoulders. In fact, despite the guidance counsellors' constant use of the term "anonymous tip," everyone assumed I'd ratted Allison out. While Allison lost her title, I gained a new one. Now in addition to being a skank, I was a dirty nark.

Awesome.

Chapter 13

The Dawn

AFTER SPENDING ANOTHER long night thinking back on the events of January—trying to guess what Lucas thinks he might get from me—I feel even more defensive when I arrive at school on Friday morning. It was stupid of me to accept a ride home from him. Now he'll think he's making inroads.

Luckily, he isn't hanging around in the front lobby waiting for me. Maybe he's given up for good. A sliver of guilt flickers in the back of my mind for the way I treated him after he'd gone to all the trouble of driving me home. Feeling guilty won't accomplish anything, though. Guilt makes me vulnerable. Vulnerability is unacceptable.

Lucas was right on the money with his door metaphor. I am so afraid of feeling exposed, it actually seems kind of understated. I'm not simply hiding behind a locked door. I'm in a locked room surrounded by a fortress, quite content to be left alone.

When I turn the corner after visiting my locker, Lucas is leaning against the wall outside Mr. Murray's room. My contentment fizzles.

He smiles and waves. How does he do that? How can he cast aside the way I treated him yesterday and smile at me as if I'm the most awesome person he's ever met? He can't be real. He must be desperate. "How did you know I'd be here?" I ask him, holding my books protectively against my chest.

"My people kick ass. They're totally on the ball. You always come straight here in the morning."

"In other words, you've been spying on me."

"Noticing someone doing something and spying are very different things."

"So you're all about the semantics?"

"And you're all about the big words. Must be all the reading."

"Must be." I need to escape. I want to get into my classroom, but he's blocking the door.

"Hey, speaking of reading, I have a book recommendation for you," he says. "Something to read at lunch hour today."

He takes a folded piece of paper out of his pocket and hands it to me. In his careful printing are three numbers and three letters. 821 DIC. "I was going to slip it into your locker," he says, "but I thought that might freak you out."

"Gee, you think?" I look at the paper again, curiosity getting the better of me. "What's 821 DIC?"

"It's the Dewey Decimal number for a library book. Check it out. You'll like it."

The fact that he knows the term "Dewey Decimal number" further fuels my interest, but I won't let him get his hooks into me. Besides, today's book is already established—331.1.

I hand him back the slip of paper. "Thanks, but I don't need it."

He huffs out a ragged breath. I'm frustrating him to no end. This is good. The warning bell rings, and without looking at him, I duck through the door, anxious to settle in before everyone else arrives.

I keep my sights set on the clock for the duration of math class. The minute hand moves in slow motion. I'm clicking my pen by 9:15. It's going to be a long morning. I occupy myself with calculations that have nothing to do with curvilinear asymptotes. If I click my pen for every second that passes between now and lunchtime, I'll have to click it 7,200 times. Either my pen will break, or someone in the class will kill me.

I'm already getting dirty looks, and I've only been clicking for three minutes. That's a mere 180 clicks. I glower at the dirty lookers, but I put my pen down because honestly, I'm even getting on my own nerves.

I need to find 331.1. That's what I've been thinking about all morning. As I dodge around clumps of people loitering in the hall, 821 DIC chirps in the back of my mind. I ignore the chirping and loitering clumps. "331.1," I mumble, pushing open the library doors and crossing to the stacks.

I find myself in the 800s. What am I doing in the 800s?

821 DIC. That's why you're in the 800s.

The chirping voice is aggravating as hell. It's right, though. I'm all about 821 DIC. I can tell myself I'm in a locked room in a fortress as much as I want, but the truth is, Lucas is scaling the wall of my fortress. He probably has a key to my locked room clamped between his teeth.

I wonder if he's somewhere in the library watching me. I do a quick perimeter walk and look down each row of stacks, but I don't see him anywhere. Good. I return to the 800s, quickly locate the 821s and scan the alphabetical collection of books. 821 DIC is a tiny book jammed between two huge anthologies near the end of a shelf. I don't touch it. I tilt my head to read the spine. It's a book of poems by Emily Dickinson.

The voice in my head chirps again. *Check it out. You'll like it.*

That's when I realize the chirping voice belongs to Lucas. If his voice is in my brain, maybe he's not climbing the walls of the fortress, after all. Maybe he's already inside. Or maybe I'm developing some sort of multiple personality disorder.

I shake my head to quiet the voice and pull the book from the shelf. It's falling apart, the pages yellow with age. A folded piece of paper sticks out of the middle, and I flip to it, looking around again to make sure I'm alone.

The paper marks page seventy-six. It's a handwritten note:

> *I like this poem. I read it at my old school. It reminds me of you, especially the first two lines. If you decide to open the door, feel free to text me to let me know. I'm probably still on the porch, but I might be napping (you tire me out).*
>
> *Lucas (aka Sorry-lost-boy)*

At the bottom of the note, he included his cellphone number. I smile. Shocking, I know, but I can't resist. I also can't resist reading the poem. Right there in the stacks, leaning against the bookshelf, I read the poem Lucas remembers from his old school—"Not Knowing When the Dawn Will Come"— a poem that reminds him of me. I read it a couple of times, but then I focus on the first two lines.

Not knowing when the Dawn will come,
I open every Door....

I stagger backward against the shelf and close my eyes to see Lucas's face. I imagine his expression—the one that makes my heart clench. A guy who's looking for an easy score with a girl doesn't make a special trip to the library early in the morning to find a book and mark a page with a note about lines in a poem that remind him of her—two lines that practically beg the girl to let him in and give him a chance.

I'm struck with the overwhelming realization that I don't care if he knows I wore a hot pink bra on New Year's Eve. I don't care that he got in trouble at his old school, I don't care that he has a learning disability, and I don't care that he has a cousin with autism. Lucas looks after his cousin—is fiercely protective of her. If I'd let him, Lucas might pull me into that bubble of protection.

Lucas has scaled the wall and landed safely on the other side. The key to my locked room—the one that was clamped between his teeth—is now wiggling in the lock.

I head straight for the circulation desk. Mrs. Fry smiles as I slide the book across the counter.

"You're the second person today who's asked about Emily Dickinson books." She scans the barcode and slips a due date card in the back.

"Really?"

"Yes, this morning, the boy you were in here with yesterday—your friend, Lucas—he was trying to track down a book of Dickinson's poetry as well. He was very intent on finding something."

My friend, Lucas.

"He seems like such a nice boy," Mrs. Fry adds as she hands me the book.

I nod. "I think maybe you're right."

The key turns, and with a loud click, the bolt slides open.

For the first time in a few months, I don't spend the entire lunch hour in the library. Instead, I slip the book of poetry into my bag and venture out into the hall in search of Lucas.

I have no clue where Lucas spends his lunch hour. Maybe he goes out for lunch. Maybe he goes to his aunt and uncle's house. That seems unlikely. He'd barely make it back in time.

The cafeteria? Oh God, I haven't been in the caf since . . . yeah. Then.

I navigate the halls warily, my confidence crumbling at the bottom of the stairs, where the smell of fried food and something spicy assaults me. It's an odour I used to associate with belonging. Mr. Vesters would call that an "incongruous correlation."

I cling to the stair railing to steady myself, visualizing what I'll do when I'm inside the cafeteria. Will I shrink invisibly against the wall, scanning the room for Lucas's face, or walk boldly between tables, hoping to find him sitting alone and eager for company?

I take a few cautious steps forward. A commotion of shouting and garbled voices at a table near the entrance slows me. I stop just inside the doors. People peer across crowded tables toward the source of confusion, a table a few feet away from the entrance filled with Spec Ed kids. Lucas's cousin is standing at the end of the table trying to pull her arm free of the educational assistant who's hanging on to her. I quickly scan the table, but I don't see Lucas anywhere.

"Let me go!" Nancy shrieks. "I have to go!"

This is exactly what happened during the Christmas assembly. I have no clue what caused her to wig out that day, but this time, I know exactly what's going on. She's rubbing a wet patch on her pant leg and an empty water bottle lies near her feet.

"I have to go!" she shouts again.

The EA holding Nancy's arm splits her attention between Nancy and the Spec Ed kids at the table. One of them stands and rocks back and forth, saying, "Sammy didn't do it," over and over again. The educational assistant tries to hold on to Nancy and sooth the rocking kid at the same time.

"Don't touch me," Nancy pleads, still plucking at the woman's hand, trying to pry it off her arm. "Stop touching me! I don't need your help!"

I take two steps forward, but then I see Allison, Marla, Dallyn and Brett laughing and pointing at Nancy from the cafeteria lineup, as though her hysteria is highly entertaining. Brett holds up his phone. Is he taking pictures?

What a jerk.

I hear Lucas's voice. *I know how it feels, that's all. To be made fun of. For something you can't help.*

Nancy can't help wanting to crawl out of her skin when her clothes get wet. It's not her fault. I take another quick look at my former "friends" in the caf line. Brett has disappeared into the servery to get food. But Allison and Marla still look my way, chins lifted.

I'm desperate to do something. I should help Nancy, but Allison and Marla stare at me, and I can't move. It's as if their eyes are nailing me to the spot.

"Didn't you hear me? I said don't touch me!" Nancy screeches and stomps her feet. "I want to go home. I need to go—"

She wrenches her arm free and bolts past me and out the door. The educational assistant meets my gaze and casts me a pleading look. "Hey, can you follow her?" she asks. "Try to make sure she gets to the office or the Special Education room or somewhere safe?"

I lift one foot and then the other, happy to discover I'm not bolted to the floor after all. I nod at the EA and turn, running after Nancy. I have to run. I have no choice. Nancy's not exactly strolling. I remain a few paces behind as she clomps up the stairs. On the main floor, she makes a beeline for the Special Education room, but instead of going inside, she paces in front of the lockers spanning the wall to the left of the Spec Ed room door.

Nancy seems completely unaware of my existence as she strides back and forth. She flaps her hands around and mutters to herself about being wet and itchy. People peer over their shoulders at her as they pass by. I can't just stand there while she behaves like a raving lunatic. I glare at a few of the gawkers, and they shrug and move on.

I point to the Spec Ed classroom. "Nancy, do you want to go inside, or do you want to go look for Lucas?"

She ignores me like I'm not even a blip on her radar. If I grab her to try to get her attention, she'll wig out again. I'm out of my depth. Keeping an eye on Nancy, I peek through the Special Education room door. A few kids work at a small bank of computers along the windows, and a teacher moves between them, pausing to point at one screen or another. More importantly, though—and praise God!—Lucas is at the front of the room, collecting pages from the printer.

His lips are pursed like he's whistling, blissfully ignorant of the fact that his cousin is out here in the hall having a hissy-fit. Before I can turn the doorknob, he looks up and smiles at me. The smile transforms his whole face. Actually, I think it transforms his whole body—his shoulders lift as he grins.

He abandons the pages at the printer. I open the door, and he leans on the frame and crosses his arms. "Hey, you. Aren't you supposed to be in the library?"

"I went to the caf. I was looking for you."

His face registers surprise and then genuine pleasure. "You were?"

"Yeah, but I found Nancy instead." I step back and beckon him out. Nancy has ceased doing laps. She's leaning against the lockers, scratching frantically at the wet patch on her pants. The traffic in the hall has returned to a normal pace, interest in Nancy's activities waning now that she's abandoned the pacing and shrieking.

Lucas brushes past a couple of people to reach Nancy's side. I follow.

"Nance, what happened?" he asks.

"Idiot Sammy poured her idiot water all over me!" Nancy wails. "I'm itchy. I want to go home."

I gather Nancy's word of the day is "idiot." I can't help approving, having a bit of a soft spot for that one as well—second to "pinhead," of course.

"I'm sure it was an accident." Lucas bends down and uses the same calming tone he'd used in the car. "Sammy didn't mean to spill water on you."

Nancy looks up at him with fire in her eyes. "She didn't spill it. She poured it! She's an idiot!"

"Okay, well, maybe we can get you dried—"

"I want to go home. You have to take me home."

"I have classes this afternoon, Nance," Lucas tries to explain. "I can't just pick up and—"

"I'm all wet! I want to go home!"

Nancy's shriek is deafening. Like, a cats-and-dogs-in-the-neighbourhood-are-covering-their-ears-and-whimpering kind of deafening. I take two steps backward, my shoulder blades crashing into the locker behind me. My horror comes to complete fruition when Marla, Brett, Allison and Dallyn emerge from the stairwell in time to hear Nancy's ear piercing shriek echo up and down the hallway.

"Holy crapballs, shut up, freak," Brett says, grimacing as the four of them make their way toward us.

Allison and Marla laugh into their hands. Dallyn throws his arm around Allison's shoulder, looking back at us blankly as they pass.

Lucas scowls, his hands tightening into fists. "Asshole." He clenches and unclenches his hands a few times, and then he shakes his head, takes a few deep breaths and returns his attention to Nancy.

"I'll take you home, Nance. Go to your locker and get your stuff, okay?"

Nancy nods and speed walks down the hallway, stopping at a locker in front of the science labs.

Lucas watches her rummage through her locker. He sighs and crosses his arms again. "Sorry if that embarrassed you."

"It's okay." *I'm used to it.* I look at the floor, the wall, his crossed arms, and finally, up. At his eyes. "I read the poem."

His eyes open wide, his eyebrows arching above them. "You did? I didn't think—"

"I liked it." I barrel along, wanting to get the words out before I lose my nerve. "I mean, I'm not sure I get it, but I liked the first two lines."

"That's cool. I didn't think you were interested."

"I was curious, I guess."

"I guess. Well, that's good."

Nancy slams her locker and starts walking back and forth and scratching again. Lucas rubs the back of his neck. "Sorry. I have to go."

"Do you think she's okay?"

"She'll be fine as soon as she's home and she can get changed."

"Will you be back? In time for Writer's Craft, I mean?" I'm trying to use my just-out-of-casual-interest tone, but I sound much more than casually interested.

And there you have it. In the blink of an eye, I've made myself vulnerable. He could hurt me so easily now.

I wait for him to wield his upper hand—to lord his new power over me—but he doesn't. He simply frowns and says, completely matter-of-fact, "I'm not sure. It depends if my uncle's too busy to deal with Nance. Look, hang on a sec."

He darts back inside the classroom, retrieves his pages from the printer, taps them into a pile and staples the corner. He hands me the clutch of papers. "Can you give this to Mr. Vesters for me if I don't make it back? It's due today. I don't want him to think I'm ditching or something to get out of handing in my work. Maybe you could explain what happened?"

"Sure. I guess."

"Thanks. So, I'll talk to you later?"

"Yeah, later."

"Hey, did you keep the note I left in the book?" He takes a few steps backward.

"Yeah, I think." Ha! I try to look noncommittal, like I don't know that the note is pressed carefully between pages seventy-six and seventy-seven in Emily Dickinson's book of poetry—like I can't still feel that thin sheaf of paper between my fingers, recalling with vivid detail the way his words and the poem had affected me, literally making me stumble against the bookshelf.

He holds out his hands, his thumbs typing on an imaginary phone. "Text me." He turns and collects his cousin, coaxing her down the hall.

I shake my head and then nod, and then shake my head again as the two of them disappear around the corner. I open my mouth and close it a couple of times, no words coming out. I'm glad he can't see any of this. I must look like a confused fish.

Lucas doesn't come back to school. I can't resist the temptation to flip through his assignment before I hand it to Mr. Vesters. Even a quick read-through confirms what I already suspected. Lucas is no dummy. His spelling is all over the place, but he knows what he's talking about. After explaining why Lucas isn't in class, I retreat to my computer, grateful that it's up and running again so I can write.

Without Lucas beside me to jiggle his leg, shake the mouse and be a general all-round distraction, I can focus the way I used to. I'm not implying that I don't wish he was here. There's no point pretending anymore. I feel his absence acutely, so I seek refuge in my writing, disappearing amid the flow of words.

By the time class winds down, I've basically finished my portfolio assignment—three solid rough drafts ready for revising and editing over the weekend. In the end, I decided to write about how my dog died when I was eight years old, describing the events in an interview, a news report and a eulogy. I know it's not the best portfolio I've ever done, but it's definitely my most inventive.

I've never had a dog.

Chapter 14

Paranoid

I'M USED TO weekends that stretch endlessly before me in the same way a long, white page taunts me when I've got writer's block. Friday nights are the worst. On Friday nights, I'm at the very, very top of that blank page. Saturday nights are awful too, but at least by then I'm halfway down the page. The boredom of several months of empty weekends makes me look forward to going back to school on Mondays.

Now that I've let down my guard, and Lucas has his foot stuck in the door, I'm even more eager for the weekend to be over, so I can speak to him again. Although, really, I don't need to wait until Monday to speak to him again. I have his cell phone number. Etched in my memory.

The ball is in my court.

I'm on deck.

I'm all teed up and checking my grip . . . .

Why am I defaulting to sports analogies? I'm watching *Jeopardy!* and one of the categories, "The World According to Sport," is apparently driving my thought processes. I'm not super-interested in sports trivia, so while some guy named Carl knocks the category out of the park, I throw on some comfy sweats and then root around in the fridge for something to eat for dinner. Mom left me sloppy joe fixings, but I'm not in the mood for slop. Go figure.

I'm chopping veggies for a stir-fry when the doorbell rings. Friday night. Must be the paperboy. Munching on a slice of red pepper, I fish around in the slush fund jar on the counter and come up empty. I schlep to the door and swing it open, prepared to tell the kid he'll have to come back another day.

It's not the paperboy who's standing on my porch.

It's Lucas.

Lucas is on my porch, and I'm standing there in my Friday night special—holey track pants and an extra-large hoodie. My hair is in the messiest ponytail ever and a piece of red pepper hangs out of my mouth. I look like a red-pepper-eating bag lady, and Lucas is standing on my porch. I've probably looked like a bag lady for the entire time I've known Lucas. The difference is, now I care.

He smiles and taps on the storm door glass. "Anyone home?"

Oh God. I push the pepper into my mouth, wipe my hand on my pants and open the storm door. I'd speak if I didn't have a slice of pepper jammed in my mouth. At least I think I would. I have no idea what I'd say, but something fantastically clever would come out, I'm sure.

He waves. "Hi. I took a chance you'd be here. Kind of a long shot on a Friday, I guess."

"Not really," I say, as I choke back the pepper.

"Can I—I mean would it be okay if . . . ?" He holds up a textbook. "I missed a whole chapter of history third period. I need some help . . . if you have some free time. I don't know . . . ."

Don't overthink, Hannah. Don't make a big deal out of nothing. "Um, sure. I guess."

I step back and he walks past me, puffing out a small breath that sort of sounds like "phew," as if he's surprised I didn't slam the door in his face.

I'm kind of surprised myself.

He enters the living room and drops his coat over the back of the armchair before tossing his textbook on the coffee table. He surveys the room with his hands on his hips.

Gee, make yourself at home.

"So, I thought you were going to text me," he says.

"I never said that."

"Oh. I thought you did."

"No. Well, maybe I did. I don't know. Anyway, I've been busy. Doing stuff." I look around the room.

He points to the TV. "Like getting caught up on game shows?"

"That's background noise," I scoff, waving a dismissive hand at the TV. "I was making dinner." I turn off the TV, as if I couldn't care less that the final *Jeopardy!* category is Medieval Castles, and head back into the kitchen, hoping all the vegetables lined up on the counter will be proof enough of my incredibly busy evening.

"Sorry. I guess this is a bad time," he says, hovering in the doorway.

"I can eat later. I'm not that hungry anyway."

I collect all the sliced veggies on a plate and stow it in the fridge.

"Where are your folks?" he asks me.

"My mom's at work. My dad's in New Zealand."

"New Zealand. Cool. Business trip?"

I lean against the counter and tuck a few stay locks of hair into my ponytail. "More like a life trip."

He frowns, watching me fuss with my hair. "What do you mean 'life trip'?"

"I mean my parents got divorced when I was five. He moved to New Zealand, met someone new, got married. He's there for life."

"Oh, gotcha." He settles his shoulder against the doorframe. "That sucks."

"It is what it is." It suddenly occurs to me that we're having a conversation, and I haven't said a single nasty thing in two minutes. That's got to be a record. Eager to continue, but not thrilled about discussing my parents, I change the subject. "How's Nancy?"

"Oh, she's fine. Her regular EA was away today, so Nance was a little off balance. She needs routine. Thanks again for helping her in the caf."

"I didn't really do anything." I shrug, feeling like a fraud accepting Lucas's gratitude. "All I did was follow her. No big deal."

"That's not true."

"What do you mean?" My eyes narrow automatically.

"I mean . . . ." He looks at the floor between us for a second and then back up to my eyes. "I mean, you could've taken off when she started freaking out. Everyone was staring, and you don't like being the centre of attention."

I snort. "That's kind of funny coming from someone who accused me of being self-centred a few days ago." So much for my record. It was a pleasant three minutes, while it lasted.

After a quick shake of his head, he pushes his shoulder off the doorframe and shoves his hands in his pockets. "When I said you were heliocentric, that's not what I meant, you know."

"No, I don't know." Yep, the snark is back.

"There's a difference between wanting everything to be about you and thinking everything's about you."

"Oh, so you're saying I'm paranoid? That's much better. Thank you."

Sighing deeply, he crosses the kitchen and leans against the stove. Now that he's mere feet away from me, I smell cologne. Why is he wearing cologne? He taps the counter, watching his fingers bounce on the laminate surface.

"Sometimes when bad shit happens to people, they assume everyone is out to get them," he says. "Paranoia is probably a logical response."

I cross my arms over my chest, trying to forget about his cologne and focussing on his words instead. "Bad shit? Meaning . . . ?"

"Meaning . . . ," He lets a beat pass then his eyes lock onto mine like a tractor beam. I can't look away. "Meaning, I know what those assholes did to you. On New Year's Eve."

There. He said it. He said it really quickly, as if he were afraid he might chicken out halfway through the sentence, but now it's out there. Confirmation. He knows. My mind races and freezes at the same time. I should say something, but I can't bring myself to be flippant with him. The alternative is honesty, but I'm not ready for the vulnerability associated with honesty.

"They are assholes," I say. Nice. Flippant honesty. Or is it honest flippancy? I'm not sure. Either way, it's a fabulous compromise.

He smiles, but there's a sadness behind his eyes. "They were your friends, though, right? The tanned twins and their blockhead boyfriends, I mean."

I don't tell him Dallyn and Allison are the only ones actually dating. It's not important. I probably shouldn't commend him for his excellent use of alliteration in describing the four dumbasses either, although I do take a few seconds to appreciate his description.

"Depends on your definition of 'friend,' I guess," I finally say.

"I guess. You know you're not the first person who's been screwed over because of the people you hang around with, right? I bet you won't be the last."

The energy in the room shifts. He's basically told me he doesn't care about what happened in January and that I should get over it—all without saying the actual words. His tone says, "been there, done that," and it reminds me of the problems he had at his old school. He got into trouble—had some sort of "misunderstanding" that I know nothing about. We're on an uneven playing field now. He knows about my past, but I don't know about his.

I'm not a fan of this dynamic.

"I'm sorry they did that to you," Lucas adds. His voice is gentle. Compassion rolls off him in waves. It's not just heart-clenching. It's gut-wrenching. He's killing me. I shake my head at the floor, swallow hard and look up again. "I don't really want to talk about it."

"I don't blame you." He clears his throat and tilts his head toward the family room. "So, my mom is picking me up from my aunt and uncle's at nine thirty to take me home for the weekend. Do you want to help me with history?"

He wanders out of the kitchen, and I follow him, thinking, *Is that it?* He knows everything. He doesn't care. I shouldn't care either. Let's not talk about it anymore. The End?

He picks up his history book and flips it open. "So yeah, if you could read over Chapter Eleven with me that would be great."

Yep, the subject is closed.

Lucas doesn't seem to care about what happened on New Year's Eve. He thinks Allison and Dallyn are assholes. On top of all that, he's looking at me with those eyes, and he's wearing cologne. I sit on the edge of the couch and shrug.

"Yeah, if you want. I mean, I'd love to help you." My voice sounds all breathy. What's going on? I'm so surprised by the sound of myself that I shrug again. The shrugging has to stop. He'll think I have some sort of tic. I already have enough off-putting mannerisms. Surely a tic would be the last straw.

He frowns and then moves swiftly to sit beside me. It's a decisive move, but the surprised expression on his face suggests that his legs have betrayed him. Now his whole body must be betraying him because, out of nowhere, he tosses the book on the coffee table, leans over and brings his face close to mine. His eyes flit down to my mouth, and then his lips press against mine softly.

Lucas is kissing me!

Lucas is kissing me and I'm not panicking. In fact, my arms snake around his neck, which is probably the exact opposite of panic. I'm fairly certain there's no one hiding in my hall closet, camera at the ready. That's most likely why I'm not panicking.

Lucas keeps kissing me, his face turning this way and that with each soft peck. His lips are soft and gentle. When I open my lips slightly, his tongue slips inside my mouth, taking me by surprise.

At first, I forget how to breathe, kind of like those first few seconds when you're snorkelling and you have to convince your brain that breathing through the tube won't result in imminent death by drowning. His tongue, a warm foreign wetness in my mouth is strange . . . but not bad. I take in some air and fit my mouth to his mouth, our tongues continuing to move together. I begin to feel warm. Very warm.

I lie back on the couch cushion, bringing him with me, still kissing him, pressing my chest against his at the same time. I'm getting dizzy, and a rolling heat moves through my body. I press against him, gasping for breath between kisses. I'm embarrassed by how loudly I'm breathing, but I can't stop myself. It's an amazing feeling. It's like eating birthday cake and opening Christmas presents and having tons of friends and getting an A in every subject on your report card, all rolled into one.

Our tongues find a comfortable rhythm. Miraculously, my nose isn't getting in the way as I always assumed it would. It's true what they say. This stuff does come naturally. I can't even bring myself to be self-conscious about my lack of experience. I keep on mindlessly rubbing up against him, and he certainly doesn't seem to care.

After kissing like this for a few minutes—or maybe it's hours, time has become irrelevant— Lucas's hand slips under my sweatshirt, his fingers tracing a line under my ribcage. I shiver and his mouth moves to my cheek, where his lips hover, warm breath fanning across my face. I clutch at his hair and open my eyes, suddenly curious to see his face. His eyes are scrunched shut and his cheeks are red. As he moves his hand higher, he finds my bra and slides his fingers across the fabric, squeezing gently. Before I have a chance to freak out or tell him to stop, he moves his hand back down to my stomach.

He swears quietly and shudders. Then he pulls away. I don't want him to pull away. I want to fit my curves to his taut muscles and feel him press back, but he's already gone, sitting up with a disgusted look on his face.

The shudder and his expression say it all. He's changed his mind.

I'm not good enough.

I try to disguise my disappointment, looking at him blankly, even though I'm still breathing heavily, and I can taste his mouth when I lick my lips.

"I should go," he says, clambering off the couch, tripping over himself and straightening his T-shirt as he moves.

I want to say, "Please don't go." That would reveal desperation, though, so I draw my knees up and wrap my arms around them.

"Yeah, totally. You should go," I say.

He grimaces and leans over to grab his history textbook. "It's okay. You don't have to show me out. I know the way."

I pull my knees even closer to my chest, but I don't bother to respond. Of course he knows the way out. No doubt, he planned his exit strategy the minute I opened the door.

If Nancy were here, she'd tell me I'm such an idiot.

Chapter 15

Apples and Trees

IT TAKES ME forever to fall asleep. I've barely nodded off when something bashes into the wall outside my door and jolts me awake. Mom. She giggles.

"Hey, be careful, Leanne," a man's voice says. She giggles again. She must be drunk.

My mother doesn't drink much. She doesn't hold liquor well at all, so when she is drunk, she's sort of useless. The idea of a strange guy being in the house while my mom's not in her right mind freaks me out. I've read books where girls have been molested by their mom's boyfriends. Those kinds of stories pop up in the news all the time, too.

Not one of the guys she's brought home has ever touched me, but the chances of something like that happening are probably higher if she's drunk. I crawl out of bed and prop my desk chair under the doorknob like they do in movies. I have no idea if it really works, but it's worth a try.

So much for sleeping now. Every sound becomes a strange man in the hall, creeping toward my room. Plus, in the darkness, I keep seeing the same thing: Lucas, his cheeks flushed as his warm hand reaches under my sweatshirt and then the look of disgust on his face afterwards. I roll over to escape the image, but Lucas's grimace merely follows me to the other side of my pillow.

I should have pushed him away as soon as he started kissing me.

I thought I couldn't hate myself more. Wrong again.

I don't feel at all rested on Saturday morning, and I can't figure out why I'm awake so early. Until an empty, painful sensation gnaws at my stomach. I'm hungry. All I ate last night was a slice of red pepper. And then Lucas rang the doorbell.

The ache in my chest amps up, rivalling the one in my stomach.

I unhook the chair from under the doorknob, feeling foolish for putting it there in the first place. Things always seem so dramatic in the middle of the night. Mom's snores rumble through the door as I pass her room on the way downstairs. She'll have a wicked hangover. . .

I stop at the bottom of the stairs. An unfamiliar leather jacket is draped over the armchair. It must belong to Mom's "friend."

That's where Lucas threw his coat last night.

Nope. I push that thought into the farthest corner of my brain. No thinking about Lucas allowed.

I won't think about his cologne or his eyes or his soft lips. I definitely won't think about the way he looked at me right before he left. Absolutely not. Breakfast is the first order of business. Breakfast and mindless TV shows.

Excellent plan.

I step off the last stair, turn toward the kitchen and freeze. My mother's "friend" stands in our kitchen, making a cup of instant coffee. Horror-stricken, I take a step back toward the safety of my room, but the floor creaks under my weight. The guy spins around and gapes at me. Bet he thought he'd see my mom and was on the verge of saying, "Hey, baby. Want some coffee?" Now there's no point trying to escape. Plus, my empty stomach is groaning for nourishment.

Wide-eyed, he makes a quick head-to-toe inventory as I walk into the kitchen. Did Mom even mention she had a kid? I pour a glass of juice and drink it, staring at him over the rim. Man, he's young. What is my mother doing? He is good-looking, though. I have to give her props. If I had one-tenth of her luck with guys, I'd be happy as a clam.

I sip the juice silently. It's kind of amusing to watch him squirm.

"Hey," he says finally, scratching the back of his head. "Sorry about this. I guess I kind of made myself at home. I really needed a coffee."

As soon as he speaks, I'm blindsided by the truth. I should have recognized him right away. I only met him briefly on New Year's Eve when he dropped some booze off at Allison's house, but he's an older version of his brother. He has the same mop of curly blond hair. He has his brother's eyes, too. I got a good look at those eyes when I sat on Dallyn's lap on New Year's Eve. And now his older brother stands in my kitchen staring at me with the same eyes.

I'm screwed.

"Sorry, if I seem a little shell-shocked," he says. "I thought you were Leanne."

You think you're shell-shocked? Dude, don't get me started on the landmine metaphors. "My mom doesn't really do mornings," I say, scrambling to figure out how to get him out of the house, pronto. "Give her another four hours."

"Yeah, she was kinda drunk last night. So, uh, she told me she had a kid, but I guess I didn't think—"

"I'd be closer to your age than she is?"

He half-snorts, half-chuckles. I turn around, grab the loaf of bread and put a couple of slices in the toaster. I don't want toast, but I have to eat something. Plus, I need a second to compose myself.

He has to leave, and he can't ever come back. Before he goes, though, he has to promise not blab about this to Dallyn. I've got no clue how to proceed. While getting hysterical and screaming, "GET OUT!" would be mighty cathartic, that likely wouldn't be the most effective approach.

"So, I guess this is weird for you, huh?" he says.

He's got a knack for understatement. "I'm not surprised to find a guy here, if that's what you mean. I heard your voice last night. And Mom tripping up the stairs."

"Yeah. She had some trouble walking."

You don't say. "She doesn't normally do that," I tell him, feeling the need to defend her, although God knows why.

"I didn't think so. She was a bit of a mess at the club. I drove her back here. Her car's still there. That's probably not very convenient for you guys. Maybe I should have left my car there instead . . . ." He trails off. I wish he'd keep rambling. His awkwardness is entertaining.

"Don't worry about it. She's working later. She'll probably take a cab in." See? I can be nice if I try really hard.

"Okay," he says. "That's good."

I butter the two pieces of toast and hand him one. He looks at it as though he's checking for mold. He's got good instincts. He finally takes a bite, washing the mouthful down with a swig of coffee.

"By the way, nothing happened last night. I slept down here. Your mom was drunk, so I just wanted to make sure she got home okay. I wasn't planning to stay. Guess I passed out on the couch . . . ." He waves the toast around and then takes another bite. His face turns red. "I wouldn't want you to think I took advantage of her or something."

"Well, that's very decent of you, Dean."

He stiffens and puts his mug down on the counter. "How'd you know my name?"

I immediately regret catching him off-guard. That won't earn me any brownie points, and he seems like a decent guy. I backpedal.

"Sorry, I just figured out who you are," I say. "I go to school with your brother. You look a lot like him."

His toast sort of wilts in his hand. "Seriously? For real?"

No, I'm making it up. Good one, right?

"Jesus." He gapes at me. "You're friends with Dall?"

"I said I go to school with him, not that we're friends."

"Right. Can't blame you for steering clear of him. That kid can be a real piece of work. Gets himself into all kinds of trouble. I keep waiting for him to grow up, you know?"

I don't know what to say, so I don't say anything. He misinterprets my silence.

"No, seriously, he can be a pain in the ass sometimes, trust me."

Sometimes?

"I'm not disagreeing. I do know him. He's a dick."

Dean guffaws, then clamps his hand over his mouth and glances at the ceiling, like he's afraid of waking Mom. His concern is totally unnecessary. You could swing a wrecking ball into her room, and she'd snuffle and roll over.

"You've hung out with him. So you do know what I'm talking about," Dean says, lowering his voice.

I turn to throw two more pieces of bread in the toaster. "It's been a while, but yeah, I know what you're talking about," I say, still addressing the toaster. "I haven't hung out with him since New Year's. I met you that night. You brought beer to Allison's house."

"Oh, right. You were there? I don't really remember. There were kids everywhere. They really trashed the place. I shouldn't have agreed to get Dallyn that beer. I figured if he had beer, he'd stay away from the harder stuff. He got wasted anyway. Allison did, too. Her parents went ballistic when they got home."

I shrug and butter the toast. "I wouldn't know. I left before the trashing started. That was . . . not a great night for me."

I hand him a second piece of toast and inspect my slice before taking a careful bite. When I look up at him, he's examining my face. He takes a swig of coffee, and then he slowly swings his mug forward, using it to point at me.

"Wait a second. You're that girl. The Twitter thing with the pictures. It's you."

I don't say anything. I look at my toast again. It's all the confirmation he needs.

"Jesus." He whistles and puts down his mug again, still staring at me. His eyes drop to my chest. A reflex, I'm sure—apparently one that runs in his family. I cross my arms. "Did you . . . I mean . . . Are you okay?" he asks.

Am I okay? So few people asked me this question in the wake of New Year's Eve that I have no idea how to answer it.

Am I okay?

Dean shakes his head as he looks me up and down. "I mean, it must have been embarrassing. High school's bad enough without someone doing something like that to you. In your graduating year, too."

"It was months ago. I'm over it. I go to school, mind my own business, come home. It's all good."

"That doesn't sound so good to me."

"No, you're wrong. The status quo works. Not rocking the boat. Staying under the radar is cool, you know?"

He looks out the window and snorts. "If Dallyn was here right now, I'd punch his lights out. He's such a prick."

"Look, don't tell him you were here—that you brought my mom home. It wouldn't be good. For me, I mean."

"He should know what he's done to you. How he's ruined your graduating year. He doesn't think about anyone but himself. Well, himself and his bitchy little girlfriend."

No, no, no! You don't understand! I blink at him desperately. "Please? Don't say anything." My tone is plaintive. I'll cry if I have to. Hey, if I can write about my eight-year-old self mourning an imaginary dog, I'm sure I can fabricate a few tears at the prospect of very real humiliation.

He frowns and shakes his head. "Someone should put him in his place."

I could suggest a few places I'd like Dallyn put. Hell ranks high among them. But I have to consider my life—my day-to-day existence for the rest of the school year. It's not worth it. "Can you let it go? I'm fine. Really."

Dean relents. Reluctantly. He says he'll keep quiet about his sleepover date, and I convince him that he'd be better off leaving right away, assuring him that my mother won't wake up until noon and that she'll be hung over and not the best company. After chugging back the last of his coffee, he retrieves his coat and shoes, perhaps seeing the benefits of a quick getaway.

He's way smarter than his brother.

By the time my mother emerges from her booze-induced coma, I've had plenty of time to think through what to tell her, and what to withhold. I have to play my cards carefully. She needs to know I'm angry, but I don't want to spook her by telling her exactly how last night's choice of "overnight guests" affects me. "We're moving!" is the last thing I need to hear right now.

When she staggers down the stairs, I'm on the couch with my laptop perched on my knees, editing my portfolio. She holds her head and moves her mouth around like she's swallowed something disgusting. Her eyes flicker to the front hall and then over to me.

"If you're looking for your little friend, he's gone." My eyes stay glued to the screen.

"Don't patronize, Hannah. It's not cool."

Is she freaking kidding? I abandon my laptop and follow her into the kitchen. She fills the kettle and plugs it in. Then she looks out the window, rubbing her neck and tilting her head from side to side.

"You know what's not cool, Mom? Lying in bed all night wondering if the guy you've brought home might wander down the hall to pay me a visit because you're too drunk to entertain him yourself, that's what's not cool."

She gapes at me, her eyes open wide. Now I know where I get my confused fish look. The apple really doesn't fall far from the tree.

I return to the living room and plonk back down on the couch. She follows, stopping behind the armchair and curling her fingers around the chair back.

"Did something happen to you last night?"

I roll my eyes. "Nothing happened. But it's not okay to do stuff like that, Mom. You totally passed out. What if you brought home a maniac? I jammed a freaking chair under my doorknob. That's not normal."

My mother drops into the armchair. "God, I can't do anything right."

Great. She's taking the pity-party approach. Too often the pity-party is followed by the "I'll make it up to you" speech. The "let's move and have a fresh start" announcement is sure to follow. I have to proceed with caution.

I perch on the edge of the coffee table, close to her chair. "That's not true."

She narrows her eyes at me suspiciously.

"Honestly. You work hard," I say. "You keep a roof over our heads. You pay bills and make food."

"I'll get a lock for your door," she offers, like doing that will somehow solve everything. This isn't the solution I'm looking for, but it's typical of her to shove the real issue under the rug and cast about for the easiest way to address the problem.

"I don't need a lock, but you can get one if you want. Just promise me no more bringing guys home after binge drinking."

She nods. I grab my laptop, snap it shut and take it upstairs to my room. I allow myself a few moments to bask in smugness. I handled things with Dean and my mom like a boss.

As a reward, I unfold the note Lucas left between pages seventy-six and seventy-seven of Emily Dickinson's book of poetry. Rereading it tortures me, but I can't help myself. The note reminds me of that feeling in the library—the moment when I felt like it might be okay to let down my guard. It's a good feeling. Unfortunately, the post-reading rush of regret isn't at all pleasant.

I try to bury both feelings, somewhere out of sight, my heart throbbing as I scan his cellphone number for the millionth time.

That's when I realize I'm just as bad as my mother.

Mom knocks on my door while I'm holed away doodling in my math binder.

"Is there anything special I can bring home from work for us to have for lunch tomorrow?" she asks.

"Not really."

"Well, I made great tips last night. Do you need some money to buy clothes for school?"

"I don't need anything."

"Okay, so how about we plan a mother-daughter mani–pedi next weekend?"

"We'll see."

She crosses her arms and leans against my bookcase.

"Is your homework going okay?"

"It's fine."

I flash her a quick smile over my shoulder. She's trying too hard, but at least she's trying, and thankfully, she doesn't suggest I start packing my belongings.

Eventually she calls a cab and leaves for work. I'm happy to be alone again. What happened to my quiet weekend, my endless blank page? Somewhere along the line, the vast white space filled up with random, chaotic scribbles, which is all the more frustrating because I'm not the one wielding the pen.

I need to regain control of that pen. I open my laptop and compose a text message to Lucas, aiming for precisely 160 characters. This writing exercise—arbitrary as it may be—requires economy of expression and careful concentration. It's like yoga for the brain.

> I knew I shouldn't have trusted you. You pretended you wanted to be my friend. Then once you had weaseled your way in, you changed your mind. Thanks for nothing.

This almost perfectly sums up my feelings about what Lucas has done to me, but it's 161 characters. I start a new line.

> What was the worst part? Was I a bad kisser? Maybe I was breathing too heavy. You thought my boobs looked way bigger in the pictures, right? Sorry to disappoint.

Hmm, close. I could leave it at that, but I hit 161 characters again. Back to the drawing board.

> 'Not knowing when the Dawn will come, I open every Door.' So poetic. Too bad you turned out to be an ass. Consider the door LOCKED. With you on the other side!!!

Now that's great. The right length and the right message. Perfectionist that I am, though, I have to try another one.

> I wish I knew what I did wrong, Lucas. I thought you were different. I want to talk to you because none of this makes sense to me. Are you as confused as I am??

This sudden surge of raw honesty surprises me. I slam my laptop closed. Then I close my eyes. What would happen if I sent any of those messages to Lucas? No. Texting him, even in anger, would let him back in. That can't happen. I'll never let myself be vulnerable to him again.

That's what I tell myself, but making those kinds of absolute statements is like reading a book and claiming to know with certainty what will happen at the end. You can't be sure what's going to happen until you reach the last page.

Chapter 16

The Same Mistake

ON SUNDAY NIGHT after Mom leaves for work, I survey my new clothes—two outfits she insisted on buying for me. "Retail therapy," she called it. I'm rarely in the mood to shop, but my mother loves shopping, and there hadn't been any strange shoes in the front hall when I woke up on Sunday morning, so I felt generous. We hit the mall together and came home with two new shirts, a pair of leggings and some new jeans.

I try on the black leggings and one of the T-shirts. Perfect for school tomorrow. The doorbell rings. I freeze. It could be the paperboy, but what if it's not?

Lucas?

Has he come back for another crack at second base?

Can we make out again, Hannah? I mean, I'm pretty sure you totally repulse me, but I hate to leave room for doubt....

I have no intention of letting Lucas in, but I run down the stairs anyway to sneak a look through the peep hole in the door. I just want to see his face. That's the lie I tell myself. I align my right eye with the hole and peer through. There's no one there.

Was I imagining the doorbell? Wishful thinking, maybe? I turn to go back upstairs, and this time, someone knocks. Loudly. I spin around and take another peek. A mop of curly blond hair moves in and out of the peep hole's range. It's not Lucas. It's Dallyn.

What the hell is he doing here?

I swing open the door, lock the outer storm door and glower at him through the glass. "What do you want, Dallyn?"

He reaches out to squeeze the storm door handle. His movements are jerky and imprecise. He looks like a chopped tree waiting for gravity to bring it down. He's drunk. Who gets drunk at six thirty on a Sunday night? What a loser.

"What do you want?" I ask him again.

He places his hands flat on the glass. "Hannah, I can't hear you!" he shouts. "Open . . . open the door!"

There's no way I'm opening the door. I raise my voice instead. "What are you doing here?"

"Hannah, I'm a . . . I'm real need talk to you," he slurs.

I shake my head. "I don't want to talk to you."

"Just for a sec. Lemme in for a sec."

"You're not coming in. No way."

"Okay, then . . . you . . . you come out here."

"No. You're drunk. I want you to leave."

He presses his forehead against the glass. "Allison and I had . . . big fight. I need to talk to you."

Gee, where have I heard that one before? "I don't care. That's not my problem."

"I told her the only reason . . . the only reason people stay friends with her's 'cause they're scared of her. She slapped me." He laughs.

God, he's plastered. "I don't know why you're telling me this, Dallyn. I don't care. Can you please leave?"

He takes two stumbling steps backward. "I'm gonna puke," he says.

He drops his keys on the porch where they land with a jangle, and I notice a car parked crookedly in the driveway. Dallyn drove here, wasted. Now I want to slap him.

He groans and lurches sideways, leaning over the railing of the porch. He barfs all over my mom's attempt at a garden. He's too busy chucking his dinner to notice me quickly pull the storm door open and scoop up his keys, and I'm too busy wondering what I'll do next to worry about him hurling all over the tulip bed.

As I retrieve my phone from the coffee table, he continues to heave and wretch, a revolting sound which makes me gag and wonder if I might need to take a quick hurl over the railing as well. When I return to the door, he's standing in the middle of the porch with his hands on his knees, gasping for breath.

"I'm going to call your brother to come get you. What's his number,

Dallyn?"

He waves me off. "Don't wanna see my brother."

"You can't drive."

"I drove here. I'm fine." He pats his pockets and spins clumsily, scanning the ground at his feet. I hold his keyring up, and he lunges for the door handle. "Gimme those!"

"You're not driving, Dallyn. You're too drunk to drive. I'll call your brother. He'll come and get you."

"I said I don't wanna see him. He's why I said that stuff to Allison. Gave me this stupid lecture about 'taking responsibility for my actions.'"

Dean lectured his brother? Did my name come up?

Dallyn's expression darkens. He yanks on the door handle so hard, I'm afraid it'll come off in his hand. Dean's possible indiscretion becomes the least of my worries.

"Gimme my keys, Hannah," he shouts.

"Tell me your brother's number, Dallyn."

His features twist with anger, and he punches the door. The glass rattles, and the window slips open a few inches.

Oh shit.

Hands pressed to the glass again, his eyes lock on mine. "Hannah. My keys."

I shake my head. "No."

He wrenches the door handle and bangs on the glass with his other fist. Either the glass is going to smash or the window will fall all the way open, and he'll rip the mesh screen and climb through. It would be so easy to throw his keys out the door and tell him to get lost, but what if he got in an accident? Someone could die. Someone innocent. I don't need that on my conscience.

I need help, and my options are limited. I slam and lock the door and then press ten numbers into my phone, recalling them from memory. I've looked at this phone number so many times over the past few days, I could probably dial it in my sleep.

With the phone pressed to my ear, I retreat to the bottom of the stairs, gripping the banister as Dallyn continues to bash on the door. He's found a rhythm now. He's not really knocking as much as drumming a steady beat, my name—a low feral growl—thrown into the mix occasionally.

After six rings, I formulate a plan B which involves selling my soul to the Devil—more specifically, phoning Allison. This isn't a pleasant prospect. I'm more inclined to jump straight to plan C—calling the police, and making good on my title of "dirty nark" once and for all. In fact, I'm panicking and on the verge of hanging up and dialling 911 when he answers.

Finally.

I've never been so happy to hear someone's voice, even if the person attached to the voice finds me despicable.

"Hello?" His voice is wary. I'm an "unknown caller."

"Lucas?"

"Yes. Who's this?"

I sigh, relief buckling my knees. I sit on the bottom stair.

"Lucas, it's me. It's Hannah."

"Hannah?"

I've caught him completely off-guard. Of course I have. I'm the last person he'd expect to hear from.

"Wow. I didn't think you'd call after . . . ."

Friday.

He doesn't say that, but I know the word is there, suspended in the silence like a piñata waiting to be bashed to pieces. I have a bat at the ready, but I don't have time to swing it. Right now isn't the time to get into what happened on Friday. The piñata will have to wait.

"I need your help," I say. "I didn't know who else to call."

"Are you okay?"

The concern in his voice surprises me. Whatever he thinks of me, whatever his feelings are about the events of Friday night, his bat isn't poised either.

"No, I'm really not okay," I admit.

The drumming on the door stops. This should be comforting, but it isn't. What's Dallyn up to now? I quickly cross to the window and pull the living room curtains aside. He's at the end of the driveway, bowed at the waist, throwing up again, this time into the gutter.

Gross.

"Hannah?" Lucas says. "Are you still there?"

"If I needed you to come over, would you be able to?"

"What's going on? Are you hurt?"

I sense movement. That might sound weird, but I can tell Lucas is moving.

"I'm not hurt, but Dallyn's here," I say. "He's outside. He's drunk. I took his keys so he can't drive, and I'm locked in the house. He's kind of freaking out—and puking. I can't drive him home. I don't have my license."

"Jesus." I hear rustling. Yes, Lucas is definitely on the move. "I'll be there in ten minutes. Don't let him in, whatever you do."

I watch the seconds tick by on the ugly sunburst clock on the wall by the stairs. I perch on the edge of the couch, my cellphone in my hands, rocking the minutes away, while outside, Dallyn shouts and bangs on the screen door and pukes and does whatever else he's doing that doesn't have some sort of sound associated with it. I'm afraid to look out the window to see what that might be.

A car screeches to a stop outside, and I breathe. Nine minutes. That's how long it took Lucas to get here.

I watch through the living room window as Lucas leaps out of his car. He goes straight to Dallyn, who's flaked out on the curb.

If I hadn't taken his keys, he'd be behind the wheel of his car right now. I did the right thing. I did an amazingly right thing and would spend more time patting myself on the back, because I don't do amazingly right things all that often, but the action outside demands my attention.

Lucas grabs Dallyn under the arms and tries to haul him to his feet. Once Dallyn realizes what's going on, he loses his passivity, pulling away from Lucas's grasp and staggering around on the road, yelling. I slide the living room window open so I can hear their exchange.

"Get your hands off me, sped!"

Lucas responds, but his voice is too low to hear. Dallyn lurches around, ranting and raving at the top of his lungs. I'd lose my mind right about now if I were Lucas, but he simply waits, hands on his hips, until Dallyn runs out of steam. Lucas points at the house and then at the car. He crosses his arms. He seems to be waiting for Dallyn to do something. To react.

Then, wonder of wonders, Dallyn's shoulders slump, and he weaves toward his car where Lucas helps him roll into the backseat. When the car door slams, Dallyn immediately disappears from view. I can only assume he's fallen flat on his face.

How the hell did Lucas convince Dallyn to get into the backseat without knocking him senseless? He must be an asshole whisperer. There's no other explanation.

Lucas immediately heads toward the house. I dash to the front door and open it as he lifts his hand to knock. Our eyes meet. His cheeks redden, likely mirroring the heat in my face.

Anyone home?

"Hey," he says. He lifts his shoulders, hands fisted at his sides as if he's bracing himself, not sure what I'll say. Doesn't he realize he has the upper hand? I'm completely at his mercy.

"Hey."

I don't get a chance to cobble together any words of thanks. He's all business.

"I, uh, I need Dallyn's keys," he says.

"Right."

I unlock and open the storm door and drop the keys into his outstretched hand.

"Oh, and I don't know where he lives." Lucas jerks his thumb at the car, "I'd ask him, but he's already passed out."

"Right. Hang on a sec."

I close the storm door. Lucas doesn't follow me. Would it be weird to turn and wave him in? There's a door between us again. The rules of this game confound me. In the kitchen, I find a piece of scrap paper and draw a hasty map to Dallyn's house. It's not complicated, but when I return to the door and hand him the paper, Lucas stares at it as if the map is written in hieroglyphics.

"I know it's messy," I say. "But it's not complicated."

"No, it's not that. It's just . . . I need a second to process it."

He frowns at the paper. Of course. Unlike Dallyn, I've completely forgotten about Lucas's learning disability. I just stupidly told him the map isn't complicated. Reading is probably always complicated for him.

"Two lefts and then a right onto Longview?" he asks, frowning as he spins the page around.

"Yeah. Number 43. The house is on the left-hand side. The garage door is kind of a reddish-brown colour." Visuals probably help.

"Okay. Sounds good."

"How will you get back? To pick up your car, I mean." That's all I mean. Of course. It's not that I want to see him again. I'm all about the car. That's all I care about. The car, the car, the car.

"Guess I'll take a cab."

I nod, and he jogs down a couple of porch steps. He stops, turning to look back before he hits the bottom step.

"Would you . . . I mean, can we talk when I get back?" he says.

Gee, Lucas, Chapter Eleven in the history text was super. Can't wait to see what amazingness Chapter Twelve has in store.

No. Better not. After all, he's helping me. Saying something that snarky would be the worst of ideas. I'll save the snark until later. "I'm not going anywhere."

This doesn't answer his question, but it does buy me some time. I'll still be here when he gets back. Whether I'll have the guts to open the door is another question.

Chapter 17

Confused

FIVE BUCKETS OF warm water. That's what it takes to wash away the putrid smell from the flower bed. I don't worry about the gutter. Gutters are supposed to reek, right? Washing the stink off the porch is relatively easy. Preparing myself for Lucas's return is harder. Way harder.

Admitting I want to talk to him is the toughest part of all. Of the four imaginary texts I wrote earlier, the last one keeps jangling around in my head.

I wish I knew what I did wrong, Lucas. I thought you were different. I want to talk to you because none of this makes sense to me. Are you as confused as I am??

Regardless of what happened on Friday, I know he's different. He's unlike any guy I've ever known. I am confused. I do want to talk to him. I need to know what Friday night was all about. It would be simple to sweep the whole episode under the rug, but after all the shame, regret and loneliness Mom has jammed under there over the years, and my feelings of insecurity, isolation and rejection squeezed in as well, you'd need an industrial-sized cement roller to flatten the pile of crap underneath.

Five minutes after Lucas's departure, I prepare in earnest for his return. I brush my hair. This makes sense. It's messy. Then I brush my teeth. This makes less sense, but I'm not about to let myself think about why I'm doing it. I cut the tags out of the back of my new shirt. They're itching my neck. This makes me think of Nancy. Thinking of Nancy makes me think of Lucas again.

He's been gone twenty minutes. He'll be back soon. Wondering how

I'll behave and what I'll say makes something—possibly my dinner—do aerobics in my stomach. I sit at the dining room table and force myself to breathe. The dining room is the only place I can imagine sitting with Lucas to talk. The kitchen's been the scene of way too many weird conversations already this weekend, and the living room . . . well, that's where the couch is.

Sitting at the dining room table and sorting the house bills and random homework sheets into piles kills all of four minutes. There's no way I can sit still. I wander into the kitchen and grab the grocery list pen off the counter and pace. In the midst of an epic pen clicking outburst, a car door slams outside. I freeze. Then I click the pen ten more times in slow succession. Once I'm sure the taxi's left the driveway, I drop the pen and cross the room.

I open the door to find Lucas jogging lightly up the porch steps. I'm getting really good at this door opening thing.

Maybe a little too good.

I let him in. While he takes off his coat and shoes, I return to the kitchen and fish money out of the jar on the counter, wishing I'd thought of this earlier. I didn't mean for him to pay for the cab to get back here.

When I turn around with a ten-dollar bill in my hand, he's standing in the kitchen doorway. Gone is the relaxed I'll-just-make-myself-at-home Lucas from Friday night. He looks totally uncomfortable, like his skin is a suit that's too small and pinching him in all the worst places.

I hold out the money. "Is this enough to cover the cab?"

He waves my hand away. "I don't need that."

"You shouldn't have to pay—"

"No, I mean, I didn't end up taking a cab."

"Oh. How'd you get back?"

"When I got to the house, Dallyn's brother was outside working on his car. He took Dallyn inside and then gave me a ride back."

"Dean?" I try to suppress the panic rising in my chest. "Dean drove you back here?"

"Yeah, Dean. Seemed like a decent enough guy. You know him?"

"Sort of," I hedge. "What did he say when he dropped you off?"

What a coincidence. I slept on the couch here on Friday night. I was gonna bang Hannah's mom, but she was too drunk to remember I was there. Maybe next time.

Lucas shrugs. "What did he say? I don't know. He thanked me for having Dallyn's back. We didn't talk much."

I inspect his face. He doesn't seem to be lying. They didn't talk much. Good. Not talking much is good. I stuff the bill in the jar and turn around. That awful "now what?" feeling fills the space between us.

Lucas slips his hands in his pockets and looks around the kitchen. We're both lost. I'm utterly floundering, with no clue what to say or do. I've abandoned the idea of laying into that piñata. My anger must have wandered away with my vocal chords. Maybe they're off somewhere doing a Mexican hat dance all over the piñata. Luckily for me, Lucas hasn't entirely lost the ability to speak.

"I meant what I said earlier. About talking," he says. "What I really meant was, I should apologize. For what happened Friday."

I must have the confused fish look again because this was the last thing I expected him to say. He wants to apologize?

He shakes his head and smiles grimly. "There I go again, huh? You're right. I do spend most of my time saying sorry to you." He draws his eyebrows together and bites his lip. Then, he flashes me a look. That look.

Heart clench.

Experience tells me the best way to cope with the heart clench is to move, so that's what I do. I cross to the door that leads to the dining room and look at him quickly over my shoulder.

"Let's go in here," the look says. I don't trust myself to speak. Not yet. I drop into a chair at the dining room table and clasp my hands together in my lap. He follows, sitting at the head of the table. Beside me, but not beside me.

Close, but not close enough.

"So, um, this is kind of weird," he says. He avoids my eyes now, tracing the pattern in the wood surface of the table with his thumb as bright-red splotches appear on his neck, and it occurs to me that Lucas blushes a lot.

A girl in my sociology class used to get blotchy when she did presentations in front of the class. Nerves. That's all it was—an involuntary physiological reaction to anxiety. It's not surprising that Lucas is nervous right now. Feeling like he has to apologize for coming on to me and then bailing without a word of explanation would be super awkward. I decide, against my better judgment, to make things easier for him.

"You don't have to apologize for not liking me," I say.

"What?" His thumb stops mid-pattern. He looks up at me from under furrowed brows. "Not liking you? Who said I didn't like you?"

Okay, now I'm confused. I frown back at him. Our eyebrows are having a duel, and his eyebrows are giving mine a serious run for their money. Very impressive. "No one. No one said it. I'm talking about Friday. The way you left."

"I'm confused," he says, leaning back in his chair slowly.

"So am I."

"You think I left because I didn't like you?"

"Well . . . yeah. You looked . . . completely disgusted."

"I was disgusted, but not with you. I was disgusted with myself. I figured you'd want me to leave . . . because of what happened . . . ."

The splotches are creeping upwards. They've reached his cheeks, as if he's dying inside. I must be missing something. Or maybe I'm not giving him enough credit. Does he think he took advantage of me? Is that why he's raking himself across the coals?

"Did you think I was mad that you kissed me?" I shake my head. "Because I wasn't. I was surprised, but not mad. And then you left . . . I don't know . . . I thought you didn't like me." My voice gets smaller and smaller as I speak, and by the end of my sentence, Lucas's face is in his hands, and he's shaking his head.

"Oh crap." That's all he says. "Oh crap."

"What? What's going on?"

He gets up and walks into the kitchen. Then he comes back, his hands laced on the top of his head. "You don't know. You don't know what happened. I've been beating myself up all weekend and you don't even know. Oh my God." He slumps down in the chair, covering his face with his hands again. "I can't believe this is happening."

If I understood what was happening, I might not be able to believe it either, but I'm well beyond confused now. "Would you care to enlighten me?"

He stares at the table for a few seconds, and then he scrunches his eyes closed. "You thought I left because I decided I didn't like you. That's not true." Now he looks at me.

"Okay." That's the best I can do. I still don't get why he's freaking out.

"I like you. I do. I liked making out with you . . . and stuff." He pauses.

"But?" I prompt.

"There is no 'but.'" He sighs heavily. "See, the thing is, I really liked making out with you. I, um, I guess I liked it a little too much. That's why I had to leave. God, this is the worst." He pushes himself away from the table and escapes to the kitchen again.

This time I hop up and join him at the counter, thinking I'm finally starting to understand what he's trying to tell me.

"You're afraid to get too close to me because of all the rumours, right?" I say. "I have a bad reputation? I'm a slut. A nark. Guilt by association and all that? Is that what's going on? You like me, but you hate yourself for liking me, so you're pushing me away?"

He chuckles and shakes his head at me. "It's not that. Not at all. I don't care about rumours and reputations. I thought you'd know that by now."

"Then what?"

He stares out the window. "You're going to make me spell this out, aren't you?" he asks.

I grab the pen off the counter and start clicking it. "Yeah, I guess I am."

He glares at my hand. "Can you stop that?"

"Tell me what's going on and I'll stop."

"Just stop it." I keep clicking and look up at him defiantly. He lets me get away with about three more clicks before he closes his hand over mine.

"Hannah, stop!" He takes the pen out of my hand and places it on the counter. The ensuing silence startles me. He takes me by the shoulders and turns me to face him. Then he drops his hands to his sides.

"I'm going to say this, and then I'm going to leave. You can think about it and decide if you still want to be friends, or whatever. Okay?"

"Okay." My voice is small again.

The blotches on his neck are fading, but he still looks so serious. My imagination goes into overdrive. He doesn't want to get close to me because he and his family are moving to Russia any day now. Or cancer. Maybe he's got cancer, and he only has a month left to live. That must be it.

"I don't care about Dallyn and all those idiots," he says. "They're not important. I like you. I really liked kissing you. And touching you. I guess I'm a loser or something because I've never done that with a girl before. And you're really hot. I guess my imagination got carried away.

I don't know . . . ." He holds his hand up to the side of his head and flicks his fingers, miming an explosion. "I lost it. That's why I had to leave. Because I REALLY enjoyed it."

He puts such heavy emphasis on these last four words that I can't help but understand what he's telling me. He's not moving to Russia. He doesn't have cancer. He just really enjoyed making out with me. Like, REALLY enjoyed it. I have a sudden vision of him swearing and shuddering before he sat up with that look of horror on his face.

Oh my God.

Holy crap is right. No wonder he was embarrassed. I bring my hands to my mouth.

"You get it now?" he asks me.

I nod, my hands still covering my mouth.

"I wanted to die," he says. "You looked disgusted. I figured you knew—"

"I didn't know." I shake my head violently. "I didn't know. I'm sorry. I had no idea."

"What are you sorry for? You didn't do anything wrong. It was my fault. When I got home, all I kept thinking was you'd figure I was like all those other guys. I mean, we'd just finished talking about what they did to you and the next thing you know—" He shakes his head. "I'm honestly not like all the slimebags who just want one thing. I mean, I didn't . . . I've never . . . ." He huffs. "Look, why don't I go, and you can think about everything?"

"You don't have to go."

He steps back, his expression uncertain.

I clench my fists at my side. "I don't want you to go, Lucas."

He looks at me with those amazing hazel eyes, and then he smiles.

I breathe out slowly, wishing I'd had the nerve to say those words on Friday, instead of letting him walk out the door.

He can't stay long. That's what he tells me. He probably wants to escape to recover from his epic confession. But then he says his uncle is picking up his aunt at the airport, and he needs to get back to help Nancy with her Sunday night routine so she doesn't flip out. I can tell he's not lying. He explains this to me while staring at the pictures magnetized to the fridge.

"Is this your mom?" he asks me.

"Yeah. That was last summer."

"She's really pretty."

So she's been told. And told.

"You look like her," he adds, smiling at me before scanning the other pictures.

I smile too, on the inside. This is a roundabout compliment, and the way he's looking at me tells me he meant it that way—intended for it to be indirect, but complimentary anyway—like he knows I'd make some incredibly smartass remark if he came right out and said, "Hannah, I think you're pretty."

I don't make a smartass comment. I don't pretend to disagree with him either. I'm not one of those girls who thinks she's ugly when she's really not. Problem is, I ruin most of my chances of being considered a pretty girl since my go-to expression is usually a frown. That's what my face wants to do. Then there's all the other stuff I'm lacking—stuff that most guys are drawn to, like a bubbly personality, a good attitude, flirtatiousness—yeah, I'm a lost cause. And yet, Lucas likes me.

Then again, Lucas isn't "most guys."

Since the appropriate response to his roundabout compliment eludes me, I decide to change the subject. "Can I ask you something?" I say.

"Yeah, sure." He leans against the dining room doorway.

"How'd you get Dallyn into the car? One minute he's freaking out and the next minute he's flopping into the back seat. What'd you say to him?"

"I told him he could get in the car and let me drive him home or wait for me to call the police."

"Yeah. Dallyn's irrationally terrified of the cops."

"Probably not that irrational. I bet he's had his fair share of police run-ins."

"Why do you say that?"

"I don't know." His eyes flicker away from mine. "Gut instinct, I guess."

"You know, when I first met you, I thought you knew Dallyn."

He pushes his shoulder off the doorway. "What would make you think that? Do I seem like the kind of person who'd hang with him?"

"The way you kept aggravating me. I thought someone put you up to it. Allison and Dallyn hate me. It made sense. Plus, I saw you talking to Dallyn in the hall and stuff."

He shakes his head and chuckles. "I didn't need Allison and Dallyn to tell me to aggravate you. I decided to do it all by myself."

"Gee, thanks."

"Don't mention it."

He settles back against the doorframe again. I lean on the counter, the awkwardness from earlier almost forgotten now.

Almost.

"So, if Dallyn hates you, how come he came over here?" he asks.

"I'm not sure. He said he got into a fight with Allison, and he wanted to talk. He said the same thing on New Year's, right before he . . . well, you know."

"Yeah. I know. Look, I'm glad you called me tonight."

"I am too. Thanks. For taking him home, I mean. That was nice of you."

He waves it off. "Forget about it. That's what friends do." He examines my face. "We are friends, right?"

"I guess so."

"What, you're not sure?"

"It's been a while for me with the whole friend thing." I shrug. "I'm kind of rusty."

"Really? I think you're doing great. You haven't given me 'the look' in about ten minutes. That's progress."

"What look?"

"You know. The one where your eyebrows scrunch together, and you shoot lasers out of your eyes? It's scary."

"Shut up." I smile when I say this. I knew it. My eyebrows are fierce. I love them more than ever.

"Shutting up." He grins back at me and raises his hands like a criminal who's just been arrested. "So, look, I'm glad we talked and cleared everything up, but I do have to go."

"Yeah. For sure." A pang of disappointment echoes through my chest cavity. *Of course. Leave right when I'm getting my footing.* I lead him back through the kitchen to the front door.

"I'll see you tomorrow, okay?" he says, dragging on his coat.

"Yep. Great. See you tomorrow."

As he reaches for the door handle, he almost seems to waver, but I can't be certain. I'm probably imagining things. But then he's gone, jogging down the porch steps and climbing into his uncle's car. I stand on the porch to watch him pull out. I even wave as he drives off.

I know, right? It's crazy.

I'm alone a lot. Being alone is boring, but it doesn't usually bother me, perhaps because I've never missed the presence of anyone in particular in my day-to-day life. That changes after Lucas leaves on Sunday night. The house is empty and way too quiet. I miss him. It's not the same feeling as when he's not beside me in Writer's Craft. That's a vague bleakness. This is worse. It's not vague at all. It's specific, and I can pinpoint its location with alarming accuracy.

It's located in the very centre of my left ventricle. It's a dangerous feeling. The left ventricle is the biggest and strongest chamber in the human heart. When a heart breaks, that's probably where the crack starts. I'm scared. I'd like to shove this fear away somewhere, but there's not a big enough rug in the world for me to shove it under.

Ritual. That's what I need. The comfort of ritual. I shower, make my lunch and choose my clothes for tomorrow. I'll wear my new jeans and T-shirt, since Lucas has already seen my new leggings. I sit at my desk and take out my backgammon dice. But wait. Will Lucas want to hang out over the lunch hour? I mean, that's what friends do, right? They hang out. I can't be sure.

I roll two dice and write the number down.

What did Lucas say when he left? *I'll see you tomorrow.* That could mean anything. Uncertainty makes my stomach lurch.

I roll the dice again, jotting the next number.

Should I wait for him in the lobby after I get off the bus? Or maybe he'll be waiting at my locker. What if I can't find him? Should I go to Mr. Murray's room?

This is complicated.

I roll the dice one last time, record the number and stick the Post-it to my nightstand. There. Whatever happens, I'm ready.

I think about how Lucas was going home to his aunt and uncle's to help Nancy with her Sunday night routine, and I realize Nancy and I have a lot in common. I briefly ponder whether I might be autistic.

My phone vibrates on the nightstand, interrupting my self-diagnosis. My phone rarely vibrates. Sometimes Mom will message me from work, but without Twitter updates and Facebook alerts—and no connections requiring the use of social media—my phone is almost always mute, even when the volume is set to high.

Could it be? I'm almost afraid to hope. Hesitantly, I pick it up and stare at the message scrolling across the alert bar.

"I really am glad we sorted everything out c u tomorrow at school."

My heart throbs —my left ventricle in particular—as I read Lucas's words. I stare at my phone for a moment, prepared to reply right away, but not wanting to seem too eager. After two sluggish minutes creep by, I slide my thumbs across my phone's keyboard. I want to type, "I'm glad we sorted it out, too. I like talking to you. You make me feel special. I miss you, and I can't wait to see you again. I wish you had kissed me goodbye."

This, in exactly 160 characters, is precisely how I feel. But I can't say that, especially not the last part. We're friends. Friends don't kiss when they say goodbye. Instead, I text this:

Me too. See you tomorrow.

Chapter 18

Two Steps Back

MONDAY MORNING, I slide into a seat on the bus, avoiding everyone's eyes. Mondays on the bus are insane. All the weekend's activities provide plenty of fodder for the rumour mill. Today, my biggest fear is that after Sunday night's fiasco, my name will come up along with Dallyn's name, or worse still, that his brother's weekend visit will creep into the conversation. I should forget about everything else and focus on the good stuff—Lucas's Sunday night visit and the lack of strange men's shoes in the front hall this morning.

Two days in a row. Go, Mom!

I put my earbuds in, but I keep the volume low all the same, listening for my name.

"Ali and Dall broke up again."

"They had a huge fight."

"She thinks he's screwing around on her."

"I heard she punched him."

"He got wasted, man."

So far, so good. Same crap, different day. They don't seem to have a clue about the rest of the weekend's highlights—the ones that might sound something like:

Dall's older brother tried to bang Hannah's mom on Friday.

Oh yeah? I heard Dallyn went over there last night.

Maybe it was a double-date—Hannah and Dallyn were hooking up downstairs while Dean and Hannah's mom got it on upstairs.

Since I don't hear any of that, I allow myself a moment of relief.

It's short-lived.

"The sped and the nark are going out, eh? I saw her get in his car the other day after school."

I'd love to spin around. *Shut your fat trap, Calder! You don't know what you're talking about!* But I pretend I don't hear. Behind me at least ten pairs of eyes are probably aimed at the back of my head. I prepare to zone out, rooting around in my pocket for my phone, but I don't turn up the volume quickly enough.

"Someone should warn the guy that he's dating a slut-faced nark."

This proclamation made by Kelly Sparks is accompanied by something being thrown at me—something that hits the back of my head. It doesn't hurt. It's only a balled up piece of paper or a chocolate bar wrapper or something, but I flinch and slip down the seat anyway, wishing more than anything that Lucas were here beside me, telling me it doesn't matter.

I don't care about rumours and reputations. That's what he'd say. And then I'd cocoon myself in his words and live inside them forever.

When the bus is empty, I stand up.

Inside the school, I scan the lobby for Lucas, but he's not there. I cling to my routine and rush to my locker with my head down and then go straight to math class. Lucas isn't there either. Neither is Mr. Murray. I wait, tucked into the alcove outside his door. Mr. Murray only keeps me waiting a few minutes. As he opens the door, we have the typical Monday morning conversation.

"How was your weekend, Hannah?"

"It was fine."

Fine? Really? Is that the best I can do? My weekend was awful. My weekend was amazing. Amazingly awful. Awfully amazing. The beginning of Friday night and the end of Sunday night were amazing bookends to the God-awful in-between parts.

I'm about to follow Mr. Murray into the room when Lucas saunters around the corner. He smiles widely when he sees me. It's the best feeling in the world, to be the reason someone smiles like that. I wish it was a good enough feeling to wipe out what happened on the bus, but it's not.

Not quite.

I try to smile back. I don't think I pull it off.

"Hey," he says as he leans on the wall beside the door, hands stuck in his pockets.

"Hey."

"Any other issues after I left last night?"

"Nope." *Just how much I missed you. Does that count as an issue?* "Your aunt got home okay?" I ask, trying to focus on his face instead of worrying about what might be happening in the hall around us—who might be watching, what they might be saying.

"Oh, yeah. It's all good." He hitches his backpack higher onto his shoulder and clears his throat. His face looks serious all of a sudden. "Look, I've been thinking about what we talked about last night."

Great. Here we go. "Okay."

"Thing is, I'm not really sure I want to be your friend."

My heart drops. He doesn't want to be my friend. What does he expect me to say to that? I shift my weight and look around the hall. Kelly Sparks and Brett Calder walk by, staring at us. Brett wiggles his eyebrows and makes a couple of hip thrusting motions.

Oh, God.

Forget about them. Focus on Lucas. What did he just say? "You don't want to be my friend?" I repeat.

He tugs on his earlobe and sweeps his hair out of his eyes. "Um, what I mean is, I want to be more than a friend."

Oh? Ohhhhhhhhh! "You want to be one-and-a-half friends?" I say. Stupid. Stupid! Why did I say that?

He grimaces. "Why can't you take anything at face value? Why do you have to make everything so awkward?"

These are good questions. I shrug, awkwardly. I've made everything uncomfortable, including myself. I'm such a loser.

"Never mind." He sighs as the warning bell rings, summoning everyone to class. "I've got to get to art class. I'll see ya later."

And he's off, loping down the hall, leaving me in a sea of loserly awkwardness.

One step forward, two steps back.

I'd love to be more than just a friend, Lucas.

You want to be my boyfriend? Really? That sounds awesome.

You've got no idea how much I've been hoping you'd ask me.

These things. These and a million other things I could have said when Lucas told me he wanted to be more than a friend. But no. I asked him if he wanted to be one-and-a-half friends.

Idiot.

I could pretend I don't know why I said something so stupid—why I'm being difficult, making everything awkward—but I do know why. This morning's fifteen minutes bus ride brought everything into focus. I was happily invisible for two months, then along came Lucas. His attention shines a spotlight on me again. I might as well paint a bright neon target on my back—or on the back of my head. Perfect for attracting balled up wads of paper.

I try not to obsess over the bullseye burning on the back of my head as I dash through the halls at lunch hour, desperate to disappear into the library's stacks.

Focus on the floor. Tune everyone out.

Mrs. Fry catches me as I pass the circulation desk. "Oh, Hannah, I'm glad you're here. Wait there for a second. I have a book you might be interested in."

"Okay."

She disappears into her office and comes out holding up a small paperback book. *The Complete Poems of Emily Dickinson.*

"Would you like to sign it out? I bought it on the weekend and processed it this morning. That book of poetry you signed out on Friday is getting so old and ratty."

"Um, okay."

She scans my face as she slides a due date card into the back of the book. "Are you all right? You look a little pale."

"No, I'm okay." I need a new word. "Okay" isn't cutting it. "I'm fine." Yes, that's better. Now if Mrs. Fry and Mr. Murray compare notes in the staffroom, they can come to the dual conclusion that my weekend was fine, and today, I'm still fine. Excellent. "Thanks for the book." I slide the volume of poetry into my bag and head for the stacks.

At the end of the aisle, I stand and stare at the shelves of books. I'm completely blank. My number. What's today's number? I slide my hand into my pocket to retrieve my Post-it note, but then I hear a movement behind me. I freeze. Lucas. He's tracked me down.

I turn slowly, bracing for "the look." But it's not Lucas standing there. It's Dallyn. He peers around the side of the bookshelf like a criminal who's escaped from the local penitentiary. Apparently satisfied that he hasn't been spotted entering the stacks, he turns around, squinting at me. His eyes are bleary and ringed with dark circles. He must be hung over.

"I need to talk to you," he says.

"I told you last night, I don't want to talk to you. I don't want anything to do with you." I take two steps backward, and he follows me.

"For someone who doesn't want anything to do with me, you went to a lot of trouble to make sure I got home safe."

"That wasn't concern for you. That was concern for other drivers, lunatic."

"Lunatic, huh?"

Yeah, sorry about that, dumbass. A three-syllable word is probably more than your pea-brain can process.

"What's the deal with you and the sped, anyway?" He sneers. "I don't think you should hang out with him. I don't like him."

Dallyn's dislike for Lucas is a good thing. In fact, it's the single highest indicator of Lucas's superiority.

"You should be thanking him. If Lucas hadn't taken you home last night, you could be in a ditch right now."

"I wasn't that drunk."

"You're delusional." Oops. Four syllables. His brain is probably melting.

"Whatever. Look, don't tell Ali I was at your place last night."

"Is that what you came all the way down here to tell me?"

"Yeah. I don't know . . . ." He gives me a quick sideways look.

"Dallyn, I'm not about to hunt Allison down and tell her about last night. There's nothing to tell. Why do you care, anyway? After what you said yesterday, I don't see why you'd give a crap what she thinks."

"I wasn't thinking straight last night. All I'm saying is don't tell her I came to your house. We're trying to figure everything out. Prom's coming up. You know."

Oh yeah. I know. What Dallyn isn't intelligent enough to realize is that one word from me to a guidance counsellor about how he came to my house drunk, and he won't be going to prom at all. Girlfriend or no girlfriend. I cross my arms. "I think you should go now."

"Does that mean you won't say anything?"

"Whatever, Dallyn. Leave me alone."

"I mean it, Hannah." He leans in close. "Don't say anything, or I'll tell her—"

"I think she'd like you to go away now." Lucas's voice floats over my shoulder, and I back up, bumping into his chest in the process. I swear I feel his bubble of protection billowing out and around me.

"What are you gonna do about it, sped?" Dallyn scoffs.

"Don't . . . try . . . me," Lucas says quietly. His chest rises and falls rapidly against my back and his deep breaths tickle my neck.

"I'd like to see that." Dallyn retreats a couple of steps, despite his taunt. "I'm out of here. Have fun doing whatever losers do. I hear the library's got some great Dr. Seuss books, sped."

I turn around and look up at Lucas. He watches Dallyn leave, his jaw twitching erratically. Once we're alone, he searches my face. "Are you okay? Did he hurt you?"

"He didn't hurt me. He didn't touch me. I'm okay."

"What did he want?"

I shake my head. "He was trying to cover his butt. He doesn't want Allison to know he came to my house last night."

"He's such a jackass."

"He is a jackass." I pick absently at the spine of one of the books beside me, avoiding Lucas's eyes. "So am I. I'm sorry about this morning. That was a stupid thing to say. I don't know. Sometimes, I—"

"Don't worry about it."

"No, I am worrying about it. I'm so stupid."

"You're not stupid. I get it. I heard what happened on the bus this morning. Some girl was blabbing about it in art class. Redhead—Kelly, I think."

"Kelly Sparks."

"Yeah, maybe. Anyway she said the ride to school this morning was hilarious. People threw stuff and made fun of you because we're friends." His jaw twitches. "It's my fault. I stirred everything up for you. I came to tell you not to worry. I'll back off."

"I don't want you to back off."

"I don't want to make your life miserable."

"You're not."

"I don't know. I'll just get you in trouble."

"In trouble? What are you talking about?"

"It's just . . . my problems." He shrugs, clamps his jaw closed and stares at the bookshelf. He rests one of his balled fists on the shelf. "I've got too much crap to deal with. I don't want to drag you down with me."

I shake my head, trying to make sense of what he's talking about.

"Are you talking about dyslexia? I don't care if you go to the Resource Room for extra help."

He ravages his bottom lip with his teeth and searches my face.

"I honestly don't care what all those pinheads say. Besides, you're smart. I know that. That's what matters. Isn't it?" I grab his sleeve at the wrist.

He looks at my fingers plucking at his cuff and blinks, his mouth twisting. "You really think I'm smart?"

"Of course you are. Having dyslexia doesn't mean you're dumb."

"Well, look how smart you are," he says, smiling reluctantly. "Not everyone's smart enough to understand that."

"I know, right?" I smile a little, too. "I'll figure out how to deal with the idiots, Lucas. Please don't back off."

He examines the books beside us and drums his fingers on the shelf. "Okay, how do you feel about do-overs?" he says.

"Do-overs as in second chances?"

"Exactly. Second chances."

"I don't know. Do-overs can be all right, I guess."

"Good, that's good because," he gives me a pointed look, "I've been thinking about what we talked about last night."

I know this is it, and I'd better not screw things up this time. "And? What were you thinking?"

"Well, I was thinking, I definitely want to be more than just your friend."

"You think?" I'm still fiddling with his sleeve, and now I try to bat my eyelashes at him. I feel like a fool, but he grins, so it's definitely worth it.

"No, I don't think," he says. "I know. What do you think?"

"I think that sounds amazing."

He closes his eyes and drops his head forward. "Thank God. Hannah, you're exhausting. You know that?"

"So I've been told."

He starts playing with my sleeve. We're not holding hands. We're holding sleeves. It's the most awkwardly amazing sleeve-hold in the world.

"Okay, I'm going to split before you can change your mind, or shoot lasers at me with your eyes or something. I have to go see my history teacher about the work I missed on Friday."

"Chapter Eleven, huh?" I can't help but lift my chin and look at him suspiciously.

"Yes, Chapter Eleven."

"So you really did have to read a chapter? That story about needing help with history wasn't some kind of ruse to get into my house?"

"'Ruse?' Nice word."

"Thanks."

"No, it wasn't a ruse. I could've used your help, but I got it done. I do have to talk to Mr. Napiers, though. Will you be okay here for a bit?" He squeezes my wrist through my shirt.

"I'll survive. I'll go read in my corner."

"Ah, yes. Your corner. What are you reading today?"

"Mrs. Fry bought a new book of poetry by Emily Dickinson. I signed it out. I think I'll read that."

This isn't exactly true, but I'm not about to tell him I compulsively pick call numbers every night because I got this really cool sign from the universe on January 5th. More than a friend or not, there are certain things he doesn't need to know.

Chapter 19

More Than a Friend

MORE THAN A friend. I don't know what "more than a friend" is supposed to look like. Lucas and I are an "us" now. When he arrives in class last period, yanking playfully on my ponytail before dropping into his seat, I'm sure everyone turns to look.

Everyone is staring. Staring at us.

Lucas ignores what's happening around us and calms me with his secret smile, like I'm the only person in the room worth his time. I smile back, and then I slip my portfolio from my school bag and hand it to Mr. Vesters.

"Hey, there it is," Mr. V. says, giving me a thumb's up. "You pulled everything together in the end?"

"Sort of. It's not great, but I did the best I could."

"I'm sure it's wonderful, as usual," Mr. V. says with a comforting smile.

I return to my seat. Mr. Vesters gets up and rubs his hands together, a signal that he's ready to launch into the next assignment.

"An interview," he says. "That's the first task for your next portfolio, which will be due in three weeks. You all know what an interview looks like, but in this case, your goal is to work the content of the interview into a personal essay. Find an angle, and then write a biographical exposé."

Beside me, Lucas moves the mouse around to the left side of the computer, plugs in his headphones for reading and generally fidgets, as usual.

"Can we interview whoever we want?" someone asks.

"Absolutely," Mr. Vesters says. "Ideally, I'd like you to interview a person you admire. Someone you'll enjoy talking to and writing about."

"Does it have to be someone in the class?"

"Not at all. You're welcome to interview a classmate, but that's not necessary. Take some time to brainstorm today and read the exemplars on your desktop."

Mr. V. circulates to answer any questions that might come up as people get started on the assignment. He stops when he reaches Lucas's chair and lowers his voice.

"I'd like you to give this assignment a go as well, Lucas. It fits well with the expectations of a mainstream English class. Are you up for it?"

"Sure. Sounds fine." Lucas shakes the mouse with his left hand, bumping my right hand in the process. He gives me a sly smile as Mr. Vesters walks away. Then he tickles the top of my hand with his baby finger.

More than a friend. This is what "more than a friend" looks like—at least so far—and so far, I'm enjoying it. I'm excited to find out what else it looks like.

We open the documents Mr. Vesters told us to read. Lucas puts his headphones on. We can't talk, but that doesn't stop us from communicating. Occasionally, his foot taps mine, but mostly, we send each other quiet messages with our baby fingers. His left-handedness, which up until today was a total pain in the ass, is now highly convenient.

The class passes quickly—way too quickly—not surprising, since I don't want it to end. I could stay there forever, feeling Lucas tickle my hand and my wrist with his finger and basking in his calming smiles and secret foot taps.

Plus, with stories about Lucas and me circulating, getting out of the school and making it home will feel like running the gauntlet today. What if I bump into Dallyn and Allison in the hallway? Will Kelly Sparks and Brett Calder torment me on the bus? Imagining the possible scenarios makes me queasy.

Lucas obliterates the queasiness with seven words.

"So, do you want a ride home?" He glances at me as he wraps up his headphone cord. As usual, his voice is breezy.

I try to copy his relaxed tone. "Sure. That'd be great."

"Great." He zips up his backpack and smiles, like he's celebrating a small victory.

I suppose it is a victory. Anything could have come out of my mouth. My no-fuss agreement must seem nothing short of miraculous.

Navigating the hallway is much less daunting with Lucas by my side. He doesn't put his arm around me or hold my hand. In fact, he doesn't make any show of possessiveness, but he's there, and his presence is comfort enough. If we pass Dallyn, or Allison and Marla in the hallway, I don't see them. I walk quickly, head down, relying on my legs to get me to my locker with little assistance from my eyes.

Old habits die hard.

Lucas has no trouble keeping up, taking one long stride for every two of mine. He leans against the wall by my locker while I stuff books and binders into my backpack.

"History was cool today," he says. "We started studying philosophy."

"Oh yeah? I thought that unit was kind of hard." Although the philosophy unit led me to that sign from the universe back in January, the topics and concepts gave me a headache most of the time.

"I know it might sound lame, but I like all the Taoist quotes. They make you think."

"What quotation did you like best?" I ask as we make the short trip from my locker to his.

He looks at me as he rifles blindly through his locker. "I don't know. Maybe, 'The journey of a thousand miles begins with one step.' I like that idea." He slams his locker closed.

As we walk, I consider telling him that our journey from his locker to the parking lot will probably take about seven hundred and thirty steps, but I don't want to scare him with another one of my weird habits. Besides, he's not talking about actual footsteps. It's not clear whether he's applying that quote to his life or mine, but I'd rather not trivialize his comment by making a stupid observation about literally counting steps.

In the parking lot, I grab his arm. "Hey, don't we have to wait for Nancy?"

"No, she's already gone home. The short bus arrives fifteen minutes before the end of the regular school day."

"Hey, be nice."

"What? It is shorter than the regular bus."

"You're making fun of me. I can't believe I said that to you. What an ass."

"It was fun watching you squirm."

"Gee, thanks. So how come you don't drive Nancy home every day?"

"Routine. My aunt and uncle can't drop everything to pick her up every day, so she's used to taking the bus. It's good social time for her. She likes it."

"Except when it's raining."

"Exactly."

We climb into his car. As he backs out of his spot, he says, "Hey, speaking of asses, I meant to tell you, that's another reason I knew you were a cheerleader."

"What do you mean?"

"Your ass. You wiggle it when you walk. I don't think you can help it."

"I do not."

"Oh, yes you do. You wouldn't know because you're not behind you when you're walking."

"So, you've been ogling my ass?"

"Yeah, pretty much since the day we met. You have a nice ass. I can't be held responsible for wanting to ogle it."

He's been checking out my ass.

He's been checking it out since the day we met.

I have a nice ass.

"I like your eyes," I say.

He laughs. "Well, thanks."

"It's true. I really do." *I've written some freaking inspired imagery about your eyes, let me tell ya.* "When someone asks you what colour they are, what do you say?"

"People don't ask me what colour my eyes are."

"Well, pretend they did. What would you say?"

"I have no idea. Green?"

"Really?"

"Why, what would you say?"

I think amber, but I say, "Hazel."

"Okay, hazel it is."

"I win?"

"You win."

"That was easy."

"I'm not in the mood to argue. According to Taoism, 'He who talks more is sooner exhausted.' Trying to talk to you over the last couple of weeks has tired me out. I need a rest." He smiles as he says this.

I smile too. This more-than-a-friend thing feels good. I watch his profile as he navigates a lane change. I love the workings of his face when he concentrates. "Who do you think you'll interview for the writing assignment?"

"Um, probably my aunt."

"Oh yeah? How come?"

"Because she's a really cool person. Remember Mr. Vesters said it should be someone you admire? I admire her. I think you'd like her. She's a writer."

"Really? What does she write?"

"Not novels or anything. She wrote a book last year about raising kids with autism. That's why she's been away for a few weeks. She was doing a book tour and talking at conventions and stuff. Moving in with them was good timing. My uncle is super busy with work, so I'm helping him deal with Nancy while my aunt is away."

This would be the perfect moment to ask him why he was forced to leave his other school, but I don't want to ruin the moment by pressing for more information. For once, my filter works, keeping the burning question at bay. "You love her a lot." That's what I say instead.

"My aunt? Sure, she's my aunt. Of course I love her."

"No, not your aunt. I mean Nancy."

"Oh. Nance? Yeah. I feel bad for her. For all kids like her. Dealt a crummy hand and doing the best they can. Poor Nance doesn't even have access to the full deck a lot of the time."

"Nice metaphors," I say,

"Thanks." His chest puffs up in that back-patting way that shows he's proud of himself. It's kind of adorable. "That's some serious praise coming from you," he adds.

"You know it."

We drive the rest of the way in silence. It's not the kind of silence I feel pressured to fill with mindless jabbering, which is good because when I jabber mindlessly, I never know what nonsense will trip off my tongue.

A few minutes later, we're in my driveway, and Lucas turns off the engine and spins in his seat so he can look at me. "You know, I could drive you to school in the mornings, too. You wouldn't have to take the bus at all. Do you want me to pick you up tomorrow?"

"I wouldn't ask you to do that."

"You're not asking me. I'm asking you."

"Oh. Right."

"So? Should I pick you up?"

"Well, sure. I guess."

"Cool. So I'll see you at around eight fifteen?"

"That sounds good. Thanks for the ride today."

"I'm glad you said 'yes.'"

"Me too. I wasn't looking forward to getting on the bus."

"That's what I figured." He pauses, licks his lips and thinks for a second. "Would it be okay . . . I mean . . . can I kiss you?"

Can a left ventricle smile? Because if it can, mine is smiling its butt off. That is, of course, if a left ventricle also has a butt. "I don't know if it's a good idea for you to kiss me, you know, considering how much you liked it the first time." I make a little explosion sound and flick my hand beside my head, copying the gesture he used last night when making his mortifying confession. He shakes his head and sighs, but he smiles at the same time. He knows I'm joking.

"Too soon?" I say.

"Are you kidding? I figured you'd be making fun of me two minutes after I told you what happened on Friday. You've given me a whole twenty-four hours to recover."

"I was feeling generous."

"I'm flattered. So?"

"So what?"

"Hannah, can I kiss you?"

I nod. He smiles again and leans toward me, his eyes drifting down to my lips. I close my eyes and wait for the moment of contact. When his mouth finds mine, my heart beats in double-time. My lips remember his lips, warming instantly with that recognition, but when our tongues meet, my whole body warms. No, "warms" isn't a strong enough word. "Ignites" is more like it.

I think of all the questionnaires we filled out before writing our college applications. *What do you want to do with the rest of your life?* Whatever I said, the answers were all lies. With Lucas's lips pressed to mine, his hair tickling my forehead, his hand squeezing my wrist as he kisses me again and again, I know that this right here is all I want to do for the rest of my life.

He gives me one last soft kiss, and as he pulls away, he looks down at my lips again and touches my chin with his index finger.

My heart swells so much, I think it might be crowding my left lung.

"I'm sorry I have to go," he says. "My uncle is heading in to the office tonight. I have to get the car back."

My disappointment is palpable. I'd love more time with him, but considering the alternative—a trip home on the bus, wads of paper beaming off the target on the back of my head—I can't complain. "That's okay." I lift my bag onto my lap.

"I'll walk you to the door." He follows me up the steps and watches me fish the keys out of my bag. As I reach for the door, he stops my hand. "Hey, before you go in, can I kiss you again?"

"Are you going to ask me every time? Because that—"

He grabs me and pulls me close. One of his hands slides under my ear and cups my neck. The way he cradles my neck as he kisses me makes me feel like I'm in a movie, and then he rubs his nose against mine, which is the sweetest thing ever. My heart can't swell much more. I'm sure my right lung is being squashed now, too.

"I'll text you or call you, okay?" he says.

"Okay."

He climbs into the car, waving before he slams the door.

I like the way he waves. I also like his eyes and his smile. I like how he's confident sometimes, but vulnerable sometimes, too. I like that he's left-handed and that he has a thing for philosophical quotes. I really, really like his kisses.

But most of all, I like that he makes me feel normal.

Chapter 20

New Terrain

BEING MORE THAN Lucas's friend changes the landscape of my life completely. For months, I travelled a flat, straight road with more of the same stretching ahead as far as I can see. But now hills and mountains pop up everywhere. Some I can anticipate, but others are totally unexpected. There are even a few bends in the road. Being more than Lucas's friend is all new terrain.

For one thing, being more than Lucas's friend means we text each other non-stop all evening until I fall asleep with my phone in my hand. It means talking to Lucas on the phone while *Jeopardy!* is on and not even caring if I miss an entire category of questions because I'm laughing so hard at something he's said.

It also means spending a few minutes after the phone call thinking about how great it feels to laugh.

It means being picked up in the morning and brought home after school. Not having to take the bus is sweet. Good-morning and good-bye kisses make those trips back and forth to school even sweeter. It means Lucas walking me to my locker and then to math class in the morning and him running to catch up with me between classes so he can walk me to English.

He doesn't complain about the roundabout journeys I take between classes, and I like him all the more for never questioning me and for taking every single one of my quirks in his stride.

Lucas and I reach the decision to restrict public displays of affection without actually discussing it. I can't call it a mutual decision. I'm sure he's waiting for a sign from me—some indication that I'd be comfortable flaunting our relationship. I'm not ready, so I don't give him a sign, and he doesn't press the issue.

The one part of the day that doesn't change is lunch hour. Lucas swings by my locker at noon to say "hi," and then he spends time in the Spec Ed room while I retreat to the library to find my latest call number. However, necessity sometimes dictates a disruption to my beloved routine. Turns out, I bombed a ten-point question on the last math test—not surprising since I'd spent the hour trying to imagine all the things I should have said to Lucas instead of, "So you want to be one-and-a-half friends?" Mr. Murray offered to let me and two other students from my math class do a lunch hour rewrite.

That's how I find myself making a quick trip to my locker today at lunch instead of to the library. I'm in the math wing—unfamiliar territory at lunch hour—and as I turn the corner, my least favourite people stand in a clump across from Mr. Murray's classroom. The guys are huddled together, while Allison and Marla hang back, leaning against the wall.

Brett keeps looking over his shoulder as if he's worried about who might be watching. When he sees me, a series of nudges and coughs breaks up the crowd and Brody Cooper, resident drug lord, tosses something inside his locker and slams it shut.

I duck into the alcove outside Mr. Murray's room, but hiding is useless. They've already seen me.

"So do you guys think the sped and the nark are doing it?" Kelly says.

She says this loudly, so I know the comment is entirely for my benefit. What's the point in saying it if I can't hear?

"I don't think the retard knows how to do it." Brett laughs.

"I'm sure she'd show him." Kelly's nasal voice rings out across the hallway. "She'd teach him all the moves."

"Then she'll tell everyone about it because she can't keep her mouth shut," Marla says, laughing at her own feeble joke.

"Open mouths can be handy," Brett says, with a disgusting guffaw that makes me want to take a shower.

Laughter fills the air, Allison's shrill giggle soaring above the others.

As the laughter dies down, Dallyn pipes up. "Lay off you guys."

What's going on? Dallyn's defending me?

I'm tempted to peek around the corner to see the look on Allison's face. It must be highly entertaining. Unfortunately, Mr. Murray arrives before I can look. He hands me his coffee mug to hold while he digs his keys out of his pocket.

I follow him into the classroom.

"No sign of anyone else?" he asks.

"Uh, no. Just me so far." I slide into my seat, wondering what's going on in the hallway. Maybe Dallyn's uncharacteristic defence of me has inspired Allison to smack him again. I wish for that with every fibre of my being.

"Okay, Hannah. Here you go." Mr. Murray slides a sheet of paper onto my desk. "Good luck."

I stare blankly at the page, clicking my pen. Is there any point in attempting to redo my answer? How can I focus on curvilinear asymptotes after Dallyn Wade demonstrated human compassion for the first time in his life? Shouldn't I call the Pope or something?

We're in Lucas's car after school. His eyes dart to my hands which are clamped together in my lap. "Are you okay? You seemed weird this afternoon."

"I'm always weird."

"Weirder than usual," he says. "You hardly got anything done in Writer's Craft. You totally zoned out."

I stare out the side window. It's true. My lunch hour run-in with the pinheads rattled me. Being back on everyone's radar after over two months of relative peace sucks, but I'm afraid to tell Lucas. What if he feels guilty again for stirring things up and wants to back away? "It was just a weird day."

Lucas frowns, glancing at my hands again. "If there's something wrong, maybe I can help."

"No, it's not a big deal. I can handle it."

"Okay, now you have to tell me."

I see that rug in my mind's eye—the one Mom jams all her crap under—and I sigh. I can't point out her avoidance tactics and then side-step my own issues. I take a deep breath and then explain what happened in the hall at lunch.

He slams a closed fist against the steering wheel. "Assholes," he mutters. "I'll talk to Dallyn."

His anger startles me. "No, you don't have to do anything. Dallyn stuck up for me. For us, I guess. He told them to lay off. Don't you think that's weird? Why would he suddenly be so concerned about my feelings?"

Lucas frowns. He checks each of his side mirrors in turn.

"I wouldn't spend too much time trying to figure out how his brain works. That's if he even has a brain in the first place." He glances at me. "I want you to tell me if anything else happens."

"Okay." I sigh.

"I mean it, Hannah. You know you can tell me anything, right?" he asks.

"Yeah. I know."

"Good. Just making sure."

When we get to my house, Lucas can't park in the driveway. Mom's car dominates the single space. He pulls up to the curb.

I bob my chin at the car. "My mom has the night off."

"I don't have to leave right this second. Should I come in and meet her?"

I peer at the house, trying to imagine the scene. What if Mom's flaked out on the couch in her silk robe watching some lame reality show? Or doing housework, wearing old skin-tight jeans and a threadbare belly shirt with Bon Jovi blasting in the kitchen?

Step right up, folks! Watch Hannah Forde send her boyfriend running for the hills.

I reach for Lucas's hand and squeeze. "I think I should tell her about you first, you know, before you meet her."

Lucas draws his head back. "You haven't told her about me?"

I wince. "I totally should have told her, right?"

Lucas gives me the "well, yeah" look. "I told my parents about you. My aunt and uncle, too."

"You did?"

"I told my aunt how you're into writing. She said she'd love to talk to you about it. She wondered if you'd like to come over for dinner. Like maybe even tomorrow."

Dinner? With his family? *Tomorrow?* Oh God, he's trying to kill me. This is another one of those more-than-a-friend things. Boyfriends invite their girlfriends over for dinner. Boyfriends all over the world take their girlfriends home to meet the parents—or the aunt and uncle, as the case may be. This may be a universal truth, but it doesn't make the reality of the situation any less nerve-wracking.

"Hannah?" Lucas grips my hand. "What do you think? Do you want to come over for dinner tomorrow?"

"I'll ask my mom if I can. I'll let you know, okay?" This is the most ridiculous thing I've ever said. My mother won't tell me I can't go to Lucas's house for dinner. I could ask her if she'd mind if we went upstairs to have sex, and she'd probably suggest mood music.

That night, we make fajitas for dinner. The whole time I'm slicing peppers, my phone chirps in the other room. I'm sure it's Lucas.

Did you tell your mom yet?

What did she say?

Are you coming over for dinner?

I'm working my way up to telling her. I take a deep breath, ready to spill, when she turns to me and makes an announcement.

"I changed the doorknob on your bedroom today all by myself. It has a locking mechanism. You can lock your door at night if it makes you feel safer."

"Huh. Okay. Thanks, I guess."

"I haven't had a date since that guy slept on the couch. Did you know that?"

A date. She calls what she does with guys after work "dates." I want to ask her if she has her period.

"Aren't you proud of me?" she says, hip-checking me at the sink. "Who needs men, right? We'll get ourselves a Lonely Hearts Club sign and stick it on the roof."

My phone chirps again, twice in quick succession. *Have you told her yet, Hannah? Huh? How about now?*

"You know, it's funny you say that, Mom . . . ." I take a quick breath. "I actually have a boyfriend."

"You do?"

"Don't look so surprised."

"I'm not surprised."

"You're gobsmacked, Mom."

"I am?"

"You don't have to pretend for my benefit. I know it's shocking."

"It's not shocking. You're pretty. You're smart. Any boy would be lucky to have you as a girlfriend. I didn't think you were interested in any of the boys at school, that's all. You always say they're so stupid.

Dylan and all those boys."

"It's Dallyn, and they are all stupid." Despite the four words Dallyn uttered in my defence earlier, I'm not ready to nominate him for a Nobel Peace Prize. "This guy—he's new," I say. "He's different."

He's amazing.

"What's his name?"

"Lucas."

"Ooh, I like that name. Does he take the bus with you?"

"He doesn't take the bus. I don't take the bus anymore either. He drives me back and forth to school."

"I thought you were home earlier than usual today. That explains it." She wiggles her eyebrows at me. "So is he a good kisser?"

"None of your business," I say, smiling into the sink.

"Oh come on. This is girl talk. Moms and daughters are supposed to talk about stuff like this."

"No, I don't think mothers are supposed to dig for details. I think you're supposed to ask if we're being careful and using protection, especially after what happened with you and Dad in high school."

Her hand stops moving in mid–cheese-grate. She looks at me, her lips pinched.

"Don't worry," I assure her. "He's not that kind of guy. Anyway, I'm not about to screw up my life by getting pregnant." The words "like you did" float in the silence at the end of the sentence.

She sniffs and goes back to grating.

I feel a pang of guilt for the harshness of my words. "So Lucas invited me to his aunt and uncle's house for dinner tomorrow. Since you're working, is it okay if I go?"

I tell myself not to hope she tells me I can't go.

She gives me a sideways look. "That sounds nice."

Damn it.

"His parents will be there too, right? Is it a big family dinner or something?"

"No, just his aunt and uncle and his cousin. He's living with them right now. It's temporary."

Mom raises an eyebrow.

"It's a long story." I toss all the sliced veggies into the frying pan and hope she won't ask me to tell her this long story.

That would be tricky, considering I don't know it.

Chapter 21

Progress

IT'S FRIDAY. WE'RE in the car heading to Lucas's aunt and uncle's house for dinner. I've had a blissfully uneventful day. This is a good thing. I've been way too busy stressing out about the family dinner to deal with any other crap.

"You okay?" Lucas asks.

"I'm nervous."

"Don't be nervous. Everything will be fine. Relax."

"I'm trying." I offer up a tepid smile.

I imagine myself sitting at the table with Lucas's family. Just normal human interaction. Casual conversation. No problem. I can do that.

Oh, God, who am I kidding? I'm a mess. I can't count footsteps. I need a pen to click or a clock to count away the seconds on. I resort to fiddling with my shirt, and by the time we pull into his aunt and uncle's garage, the right side of the hem is a wrinkly mess from being scrunched by my sweaty hands. I wipe them on my thighs before climbing out of the car.

I follow Lucas to the door, and he swings it open. "Hello?"

"We're in the kitchen!" a woman's voice replies.

Lucas takes my school bag, hangs up my coat over top of his and kicks off his shoes. I do the same. He gives me a quick kiss for courage—at least that's how I interpret it—and then he takes my clammy hand and starts leading me to the kitchen.

"Wait!" I grab his arm. "What should I call your aunt? Mrs. Owens?"

He frowns. "She might think that's weird."

"It would be weirder to call her 'Trudy' wouldn't it?"

"Kind of forward," he agrees, "though not necessarily weirder."

"I'm not good at this sort of thing, Lucas. Seriously. Social skills of a turtle. Help me out."

"How about you try Mrs. Gordon?" he suggests.

I give him my best confused fish face.

"She's my mom's sister," he explains. "Different last name. Though you can call her 'Mrs. Owens' if you like. That might be good for a laugh."

"You're a riot." I glare at him.

Lucas smiles and smoothes the crease between my eyebrows with his thumbs. He gives me another peck on the lips and grabs my hand again.

Passing the family room on the way to the kitchen, I take note of the shiny hardwood floors, the beautiful paintings on the walls and the general lack of clutter.

By comparison, my house looks like it could be on one of those TV shows about hoarders—where the people have so much junk piled up, they can't find their pets.

"Everything's so neat," I whisper.

"That's to help Nancy," he explains. "Messiness stresses her out."

"Right. That makes sense."

The kitchen is just as neat as the family room. Nancy sits at the table doing homework. It looks like science. She's labelling diagrams.

"Hey, Nance," Lucas says. He leans over and rests his elbows on the table until she looks up at him.

"Hi." She tilts her body sideways and glances at me. Well, not exactly. What she actually does is glance at my stomach. "Hannah rhymes with banana."

"Hannah rhymes with banana" is a weird thing to say, but it's a step up from "bah, humbug." At least she knows my name. Her acknowledgment gives me a boost of confidence, but I still stand there stupidly.

Lucas reacts for me. He laughs and says, "Sure does." Then he holds his hand out to hers ET-style and their index fingers touch. This makes Nancy smile a little. Lucas grins back at her.

His aunt pats him on the back. "Okay, let her get on with her work."

He smiles at me. "Hannah, this is my Aunt Trudy."

Aunt Trudy dries her hand on a dishtowel and reaches out to shake my hand. I'm still worried about my sweaty palms, and I wish I'd asked to borrow the dishtowel before slipping my hand in hers.

"It's nice to meet you, Hannah," she says.

She has warm eyes.

"It's nice to meet you, too . . . ." I've already forgotten her last name. Excellent.

"I hear you've been helping Lucas with his schoolwork. This changing schools business has been so disruptive. It's nice of you to help out."

"It's just some reading, sometimes. I don't mind." *He's a really good kisser. Fringe benefit.*

"Hannah's a great reader," Lucas says. "She's a good writer, too."

"Lucas, you've never read anything I've written," I say.

"Mr. Vesters thinks you're a good writer."

"Well, if he thinks so, it must be true," Lucas's aunt says. "Don Vesters has an inimitable grasp on writing conventions and style. Better than a lot of authors I know."

Lucas's aunt said "inimitable." An awesome five-syllable word. I like her already. I look up at Lucas. "I didn't know Mr. V. taught Nancy."

Aunt Trudy laughs. "Don? He's never taught Nancy. No, I've known him for years. We took some writing courses together about ten years ago. Lovely man."

Lucas's aunt knows Mr. Vesters? That means Lucas kind of knows Mr. Vesters. I question him with my eyes, and he shrugs, like he's been caught in a lie. He hasn't lied to me—not really—but even so, I feel like he's purposely kept me out of the he-kind-of-knows-Mr. Vesters loop.

"Okay, Nancy needs to concentrate. Why don't you two go watch TV in the basement or something? Uncle Ken's up in his office working. Dinner will be ready soon."

"Do you need any help?" Lucas asks. She swats him with the dishtowel and tells him to shoo. She's so motherly, and she's not even his mother.

Lucas leads me to the basement rec room. A big-screen TV is mounted over the fireplace and one of those huge couches forms an L-shape in front of it. We both flop down on the long part of the "L." Lucas reaches for my arm and plays with my sleeve.

"Well, go ahead," he says.

"Go ahead and what?"

"Ask me. How come I didn't tell you my aunt knows Mr. Vesters?

That's what you want to know, right?"

"I guess. I mean, did you already know him before you started school?"

"I had no idea who he was. He was at a meeting I had with a guidance counsellor about my timetable on my first day. Mrs. Palmer said I might have to take English in summer school because all the classes were full, but Mr. Vesters offered to take me into his Writer's Craft class and change the program so I could get my mainstream English credit."

"Summer school would've sucked."

"Totally. Aunt Trudy asked him to watch out for me. Maybe he was worried she'd think he was an ass if he didn't try to help me. At least that's what I thought at first. Now I know that's not true. He's a good guy."

"He sure wants you to do okay," I say.

"Why would you say that?"

"Because he asked me to help you."

"He did?"

I shrug, remembering too late that Mr. Vesters asked me not to tell Lucas about his request. "He said he was worried you might struggle. He made me promise not to tell you. He didn't want to make you self-conscious. I guess that doesn't really matter now."

"Huh."

"Don't be embarrassed."

"I'm not embarrassed. I think it's kind of funny actually."

"I don't get how that's funny."

"Well, it's just that he said almost the same thing to me during that meeting in the guidance office. He said I might find the class tough, but he'd make sure I got help. He told me about you—said I'd probably be sitting beside you. Mrs. Palmer agreed it would be nice if you had someone to talk to because you've had a rough semester, but not to tell you they'd mentioned anything."

"Wait, are you telling me you started hanging around with me as a favour to Mr. V. and Mrs. Palmer?"

"No, I started hanging around you because you have a nice ass."

I roll my eyes.

"I'm kidding," he says. "I thought you seemed interesting."

"You thought I seemed interesting? Me?"

"Will you stop that?"

"Stop what?" I pick at the seam of the couch cushion. He traps my hand with his.

"Stop thinking there isn't a single person in the world who'd want to get to know you. I had no idea who you were when we bumped into each other in the hall that first day," he says. "By the time I figured out you were the girl Mr. Vesters had told me about, it didn't matter. I wanted to talk to you. Not because of what Mr. Vesters and Mrs. Palmer said, but because of me. Because of you."

"That's what I couldn't understand. I still don't understand. Why me?"

"Why you? Because you're different. Quirky. Feisty. Smart. You were a mystery to me. Sure, you slammed the door in my face and gave me attitude, but that's way more interesting than giggling and flirting. No one had to convince me to spend more time with you, Hannah."

"So talking to me wasn't a favour to Mr. V?"

He puts his arm around me and pulls me close, tipping my chin up. He kisses me gently. "Does that seem like something I'd do as a favour to Mr. Vesters?"

"Uh-uh."

He kisses me again, more passionately this time. "How about that?"

"Okay, okay," I say breathlessly as I pull away. "It was a stupid question."

"Really stupid. It's probably one of the stupidest things you've said to me so far. And you've said a lot of really dumb things."

All the stupid things I've said to him flash before my eyes like neon signs. Soon, there are so many neon signs flashing before my eyes that it's a wonder I don't have an epileptic seizure. "I have said some doozies, haven't I?"

"Yep. And somehow I'm the one apologizing all the time. Go figure."

I like how he's not trying to soften the blow. His honesty reveals more about his feelings than any attempts to appease me ever would.

"You're right. I'm sorry I've been such a pain in the ass." I lean over to kiss him. It's meant to be a sweet apologetic kiss, but it ends up being one of those kisses that instantly explodes, and before you know it, I've forgotten that we're in his aunt and uncle's basement and somehow find myself clambering onto his lap and straddling him. I kiss him like a crazy woman, almost tearing his hair out at the roots. He doesn't protest, although he does groan a little as I wiggle against him. Then I remember.

Basement.

Couch.

Lap.

Happy New Year!

I scramble to the end of the couch mumbling apologies and wiping my mouth with the back of my hand.

"It's okay." Lucas reaches for me and tries to pull me back. "My aunt and uncle are all about respecting privacy. They're not gonna walk in on us. Get back over here."

I shake my head and check my buttons. They're all done up. No body parts are hanging out.

Lucas watches my fingers travel across the buttonholes on my shirt. "Oh right...." He leans forward, his eyes wide.

I cover my face with my hands.

He scoots beside me and rubs my back. "It's okay. I forgot about . . . that. We can stop."

I rock back and forth a few times, my hands still covering my eyes. "Did you see the pictures from New Year's, Lucas?" I finally ask him. "Did you see them, or did you just hear about them?"

"I didn't see them. Someone described them to me."

I peek through my fingers. He's frowning at the carpet, the muscle in his jaw jumping erratically. Is he imagining the scene? "Do I want to know who told you?"

"Does it matter?"

"I guess not." I pause, then move my hands away from my face. "Was it Dallyn?"

He shakes his head. "No."

"Allison?"

"Uh-uh."

"Marla?"

His mouth puckers. All the confirmation I need.

"Of course it was Marla." I hate her. I hate her with the wrath of a thousand fire-breathing dragons.

"She told me the day she warned me about hanging around with you. She said you tried to break up Dallyn and Allison by coming on to him.

She said Allison waited for you to make your move, and then she took the pictures."

"Bullshit. It's all lies."

He shakes his head and clenches his fists. "I know."

He says this with such authority—such blind faith—my heart does somersaults. "How do you know?"

He shrugs. "I just do."

"You sound so sure. I was there, and sometimes I'm not even sure what happened that night."

"When you hear the same rumours about yourself so many times, you start to believe they're true," he says, staring at a blank spot on the wall across the room. "Anyway, it doesn't matter. Whatever happened before isn't important, and I wouldn't like you more or feel different about you if it hadn't happened. To me, you're Hannah, both ways."

He threads his fingers through mine and draws little pictures on the back of my hand while I work at processing the words he's just said.

"You're not a bad person. You know that, right? You just have a little baggage. Like everyone," he says. "Like me."

Like you? What do you mean? For the millionth time, I wonder why he had to transfer schools in April. And now I wonder if that's how he knows exactly the way I feel. "Are you ever going to tell me what happened at your old school, Lucas?" I ask gently.

He looks at me without speaking. He has to tell me sooner or later. I'd prefer sooner. The mystery of what happened to him at his old school is starting to take on a life of its own in my imagination.

He hacked the school's computer system and changed his final marks.

He slipped a roofie into a girl's drink at a dance and raped her behind the bleachers.

He made a pass at a hot, young teacher.

He made a pass at an ugly, old teacher . . . .

These and a hundred other scenarios I've imagined, each more bizarre than the one before it and not one of them makes sense.

Lucas's aunt opens the door at the top of the stairs, and my question stays suspended in the air between us.

"Dinner is ready," she calls.

Worst timing ever, at least in my opinion. Lucas probably wants to buy her a fruit basket.

At the dining room table, Lucas sits beside me. Aunt Trudy and Nancy sit across from us. Uncle Ken's spot at the head of the table remains empty.

"Why isn't dad eating?" Nancy scowls at her plate and pushes the peas as far away from the chicken and potatoes as possible.

"Dad's on the phone with a client. He'll eat later."

"He's always on the phone with a client or working late. It sucks."

Nancy continues scowling. She may be disappointed, but I'm kind of relieved. One less set of eyes assessing me over dinner can't be a bad thing.

"My uncle is an accountant," Lucas says. "It's tax season, so he's really busy right now."

I nod and pick up my knife and fork. Across the table, Nancy continues to push her food around, grumbling that the idiot peas are tainting her scalloped potatoes. I'm with her on that. I've never liked peas. The way they explode always freaks me out. I choke them back because I'm a guest who knows how to be polite, damn it. And I don't have autism.

Dinner conversation focuses mainly on Aunt Trudy's writing. She talks about the courses she's taken and the writing process and shares some highlights from her book tour. I listen with rapt fascination. I decide there and then that I want to write a book. I have no idea what this book will be about, but it will be amazing, and I will travel all around the country promoting it.

"How was school today, Lucas?" she asks.

He swallows a piece of chicken and chases his food with a chug of water. "It was okay. Hey, I have to do an interview for Mr. Vesters' class. Can I interview you?"

Aunt Trudy smiles.

"See, Nancy?" she says. "Lucas thinks I'm interesting."

"That's 'cause you're not his mom," Nancy says, her mouth full of scalloped potatoes which may or may not have been tainted by idiot peas.

"Hmm. I guess you can't argue with logic like that," Aunt Trudy says, winking at her daughter.

Nancy gives her mom a wide toothy grin. It's the first time I've seen her smile like that. There's something else we have in common. She's a lot prettier when she smiles.

After dinner, Lucas and I help clear the table.

"So was that as bad as you thought it would be?" he whispers, as Aunt Trudy scrapes plates in the kitchen.

"I didn't say it was going to be bad. I was nervous, that's all."

"Do you really think you have—what did you say earlier?—the social skills of a turtle?"

"I have my moments."

He laughs. "We all have our moments."

Once the table is clear, Aunt Trudy asks us if we wouldn't mind entertaining Nancy until her favourite TV show starts. Nancy has a hissy fit. Apparently her dad always plays a board game with her after dinner.

"We can play something with you, Nance," Lucas says.

Okay. Looks like we're going to play a board game with Nancy.

"This one," Nancy says, grabbing a yellow banana-shaped bag from a shelf behind the table. She opens the zipper, pouring little tiles with letters on them all over the dining room table.

"Hey, is this a word game? I love word games," I say. "Is it like Scrabble?"

Board games I can take or leave, but I'm all about the word games. Crosswords, Jumbles, Scrabble, Boggle, *Wheel of Fortune*. If I didn't love word games, I wouldn't tell Nancy I did. She can probably spot a phony a mile away.

"Bananagrams," she tells me. Actually, she tells my stomach. I don't think she's looked at my face once all night—or ever, for that matter. "It's the best game. Lucas won't play. He says games are supposed to be fun. If your name was 'Hannahnagrams' it would rhyme."

"I guess it would," I agree. What else can I say?

"Your name is a palindrome," Nancy tells me.

"I know. That's my favourite thing about my name."

"My favourite thing is that it rhymes with banana."

Lucas giggles beside Nancy and me while we launch into a rousing game of Bananagrams. She has a great vocabulary. She wipes the floor with me. Granted, it's hard to concentrate because the whole time we're playing, Lucas traces swirly patterns on my back with his fingertips. It feels so good, it's a wonder I can pull together any words aside from "ooh," "aah" and "mmm."

We're in the middle of the game when Lucas's uncle finally makes his way downstairs.

"Who's watching *Law and Order*?" he calls out.

Nancy leaps up so quickly, she almost turns the table over. "Me, me, me!"

Uncle Ken pops his head into the dining room. He's agreeable-looking in that I-think-I've-seen-you-somewhere-before way that some people have. Lucas introduces me, and his uncle apologizes for missing dinner.

"The perils of April." He shrugs and sighs.

He and Nancy wander off to the family room together. Lucas and I collect the Bananagram tiles, and he puts them away.

"Thanks for doing that." Lucas stands in front of me and takes my hands in his. "You were great with her. I think she likes you."

"She's funny. Smart, too."

"She is smart," Lucas agrees. "Asperger's is an autism spectrum disorder. That's a fancy way of saying everyone who has it deals with different problems. She does great in school. The skin sensitivity and not knowing how to act in social situations are the hardest for her to deal with. She has trouble making friends. People are put off by the hand flapping and pacing and stuff."

My face warms. I'm totally one of those people.

"Hey, what was that touching-index-fingers thing you did when she was doing her homework earlier?" I ask.

"I push her a little. Try to make her interact. I make her look at me. Sometimes she does and sometimes she doesn't. Every bit of safe contact helps. At least that's what I figure."

"She sure is stubborn." I think about the small pile of "idiot peas" that remained on her plate at the end of the meal.

"Oh yeah. Once she decides something, it's really hard to budge her, especially if you're messing with her routine. Plus, she has these obsessions. Like detective stories and crime dramas on TV. She loves anything involving clues." He chuckles. "Now that I think of it, I guess she does have a hell of a lot of issues. Maybe I'm comparing her to this kid at my old school—Mark. Next to him, she seems almost normal. . . ."

His words trail off. Or maybe they don't. Maybe he keeps talking, but I don't process much after he says, "my old school." I say, "Hmmm," like I'm thinking about Nancy and her issues. I'm not. Not at all. I hesitate for a moment and then take the plunge. "Lucas, I want to know what happened at your old school."

He drops my hands and steps away from me. "I'd rather not talk about it."

"That's not fair. You know all my stuff."

"All your stuff? Are we keeping score now?"

He puts his hands on his hips, and I cross my arms in response. "Don't be like that."

He sighs and shakes his head. Thinking. He's thinking. Is he tottering? I reach out and grab a fistful of T-shirt near his waist.

"Please?" I take a step closer and slip my arms around him.

He tilts his head back in resignation, and then he makes a frustrated growling sound, resting his hands on my waist and looking down at me.

"Okay. Okay, you win."

Chapter 22

Unpacking the Baggage

LUCAS GRABS HIS laptop from his backpack as we pass through the front hall, and then he takes me back down to the basement where he motions for me to join him on the couch. He flips his laptop open on the coffee table, takes a deep breath and grimaces as he waits for the screen to come to life.

"I'm going to show you something," he says. "Before I do, I need to tell you about Mark. You know, the kid from my old school?"

"Okay. What about Mark?"

He takes another huge breath. It's moments like these that the expression "girding your loins" was designed for. Lucas is totally girding his loins. I'll be honest, I'm girding mine a little, too.

"So, this year at my old school, I joined a club called Buddy Up," Lucas says, his tone business-like all of a sudden. "It's this group that connects kids who have learning disabilities with other students who kind of mentor them. Mark was the kid I was paired with. I was the mentor." He smiles grimly.

"I bet you were a great mentor." I'm not saying that to soothe his ego. After seeing how he deals with Nancy, I figure he can mentor anyone.

"I did my best. He was autistic. He isolated himself way more than Nancy. He was so lost in his own world. I tried to get him to do stuff after school. We'd take the city bus to the arcade at the mall. He loved the bus. How sad is that?"

"That is pretty sad."

"Anyway, this one day, we were waiting at the bus stop behind the mall, and there were these two guys standing really close together. The one guy went to my school. His name was Rory. He was buying drugs from this other guy. It used to happen at that bus stop all the time. Mark was watching them, totally zoned out. You know how kids like that stare sometimes and don't realize they're doing it? So the guy selling the drugs sees him watching and says, 'What are you staring at, retard?'"

"Asshole."

"Total asshole," Lucas agrees. "Mark shouted back that he wasn't a retard. I was kind of proud of him for sticking up for himself, but you choose your battles, right? But then Rory comes at us and starts shoving Mark. The kid was so terrified, he wet himself. What could I do? I got in the middle of it and . . . well . . . ."

He gives me one last hesitant look, and then he opens a file on his desktop. It's a video file. He presses play and sits back, crossing his arms.

The video is only fifty-three seconds in total. At the beginning, the camera is aimed at Mark, identifiable by the telltale dark stain down the leg of his pants. Then the focus shifts to Lucas and the other guy—Rory, I guess—as they close in on each other. Rory shoves Lucas's shoulders, and Lucas pushes him back. Rory grabs Lucas in a headlock. Lucas rams the heel of his shoe into Rory's shin and jabs his elbow into Rory's stomach, winding him.

They're at each other again, grabbing and punching erratically. The video goes in and out of focus, and it's hard to tell what's happening.

Then something flashes in Lucas's left hand.

It's a knife.

Another blurry scuffle unfolds, and Lucas's elbow slams into Rory's nose. Rory's hands fly to his face. When he pulls them away, there's blood everywhere.

The video jerkily pans across the crowd of bystanders, and then it goes to black.

We just sit there for a while, staring at the nothingness on the screen.

"What happened after that?" I finally whisper.

"Not much. Rory took off with his buddy. I put the knife in my pocket. That's pretty much it."

Again, I can't think of what to say.

"That wasn't my knife," Lucas says. "Rory tried to cut me, and I got it away from him in the scuffle. I didn't use it, but I think I broke his nose. It looks bad, huh?"

I can't deny it. It looks bad. "How'd you get the video?"

"Some kid from school filmed it with his phone and threw it up on YouTube. I snagged it before school admin got tipped off and took it down. It was longer than that. I edited it down."

Like me with the pictures on Twitter, paring down the ten posted pictures and selecting the best ones as a keepsake. A souvenir to rage over later.

"Did you get charged?" I ask him.

"No. It didn't get that far. Rory's a rough kid. He already had a police record, and he got suspended a lot. He had a social worker helping at school and stuff. We both got kicked out."

"You weren't even on school property."

"Doesn't matter. Zero-tolerance policy. We both posed a danger to the school community. All that good stuff. 'A policy is a policy.'"

I can almost hear the voice of whatever official spouted these edicts at him. I'm irrationally angry on Lucas's behalf. Then I decide, no, my anger isn't irrational. It's perfectly reasonable.

"I can't believe you got expelled for protecting someone. That's so unfair."

"Whatever. It is what it is."

Acceptance. He's so calm. I'd be screaming my head off.

"It wasn't easy getting a timetable at a new school either. Remember when I was away for a couple of days? You accused me of ditching?"

"And you told me to mind my own business?"

"Exactly." He smiles. "I had to do a two-day anger management course before the principal would finalize my timetable."

"That sucks."

"You know what? It was a pain, but I learned a lot. Stuff's been building up inside me for a long time. I snapped that day at the bus stop. The classes helped me figure everything out."

I shake my head, trying to fathom the notion of Lucas snapping. "This is so weird. When I think of a loose cannon, I picture someone like Dallyn, not you."

Lucas shrugs. "Dallyn's got issues for sure. But I do, too."

"You're nothing like him, Lucas."

"What I mean is, when someone picks on a defenceless kid or bullies a friend of mine for no reason, I know what it feels like, and I just get so mad . . . ." He grits his teeth and shakes his head, his hands balled into fists. "So I guess that's it. That's my deep, dark secret." He relaxes his hands and flops back on the couch. "I'm kind of shocked you haven't heard about it yet, but now that you know, I wouldn't blame you if you wanted to break up."

"What?" I gape at him and shake my head. Is he serious? "None of this changes anything, Lucas. You're obviously not the kind of person who goes around irrationally shanking random people at bus stops."

"You're sure of that, even though there's proof of my crime, in full colour?"

"Don't be ridiculous."

"Well, a lot of people saw that video and think I'm a violent offender now, so . . . ." Lucas stares at his hands glumly.

I've never seen him look so disillusioned. Impulsively, I reach into my back pocket to retrieve my phone and scroll through the picture gallery until I find the file folder with the pictures from New Year's Eve. I angle the phone toward him and click on the first thumbnail, and then the next, and the next without taking my eyes off the images. It's been a while since I've looked at the pictures. Not that it matters. They're burned onto a memory card in my brain. If there were a button I could push to pop that memory card from my head. I'd eject it and drop it in the nearest vat of battery acid.

At the last picture, I exit the folder and drop my phone on the coffee table. "So there you go. Now you've seen the New Year's pictures for yourself. Does that mean the stories about me are true?"

I lean back, my hands clenched in my lap. Lucas rubs his eyes, like the pictures have scorched his retinas, and he's trying to scrub the images away. "I could kill them. Both of them, but especially him." That's what Lucas says.

Probably not the best thing to tell me after showing me that video and telling me he has anger issues.

"If Dallyn breathes in your direction, I want you to let me know. He'll be sorry."

"That's not why I showed you the pictures. Don't say things like that."

He looks at me, his eyes blazing. "I mean it. Promise you'll tell me?"

"You can't fight him, Lucas. I won't let you get in trouble for me. I can take care of myself."

He sighs, the tension slowly draining from his body. "I'm not going to fight him. I'd just talk to him, that's all. I would never purposely start a fight. Until that day at the bus stop, I'd never hit a person before. You do believe me, right?"

I move close to his side and press my lips to his shoulder. "Of course I believe you."

"And you're not scared of me? I promise I'd never hurt you."

"Lucas, I'm not scared of you at all. No one else has ever made me feel as safe as you do."

"Honestly?"

I put my hand on his cheek, lean over and give him a slow, soft, lingering kiss. "Would I kiss you like that if I was scared of you?" I ask him.

"I guess not. It's just . . . a few of my friends at my old school aren't allowed to hang out with me now. Even Mark's parents are kind of freaked out. They won't let me see him anymore. That's why I was afraid to tell you. I wanted to, though. Remember in the library when Dallyn was harassing you? Right there in the stacks, I almost spilled the whole story. Then I chickened out."

Right. Lucas had said he was afraid of stirring things up for me because of his problems. He wasn't talking about dyslexia at all.

"I thought I'd tell you what happened at that bus stop, and you'd never want to talk to me again," he says.

"Well, that's a coincidence. We both said the dumbest things ever on the exact same night." I shove him gently with my shoulder. "You're gonna have to try a little harder if you want to scare me away. Maybe start torching city blocks or pillaging entire villages."

"Pillaging, huh? You have some of the best words."

"Words are awesome."

"They can be. No words can be awesome, too."

This is his clever segue into kissing me, and I'm not about to complain. I smile against his lips. It might be strange to be smiling after he's just finished telling such an awful story, but I'm not focused on the story. I'm focused on the telling.

He trusts me.

"Can you do something for me?" he says at last, brushing my hair back so he can see my face. I search his eyes, and he pats his thighs. "Can you sit here—like you did earlier, before dinner?"

Like in the pictures.

I dart my eyes at the ceiling. "What about your aunt and uncle?"

He shakes his head. "My uncle's with Nancy, and my aunt always writes after dinner. Nothing can budge her when she's writing."

I swallow dryly and shake my head. "I don't think so."

"Hannah, do you trust me?" he says.

Oh great. This is called putting your money where your mouth is. Surely right now, all he needs to know is that my opinion of him hasn't changed. He looks at me hard, with those insanely beautiful hazel eyes, and I'm putty in his hands, a locust trapped in his amber.

Doomed.

I do trust him. Of course I do. Very slowly, I stand and move to sit astride him. He watches my face.

"Okay?" he says.

I nod.

He slides his hands along my legs, resting them at my hips. Then he gently pulls me forward. Closer.

"This okay, too?"

"Uh-huh," I say, trying to sound brave. Tentatively, I run my fingertips up his forearms and across his biceps. I love his arms. Lucas's muscles don't scream "brute force" like Dallyn's do. Lucas's strength is quiet. When my fingers slip inside the sleeves of his T-shirt and tickle at his shoulders, he closes his eyes and swallows.

"That's nice," he whispers.

I lean close and kiss him. Like his strength, his passion is quiet. I can tell he's trying to stay in control. When I finally pull away, we're both breathing heavily.

"Still good?" he asks me. I nod again and he smiles, rubbing my arms.

His eyes don't leave mine. I recognize his expression. I know what he's doing. This is how he looks at Nancy. This is just like him holding his hand out and trying to get her to touch his finger with hers.

Every bit of safe contact helps.

I slowly reach down and undo the top three buttons of my shirt. Lucas blinks, but he doesn't look down. He keeps his eyes locked on mine.

I'm not wearing my pink bra. That bra is stuffed somewhere in the back of a drawer. I only wear white cotton bras now. I don't care about my undergarments. All I care about is Lucas.

I bring his hand to my chest, guiding his fingers inside my shirt. Now his eyes move. He watches his hand slip under my bra, his left hand tightening at my waist. He pulls me forward, and I think he's going to kiss me, but he doesn't. Instead, he rests his forehead against mine as his hand moves gently under the cotton of my bra.

Lucas's hand is inside my bra, and he's touching my boob. No. That's not what's happening at all. Lucas is touching my heart.

After a few minutes, he slowly withdraws his hand and re-buttons my shirt. Then he pulls me close and hugs me.

And I burst into tears.

I escape to the basement powder room where I work my way through several Kleenexes, dropping them in the garbage can, one after another. He stands outside the doorway watching me, rubbing the back of his neck, shifting his weight, following my movements with his eyes. Guys have no clue how to deal with crying girls. It's actually kind of funny.

At last he finds his voice. "Are you okay?" he asks me. "Are you mad at me? Is there something I can do?"

I'm fine.

No, I'm not mad at you—you're awesome.

Nothing.

I shake my head. Blow my nose again. "Give me a second."

That's all I can squeak out. There's nothing a guy can do when you're crying like that except wait. Lucas either figures that out or runs out of questions. Finally, I wash my hands and take a huge cleansing breath. We meet in the doorway, and I dissolve into his arms, melting against him gratefully as he rubs my back.

"Are you okay?" he says again.

"I'm great."

He leans his chin on the top of my head. "You're great?"

"Yep."

He sighs. "Girls are crazy."

We end up back on the couch, and I snuggle up to Lucas's chest while he wraps his arms around me. For the longest time, we just sit there. We sit and we breathe.

Breathing is good.

Leaning against him, the rhythmic rise and fall of his chest soothing me, I sift through the details of the last few weeks, seeing Lucas through this new lens. Expelled and forced to switch schools—obliged to move in with his aunt and uncle for the sake of convenience, helping them out with Nancy, traipsing back and forth to his house to see his parents every weekend. He's had his life turned upside-down and lost his friends, all because he tried to protect a kid who didn't know how to protect himself. I'd be spewing rage balls.

Every. Single. Day.

But not Lucas. He takes everything in stride, grateful for the opportunity to take an anger management course and still watching out for kids who need someone to stick up for them. Kids like Nancy.

Or like me.

"Hey Lucas?" I say into the semi-darkness.

"Uh-huh?"

"Is everything you told me tonight off the record?"

"What do you mean, off the record?"

"I mean, I'm kind of stuck on my portfolio assignment. The interview part. I'd like to write my article about you."

"Me?" He draws his head back.

"Yes, you."

"Why would you want to write it about me?"

"Isn't it obvious?"

"I'm not that interesting."

"Sure you are. But that's not the point. Mr. Vesters said we have to pick someone we admire. I admire you. You're amazing."

"So are you."

He pulls me close and rubs my back.

"Does that mean I can do my article about you?"

"I don't know what you'll find to write about."

He has no idea that his eyes alone could inspire an entire essay.

"So, is your mom working tonight?" he says, threading our fingers together.

"Yep."

"How about I take you home? My mom's picking me up here at ten. That gives us a couple of hours . . . you know . . . ."

He catches my eye and raises an eyebrow. *You know.*

Do I know?

When he leans in, sliding his hand along my thigh as he kisses me, a million butterflies break out of their cocoons in my stomach, their wings flapping madly.

If I didn't know before, I do now. I ease away and push him back gently. "Lucas . . . ."

"Sorry. Too much?"

"It's not that. I'm just . . . I've never . . . I mean I'm . . . you know."

Apparently, "you know" is the go-to phrase of the day.

"You're a virgin. So am I. That's cool."

He says this so matter-of-factly. I cringe, drawing my knees up to my chest and wrapping my arms around them.

"Hey, you don't have to be nervous. We'll figure stuff out together."

Nervous? Not a strong enough word. "Terrified" is more like it.

As we make our way upstairs, Lucas holds my hand, his thumb brushing across my knuckles every few steps and making my stomach flutter with every pass. I'm terrified, but anticipation is definitely working its way into the mix.

I take a personal inventory of my current situation. I just had dinner at my boyfriend's aunt and uncle's house, and ate all my idiot peas, and played Bananagrams with an autistic kid, and cried when Lucas touched my boob because it was like he was really touching my heart. He really likes me. Not just that, he trusts me. Me. I don't remember the last time I felt this content, this balanced. Is this how my five-year-old self used to feel before my dad took off in the middle of the night and never came back, tilting my world and leaving me feeling perpetually off-centre?

At the top of the stairs, Lucas tugs my hand, and we go into the kitchen. He was right. Aunt Trudy is writing, her fingers pecking at the keys in short bursts. Type a few words . . . think. Type a few more words . . . think. She doesn't even notice we're there. I know that feeling of getting so lost in the world of words that you become entirely oblivious to everything around you. Lucas clears his throat, and she looks up at us over her laptop.

"I'm taking Hannah home."

Aunt Trudy doesn't get up, but she offers all the appropriate parting words. It was lovely having you. You're welcome any time. She tells us not to interrupt Nancy and Uncle Ken. She winks at Lucas. I'm guessing Nancy doesn't take kindly to being interrupted during *Law and Order.*

I fumble my way through the obligatory "thank you" speech, and then we're in the hall, gathering up coats and locating my school bag. Lucas hunts around for our shoes, discovering someone has moved them from the garage entry to the front door. They sit in a row alongside the family's shoes. I bend to pull my shoes away from the wall, and that's when it happens. My world tilts again.

I catch a whiff of stinky shoes. Black Italian leather shoes, with a gold buckle.

Oh my God.

I know these shoes. And I know the face of the man who wears them. Uncle Ken doesn't just have that familiar I-think-I've-seen-you-somewhere-before look about him. I have seen him before. In my kitchen. With my mother. I only saw him once—and very briefly—but the shoes? I saw them and smelled them on several occasions.

Holy shit. Lucas's uncle is Mr. Funky Feet.

Chapter 23

Coping

I'VE NEVER BEEN happier to hold Lucas's hand. If I weren't holding his hand, I'd probably do a face plant in the middle of the Gordons' garage.

Somehow my feet keep moving, one in front of the other. Lucas still rubs his thumb across my knuckles, but the persistent butterflies-in-the-stomach sensation has turned into a gaggle of geese flapping their wings and that I-think-I-might-puke feeling.

I'm probably about to have my first panic attack. It must feel something like this. My stomach churns, my mouth feels cottony, my heart pounds, I have a strange ringing sensation in my ears, and my palms sweat profusely. I've suddenly developed hyperhidrosis of the hand. Is there such a thing as hand deodorant? If there is, I need some right now.

I topple into the passenger seat, only vaguely aware of Lucas climbing in beside me and leaning over to kiss me before he pulls out of the garage.

"You okay?" he says, holding up our joined hands.

Gross. I'm sweating all over him. *Well, your uncle slept with my mom. A bunch of times. So, yeah, weird right? I'm just having a heart attack over here. Don't mind me.* I assure him I'm fine and do my best to calm down and pay attention to what he's saying to me as he drives.

"It felt awesome to talk to you about stuff tonight. It's been a tough couple of months . . . I guess you know how that feels though, right? . . . Right, Hannah?"

"Huh?"

As we turn into my neighbourhood Lucas frowns at me.

"Are you sure you're okay? You've gone all quiet."

"No, I'm fine. I'm good." I sound completely unconvincing, even to my own ears. "Maybe I'm a little drained." I half-smile and pretend to roll my eyes at myself. "Bawling my face off kind of took it out of me, you know?" There. Much better. That sounds plausible. No room for argument there. In my driveway, Lucas cuts the engine and turns in his seat.

"I think I scared you tonight."

I shake my head. "You didn't. Honestly. I know you didn't mean to hurt that guy at the bus stop—"

"No, I'm talking about the other stuff. You and me . . . sex . . . and stuff." He pauses and clears his throat. "If you don't want me to come in tonight, I won't. I'm not trying to pressure you. I just thought . . . you know . . . but whatever. We can keep things chill."

I let out a slow breath. There's no need to ask him to clarify what he "just thought" and what exactly he means by "you know" this time. He's a guy. If he's not thinking about us having sex, he's thinking about us doing all the other things that will lead up to sex.

The last thing I'm thinking about is sex and the things that lead up to it, which makes me even madder because I'm seventeen, and I have a good-looking boyfriend who's caring and sweet and who makes my heart thunder. If my life were normal, I'd totally obsess over the thought of having sex with Lucas. But no. I'm thinking about how my mother had sex with his uncle. On more than one occasion. In my house.

And so I say the last thing in the world I actually want to say.

"Keeping things chill would be good."

After pacing around the house for three hours, texting Lucas non-stop and trying to pretend everything is dandy, I fall into bed at eleven, pull my blankets up tightly under my chin and stare at the shadows dancing across the ceiling. My imagination has always been far too fertile, and the worst thoughts have a way of rearing up in the dark hours when you're supposed to be sleeping. Would anything good come of telling Lucas about my mom and his uncle? There's no way he'd want anything to do with me afterwards. He'd hate my mother. Then he'd hate me.

But how can I stand by and do nothing when I know a married man has been screwing around on his wife—and may be continuing to screw around on her? What if he's still seeing Mom? Maybe she's taken a break from bringing guys home after work, but who knows what goes on all day when I'm at school?

It's not fair. Lucas finally confides in me, and I bare my soul—almost literally—only to have my chance at happiness snatched away. I roll over and punch my pillow. I squeeze my eyes shut and pray for sleep, but I'm still wide awake when my mother rolls in at one o'clock. There's only one pair of footsteps and no whispers. She's spending another night alone. I briefly contemplate going out there now and confronting her. But something stops me—a warning voice.

Examine the present and figure out how to deal with it.

That's what I have to do. I have to think. Consider the implications of revealing what I discovered to my mother.

Telling Lucas would be bad, but telling Mom would be worse. Twice before, she blew the whistle on guys she got involved with when she found out they were married. She told their wives they were screwing around. Those four fabulous words I've grown to dread inevitably followed.

We have to move.

We moved away both times, leaving a trail of misery in our wake—two broken marriages. Two fractured families. I felt crummy both times, but mostly for myself, not for the families involved. This time, the victims have faces. How would Nancy cope with this?

How am I going to cope with it?

The next morning, I sit on my bed with my Writer's Craft binder leaning against my knees. I want to write the article about Lucas but can't seem to string together a single intelligible sentence, so instead, I doodle. Mom has been awake since nine. She vacuums downstairs, empties the dishwasher and cleans the bathroom. She seems incapable of sitting still. The endless consciousness must be getting to her. It's getting to me too. It would be a lot easier to avoid her if she were asleep.

Every once in a while, she passes my door. Finally, she stops her manic spring cleaning and pokes her head into my room.

"Busy?"

"Just studying." *Huge doodling exam on Monday.*

She drifts into my room and inspects my collection of knick-knacks, picking things up, turning them over and putting them back down. She scans the books on my shelves. "All these words," she says.

If she wants to see words, she should take a gander at the inside of my brain which is about to explode from the effort of keeping all the words I want to say to her stuffed inside, most of which I'd probably regret the second they tripped off my tongue. My filter's about to bust, Hoover Dam style. I glance at my clock. It's only eleven thirty. Staying here until she leaves for work is out of the question. I slide my binder off my lap and sit up.

"I'm going to the mall."

Mom spins around with my Grade Eight spelling bee award in her hand.

"You meeting Lucas there?"

"No. I'm going alone."

She slides the award back onto my shelf.

"I'll drive you. We could shop together."

"It's okay. I won't be long. I know exactly what I need."

She quirks an inquisitive eyebrow. It's no secret how much I hate shopping. I don't need anything is my usual answer whenever she proposes a trip to the mall. "I need new bras," I say, without even thinking.

"I just bought you three at Sears last week."

I leap up and grab a pair of socks from my top drawer and perch on the edge of my bed.

"Not those kind of bras. Nice bras. Like the hot pink one you got me for Christmas." Which I'll never wear again. Ever.

"Oh, I get it. Nice bras." She watches me wiggle my foot into one of my socks. "You and Lucas are being careful, right?"

I look at her like she's sprouted a third eye.

"Well, that's what I'm supposed to ask you, isn't it? Are you using some form of birth control? Protecting yourself from STDs? All those motherly questions?"

"We haven't done anything requiring protection." Yet.

She disappears across the hall and returns a minute later with two foil packets. She opens my nightstand drawer. "I'll just put these in here. In case of an emergency."

I am stunned into silence by the realization that my mother just dropped two condoms in my drawer. She sits beside me, grabs my ankle and rests my foot on her lap. She takes my other sock and puts it on for me. She doesn't pull it on—she rolls it on.

That's one way to make a point.

Taking the bus on a weekend is nothing like taking the bus to school. I'm surrounded by old ladies and young mothers with kids in strollers. A few rowdy teenagers sit at the back of the bus, but no one I know. A little kid spoils my peaceful ride by kicking the back of my seat the whole way. It's aggravating as hell, but I grit my teeth and glare at the seat in front of me instead of scaring the bejesus out of the kid with my eyebrows. They're ferocious today.

When the bus pulls up to the mall, I leap from my seat without a backward glance. As soon as I step off the bus, a creepy déjà vu feeling hits. Lucas's video—this is where it happened. I spin around, slowly scanning the area. This is where he wrestled a knife away from that loser druggie while defending a defenceless kid, a move which ended in his own punishment. My blood boils, and I shake my head at the unfairness of the world.

I abandon the bus stop and set my sights on the main entrance to the mall. Inside, I head straight to Victoria's Secret, and after briefly scanning the selection, I settle on a couple of lacy bras—one midnight blue, the other one black—snagging the matching panties for good measure.

Though hanging out at the mall has always seemed like a pointless activity to me, window shopping today will allow me to avoid going home to face Mom. I meander along checking out the store displays. At the card store, the Mother's Day signs catch my eye.

Because Mom means everything....

It's not hard to guess the sentimentality of the verses in the cards. I'm certain there aren't any Mother's Day cards appropriate for my mom and our current situation.

I could say you're the best mom ever,
But that's not really true.
You flirt with way too many guys
And boy, they sure like you!
Hitting on Dean at work that night
Was a crazy-ass mistake

But sleeping with my boyfriend's uncle
Really took the cake . . . .

I'd give myself props for making up this imaginary Mother's Day verse on the spot, and entirely in my head, but really, it reaffirms what I've always known: I can't compose poetry to save my life.

The aromas from various vendors blend together in the food court. It's nauseating, but my stomach grumbles anyway. I buy a giant peanut butter cookie and a lemonade and then scan the table area. There are a few familiar faces scattered around, so I snag a stool at the end of the bar-style counter facing the Taco Bell, my back to the tables. *If I can't see them, they can't see me.*

I rest the Victoria's Secret bag on the empty stool beside me, nibble on the cookie and sip the drink, trying to think happy thoughts. I have two new bras! Lucas will love them!

These happy thoughts are tainted by the uneasy feeling in the pit of my stomach, the one that's securely attached to the secret I can't rid myself of.

Lucas's uncle has slept with my mother. Repeatedly.

If I could stick my fingers down my throat and purge the secret and the sick feeling associated with it, I would. I'd run to the nearest bathroom and happily puke for hours.

Ironically, just as I picture myself retching into a mall toilet, another nausea-inducing entity presents itself.

Dallyn Wade is here. He's spotted me, and he's walking my way.

Chapter 24

The Second Circle of Hell

BEFORE MY BRAIN can send the appropriate get-your-ass-moving signal to my feet, Dallyn sidles up beside me, his hands stuffed in the pockets of his leather jacket. His lower lip is split, and there's a bluish-purple bruise beside his mouth.

Oh God. What if Lucas tracked him down and, instead of just talking to him, he ended up punching him in the mouth? But no, he promised me he wouldn't do that. And besides, Lucas knows that fighting with Dallyn would lead to another expulsion. More than likely, Dallyn and Allison had another fight, and this time, instead of slapping him, she went straight for the right hook. I'd have paid big money to see that.

He leans his elbow against the counter, bobs his chin at me and leers as if to say, "How you doin'?"

I adopt a weary tone. "What are you doing here, Dallyn?"

He gives me a once-over and shrugs. "Same thing as you, I figure."

Buying bras? Doubt it. But speaking of which, I grab the Victoria's Secret bag from the stool, hoping to move it out of his line of vision.

He's too fast for me. He tears the bag from my hands and peeks inside. "Hey, black lace. That's way hotter than the pink one."

I give him the glare and wrench the bag away, jamming it under my leg. He slides onto the stool beside me and scans the nearby tables.

"You waiting for the sped?"

"I don't know anyone by that name."

"Yeah, whatever. You got off the bus alone. Is he meeting you here?"

"You saw me get off the bus? Are you following me?"

"Maybe. It's not easy to talk to you when lover boy keeps popping up."

"I told you to stay away from me."

"Would it kill you to talk to me?"

I gape at him. "Do you have amnesia? Early onset Alzheimer's?"

He blinks. Yeah, I've lost him. I can almost see the words flying over his head. Time to dumb things down. "You can't do what you did to me on New Year's Eve and expect me to want to talk to you about anything, Dallyn. Ever."

"Aw, come on. Get over it, already. And don't tell me you didn't enjoy it."

I recoil, flames of rage threatening to spew from my mouth. "Oh yeah, I love being taken advantage of and embarrassed on Twitter so the whole school knows what happened. That was the best time of my life. I went straight home and wrote all about it in my diary."

"I wasn't talking about that. I meant, you know, when we were alone in the basement. You were as into it as I was. It was fun, right?" His eyes drop to my chest, and then he winks at me.

I bet he thinks he looks insanely sexy. At one time, I might've even thought so. If only I could go back in time and smack myself. "For one thing, Dallyn, we weren't alone. Allison was behind the stupid furnace. And for another thing, what you and Allison did ruined that entire night. Every single minute of it. You made my life miserable."

"Yeah, well, it wasn't my idea."

"I don't care whose idea it was. You went along with it."

He rests his right hand on the counter, his thumb drumming a steady beat. "That's not how it was supposed to go down."

I turn my head slowly. "What do you mean?"

"What I mean is . . . ." He cuts a quick look over my shoulder. "What I mean is I thought Allison was with Marla upstairs." He says this quietly, like he suspects I might be wearing a wire or something. "They were supposed to walk in on us. Catch us making out. Then Allison would snap and tell everyone what they saw. She told me to make it seem like you were coming on to me. I didn't know she was downstairs. I didn't know she was going to take pictures and throw them on Twitter."

"Either way, you knew she was planning to spread lies about me."

"Come on, my own girlfriend was telling me I could make out with you. What was I going to do? Say no?"

"Well, yeah." *Dumbass.*

He shakes his head. "You've got this angry chick thing going on. It's hot." He shrugs. "Free pass, right?"

"Is that your idea of a compliment? Am I supposed to feel flattered? You're such a jackass." I slide off the stool, clutching the bag at my side.

He grabs my arm. "Hey, come on, Hannah. I told Allison to leave you alone, you know? I've been trying to have your back. Doesn't that count for something?"

I shrug out of his grasp and narrow my eyes at him.

He moves closer. "I know my brother took your mom home from the club. I haven't told anyone."

My heart drops into my stomach, hitting the half-digested cookie with a sickening squelch. He knows? I can't believe Dean blabbed. I open my mouth, hoping some semblance of a clever rebuttal will emerge, but I've got nothing.

"You don't have to deny it," he says. "Dean told me what happened."

"Nothing happened." These words come out as a vehement hiss.

"Yeah, that was his story too." He lifts a suggestive eyebrow.

His story. Dallyn's got something on me. If I were a cat, this piece of information would be a ball of twine, and he'd be batting it around in front of my face. I scan his eyes, trying to measure his intent. Is he mocking me? Or is this some sort of threat?

I toss my hair, aiming for nonchalance. "All he did was help my mom get home after she had a couple of drinks. He slept on the couch."

"I can think of a few people who'd eat up a story like that."

I shake my head. "You're on a behavioural contract, Dallyn. If you stir things up for me again, you'll get suspended in a heartbeat."

"What the hell. That'll give the old man another excuse to punch me." He smiles across the food court as he says this.

I perch on the stool again, eyeing the bruise on his chin. "Wait, your dad hit you?"

"Not exactly." He shoves his hands in his pockets and shrugs. "I got in the way of his fist. He was aiming for my mom."

"What?"

His phone rings. He pulls it from his pocket and scans the display, grimacing as he answers.

"I'll be right there," he says. "Yeah, well, it took longer than I thought. I'll see you in five." He hangs up and re-pockets his phone.

"I gotta go. My brother's here." He turns and takes a few backward steps. "We could have some fun, Hannah. Maybe in the summer when the sped goes home. Think about it."

He swaggers away without waiting for a reply. Not that I have anything intelligent to say. There's way too much information careening around in my head. I don't know what to puzzle through first.

I take the scenic route home, which involves transferring buses twice. Riding around town for two hours gives Mom time to leave for work, so I don't have to see her.

When I finally get home, the crockpot is on the counter with instructions to keep the heat low and stir it occasionally until six o'clock. I open the lid and peek inside. It's a stew, and it's been cooking for a few hours already, the contents starting to blend together.

The mishmash of ingredients is a perfect metaphor for my state of mind. How can spending five minutes with Dallyn Wade create such chaos in my brain? Part of me feels sorry for him. He must have a terrible home life. My mom may be a freak, but at least she doesn't hit me. And then there's the fact that Dallyn has been sticking up for me, maybe more often than I realize. What I don't understand is why.

Maybe he likes me enough to want to protect me. But if he really liked me, why wouldn't he have broken up with Allison long before now to ask me out? The answer is obvious. Dallyn doesn't want to date me. He just wants to screw around, and he's conceited enough to think that telling me he thinks I'm hot might make me consider his offer.

Well, he's wrong. I still think he's a slimebag. A slimebag who thinks his twenty-three year old brother slept with my mother.

The question is, what does he plan to do with that information?

At five in the morning, I stumble out of bed to use the bathroom, only to discover the light is still on in the hall. My mother's door is wide open, and her bed is made. I run downstairs to look outside. Her car isn't in the driveway. I check my phone for a text message. The only messages I have are from Lucas, who continues to fill my inbox, even when he knows I'm asleep.

"Why are weekends so long?"

"I miss you."

"I can't stop thinking about all the stuff we talked about on Friday. I'm glad you trust me."

"Is it Monday yet?"

This isn't the time to wallow in Lucas's words. I send Mom a message instead.

"Mom? Are you there?"

I stare at my phone, willing her to reply. She doesn't. After a few minutes, I send another text.

"Message me as soon as you get this. I'm worried."

With my phone clutched to my chest, I sit on the couch in the darkness, my heart and my eyelids heavy. Now I know how parents feel when they half-sleep, one ear tuned to the sound of a car pulling into the driveway, a door being unlocked, footsteps on the stairs. My mother makes me crazy, but I'd feel better if she were home safe . . . even if she did have a guy with her . . . .

The front door creaks open, jolting me upright and awake. Dim light pours through the curtains. Vaguely disoriented, I untangle myself from the ancient afghan and stumble to my feet with a wicked crick in my neck.

Mom rounds the corner of the family room and gasps, jumping backward. "Hannah, what are you doing down here? It's seven in the morning."

I ignore her question. "Where were you?"

"I stayed at a friend's house. I got your message. I texted you."

Stayed at a friend's house. There's a great euphemism for "one-night stand" if I ever heard one.

Make-up smudges her eyes, her hair is a frizzy mess, and an enormous run covers the length of her pantyhose. The walk of shame has a new poster girl.

I whirl around, locating my phone on the floor in front of the couch.

"Half an hour ago," I say, reading the message she sent to let me know she was on her way home. "What about at five in the morning when I was freaking out?"

"I was asleep."

"Couldn't you have texted me last night to let me know you wouldn't be home?"

"I figured you'd be asleep anyway."

Seriously? "Mom, if I didn't come home, you'd call the police and report me missing. Then you'd ground me for six months. I had no idea where you were."

"I thought I was doing you a favour, going to his place instead of bringing him here." She peels off her coat and returns to the front hall to hang it up. "God, Hannah, I don't know what to do anymore. I can't win." She slams the closet door. "Sometimes I think you can't stand the thought of me having fun. The minute things seem to be going well for me, you get in a snit."

A snit? She thinks I'm in a snit?

She licks her fingers and rubs them under her eyes. "Maybe you should focus on the things that make you happy for a change, instead of obsessing over what I'm doing. You're seventeen years old. You've got a boyfriend. You'll be going to college next year. I can't be responsible for your happiness forever."

I shake my head. "I'm not . . . how can you . . . ? I never said you're responsible for my happiness. I just think it would be nice if you weren't responsible for my unhappiness once in a while."

She draws her head back sharply. "That might be the nastiest thing you've ever said to me."

"I'm sorry, it's just . . . ." I cast about for the appropriate words. Why am I the one apologizing and feeling defensive? "You make bad choices, that's all, and I end up dealing with the fallout from the things you do. You have no idea how your decisions affect me."

"Decisions? What decisions?"

"Like . . . bringing home someone like Dean—"

"God, that again? I got a lock for your door. From now on if I have a few drinks after a shift, I'll take a taxi home. Alone."

"It's not just that. It's . . . the guys you choose. They're bad news."

"They're not good enough for you? Perhaps you'd like to design a questionnaire for me to hand out?"

"That's not what I'm saying."

"Well, what are you saying?"

I sigh, exasperated. What am I saying? *Can you try to stay away from married men?* I can't open that can of worms, so I opt for the next best thing. "Your friend, Dean. Did you know he's only twenty-three? He's still in college. And you know what else? His younger brother is Dallyn, the guy that screwed me around in January. He knows you brought

Dean here. He thinks you two had sex. Do you have any idea what it's like to have jackasses like Dallyn talking about me because of the things you do? It's mortifying, Mom. It makes me want to crawl under a rock!"

I take in a huge breath at the end of this rant, and it's like my lungs have filled properly for the first time in forever. I can breathe. My mother, on the other hand, looks like I've punched her in the stomach. Her mouth forms the shape of an O, but no sound comes out.

"Oh my God," she finally says. She covers her mouth with her hands. "I didn't know. Why didn't you tell me? We should have moved back in January. I told you then I wanted to get you away from these awful kids, and you said no, but it's not too late, we could still move—"

"No!" I don't mean to shout, but the word flies out of my mouth. "No," I say again, this time more calmly. "What's the point of moving and then making all the same mistakes over and over again? That doesn't solve anything. It's like putting a lock on my door. If I had to choose, I'd way rather you stopped doing stupid crap that makes me want to lock myself in."

She flops into the armchair, picking at the hole in her pantyhose with her hand. "I embarrass you, right? I must be the worst mother ever." She sniffs and blinks at me. She's looking for me to contradict this statement. She's wants sympathy.

I'm fresh out.

I hole myself up in my room, a pretense of homework keeping me in there for most of the day.

While I stay put, Mom seems to be in constant motion. Ironically, in my effort to ignore her, I become acutely aware of everything she's doing. Stairs creak. Kitchen cupboards open and slam closed. Water runs, the oven door squeaks, and the fridge closes with a thud.

I wait until the shower runs before I dash downstairs to grab food, returning to my room with a plateful of snacks, so I can hunker down for the long haul. Just before she's supposed to leave for work, soft footsteps pad on the stairs, and a floorboard squeaks outside my door. The doorknob doesn't turn, but I close my eyes and imagine her flattening her hands against my door and pressing her ear to the wood. She eventually retreats as quietly as she approached. A few minutes later, my phone chimes with a text message.

"I'm leaving for work. Dinner's in the fridge. Home by 1 am. I PROMISE!"

Promises, promises.

I toss my phone on the bed and lie there waiting for the front door to slam shut. Once her car has cleared the driveway, I peek through the curtain to confirm she's gone and then fling my bedroom door open. Sweet freedom!

The comfort of routine is luxurious. I slice my celery sticks for the next day, take a long shower and then sit at my desk with my dice and Post-it notes.

Within two minutes, everything is obliterated from my mind except 363.25.

When I go downstairs to grab my lunch the next morning, Mom's in the kitchen. She opens the fridge, her movements lethargic, like every muscle in her body labours under the effort of moving. Even though she came home right after work, as promised, it's still way too early for her. She needs at least eight hours of sleep to function properly, usually more. She hands me a brown bag.

"This is for you."

I look at the bag, then at her, as if she's an alien who's just handed me a flaming piece of space debris. "You made me a lunch."

"I didn't sleep much. Thinking about everything, I guess. Figured I might as well get up and do something useful instead of just lying there."

Is this a peace offering? A lunch made at the butt crack of dawn as a sign of some sort of maternal leaf-turning epiphany? I open the bag. There's a tuna sandwich, an apple and two cookies inside.

"Well, thanks." I find my baggie of celery sticks in the fridge and drop it into the brown bag. I might not eat all the other stuff, but rejecting the gesture would be cruel, even for me.

She leans against the counter near the sink and crosses her arms. "So I'm thinking I'll ask for a night off next weekend. Maybe we could go out for a nice dinner. Have a long talk."

I pick at the rolled edge of the brown bag and shrug.

"You said some things yesterday that really hurt me, Hannah, but I said some hurtful things too. I'm not perfect, but I'm the only mother you've got. We have to talk and figure out how to get past this."

"I guess." I'd rather not talk about everything again, for fear of accidentally revealing something I'm not prepared to tell her, but at least I have time to organize my thoughts and come up with a game plan. I bob my head at the front door. "I should go. Lucas will be here any second."

She nods, her lips pulling into a grim line.

I head for the door and grab a hoodie from the hall closet. I expect to see Lucas waiting in front of the house, but he's not, so I sit on the top step of the porch, waiting. After five minutes pass, I start to worry. He's always so prompt.

What if there's been a car accident? What if Lucas is lying dead or mangled in a ditch?

I check my phone for messages. Nothing. I could text him, but what if rather than being dead or mangled in a ditch, he's stuck in traffic? If he reads my text while driving, the distraction might actually cause him to have an accident. I close my eyes and turn to face the morning sun.

Calm down. People are late all the time. Don't be a freak.

Another five minutes pass, and the sound of a car engine approaches. I open one hopeful eye and squint down the street.

Hallelujah! He's twelve minutes late, but he's here.

I dash for the car and clamber inside before Lucas has even pulled to a complete stop. He grins as I buckle myself in, and then he leans over and slides his hand under my hair.

"Sorry I'm late." He gives me a longer than usual kiss hello. His tongue is cool and sweet. "I missed you this weekend."

"I missed you too. A lot." *Navigating the second circle of hell would have been so much easier with you by my side.* I can't tell him this. What would I say?

Your Uncle Ken is cheating on your aunt. You'll never guess how I know.

Dallyn knows his brother slept over at my place. Oh, and Dallyn wants to get it on with me.

My mother has a wee tendency to sleep around. But I'm nothing like her, honestly.

He scans my outfit. "No new clothes? I thought you went to the mall on Saturday."

"I did. I'm wearing a new bra. It's black. Black lace." I throw my shoulders back and jiggle a little. He watches this with undisguised interest. "Tell me your mom's working tonight."

"My mom's working tonight."

He smiles and mimes an explosion beside his head, complete with sound effects. Best. Reaction. Ever. I've been with him all of ninety seconds, and I feel better already.

"I hope you weren't freaking out." He pulls away from the curb. "I wasn't sure if I was going to be able to pick you up. My uncle had a marathon session at work last night. All these clients leaving their taxes to the last minute, I guess."

Ha! Did he really have a marathon accounting session, or has Mr. Funky Feet been up to his old tricks?

"He got home half an hour ago," Lucas adds. "He must have slept at the office. I was holding off texting you. I didn't want you to have to grab the bus."

Whatever Uncle Ken was doing, at least I know he wasn't doing it with my mother. Thank God for small miracles.

Chapter 25

In My Corner

SINES, COSINES AND tangents. Iambic pentameters and trochaic feet. Cool words, but seriously? Some days, school can be so stupid. Today is one of those days. There's no way anything we talk about during math or English will affect me in the future.

I'm desperate for the day to be over. I've never needed to be alone with Lucas more than today. I want to tune out the whole world and not just the world of school—everything. I want to pick up where Lucas and I left off on Friday before the earth tilted, dropping me on my backside again.

My two-minute walk between classes with Lucas and the three-minute locker visit at lunch hour aren't enough to sustain me. After Friday night, walking side by side down the hall, not touching, not even holding hands, seems ridiculous. I'm too much of a coward to reach for his hand. Knowing Lucas, he's probably terrified of pushing me.

Once Lucas leaves for his noon hour visit to the Spec Ed room, I depart for the library. What does 363.25 have in store for me? *The Truth Behind Crime Scene Investigations.* Not my thing. I flip through the book as I wander off to my corner, and the word "deoxyribonucleic" jumps out at me. Hmmm. Maybe we have a winner after all. I should write that one down. I fish my pen out of my backpack. When I reach the collection of chairs in my corner, a familiar face greets me.

"Lucas, what are you doing here?" I drop into the seat beside him. "You just left to go to the Spec Ed room."

"I got sidetracked by Dallyn Wade. Did you have fun at the mall with him? He said he likes the new black bra you bought."

He crosses his arms and leans back in his chair. One eyebrow flicks up. *Talk.*

I frown and kick his chair. "I wasn't at the mall with Dallyn. I ran into him at the mall, and he snooped in my bag. If he said we were together, he's trying to push your buttons. By pushing your buttons, he's pushing my buttons."

"You said you'd tell me if he bothered you again. Why didn't you say something?"

"There was nothing to tell. Besides, if I told you, you'd probably confront him. Dallyn's not a talker. He'd rather throw a few punches around. That's the last thing you need right now."

"I guess. Looks like he was in a fight this weekend. Did you see his lip?"

"He said his dad did it. His dad was aiming for his mom, and Dallyn stepped in the middle of it."

Lucas mulls this over for a minute. "That sucks," he says. "Everyone has crap to deal with, though. Doesn't mean he should get a free pass to be an asshole."

"Just stay away from him, Lucas." *Please stay away from him. He knows too much.*

"Don't worry. I didn't go looking for him."

From Lucas's tone, I sense the subject is closed. Fine by me. Lucas picks up my book and stares at the cover, his lips moving. "I didn't know you were interested in *CSI*. You and Nancy will have lots to talk about next time you're playing Bananagrams."

"Very funny."

He points at the Post-it note stuck to the table. "What's with all this anyway? You have a new Post-it note every day. Why do you come here every day and read all these random books? They don't have anything to do with school, do they?"

Why do I do this?

Because I'm a loser.

Because I'm afraid of the cafeteria.

Because for months there's been nowhere else for me to go and no one else to talk to.

Because the universe gave me a sign . . . .

When I don't answer, he looks around, waves his hands at the bookshelves. "Seriously, what's with all this? The Post-it notes, the books, the celery eating—every day with the celery and peanut butter."

"Allison's allergic to peanut butter," I say.

Lucas laughs. "Therefore you eat it every day?"

"I couldn't eat peanut butter at school for three months while we were hanging out. I've got a lot of time to make up for." Proof that I'm not an entirely wretched person. My fantasy-homicidal tendencies aren't based on a sadistic hatred of the entire human race—just a rebellious "eff you" to one of my least favourite people in the world.

He looks at my hand as I click my pen. He lets me click a few times, and then he reaches across the table and takes the pen out of my hand, placing it on the table between us. "So tell me about the Post-it notes," he says, his eyes softening.

I could say, "I don't have to tell you anything. Who do you think you are telling me what to do?" Instead, I explain that on January 5th, the universe gave me a sign—"a really cool organic sign," is what I actually say. I tell him the whole story—how the date matched the call number of the book Mrs. Fry suggested, and how the book gave me a message: "Examine the present and figure out how to deal with it." I explain the process of using backgammon dice to pick a Dewey Decimal number every night, how that number becomes a new mantra every day, and knowing it's on a Post-it in my pocket gets me through the morning.

"Wow," he says.

"I know, right? I sound clinically insane."

He gives me a sad smile. "No, you don't."

"Yes, I do. I'm pathetic."

He picks up the Post-it note, rubbing his thumb across the numbers. "No, you're not."

This isn't at all how I expected him to react to my bizarre behaviour.

"You coming in here to read books at lunch is no different than me going to the Spec Ed room," he says. "You feel comfortable here."

"Wait, I thought you went to the Spec Ed room to get extra help."

"Sometimes I get an assignment proofread or print something out, but mostly I hang out with the kids. I tried to talk the Spec Ed teacher into starting a Buddy Up program, like at my old school. She said it's too late in the year, so I'm doing it informally. You could help me. Why don't you come down to the Spec Ed room right now? Nancy's down there with her friend, Declan. Remember the kid we saw in here with his educational assistant that day? That's him. He's a bit neurotic, but totally harmless."

"I don't know . . . ." The pen finds its way back into my hand. Click, click, click.

"These kids aren't as scary as you think."

"I didn't say they were scary."

"You didn't have to. I can see it in your eyes. What scares you more, the kids in the Spec Ed room or stepping out of your comfort zone?"

"Since when do you have a psychology degree?"

"Don't get snarky just because you know I'm right."

"On Friday, you said you liked me the way I am. Maybe this is the way I am."

"This isn't the way you are, Hannah. This is just stuff you do. Maybe there's other stuff you could be doing." He points at the book in front of me and waves his hand around at the shelves. "This might be comfortable, but what's the point? To become a Dewey Decimal guru? To collect trivia so you can be the next great *Jeopardy!* champion?"

Ouch. "Where do you get off judging me?"

"I'm not judging you."

"You're totally judging me. You're saying the thing that makes me comfortable is trivial, and what makes you comfortable is important. That's judging."

He shakes his head. "I'm just giving you a different perspective, that's all. You shouldn't have to hide in here every day."

"I'm not hiding." God, I'm totally hiding. He knows it and I know it.

"So if you're not hiding, you'd be cool leaving with me right now?"

"I just told you, I don't want to go to the Spec Ed room."

"Not to the Spec Ed room. There's a talent show tomorrow night, and Nancy and Declan are going. It's the last day they're selling tickets, and I told my aunt I'd buy them. Come with me to grab the tickets. Hey, we could go to the show as well. The four of us could go together."

"The talent show is a fund raiser for the cheer squad."

"Oh." He purses his lips and nods.

"The squad will be doing a bunch of routines. I'm not interested."

"Can't blame you for that." He slaps his thighs with the palms of his hands. "I guess I'll head out then. I'll see you in Writer's Craft. Thanks for letting me sit in your corner for a while." He stares up at the ceiling, checks out the walls on either side of us and then looks back at me.

I roll my eyes. "You can sit wherever you want, Lucas."

He stands and drags his backpack over his shoulder, moving beside my chair. "That's good, because I've been in your corner since the first day we met. I'm not about to give up on you now." He tickles my forearm through my shirt, a smile nudging the corner of his mouth.

Damn it. Why does always know exactly what to say? And does he have to be so cute when I'm at my most vulnerable? I sigh. "I guess I could come with you. To buy the tickets, I mean."

He lifts a hopeful eyebrow. "Oh yeah?"

I scrunch my eyes closed, already regretting my words. When I re-open them, he's holding his hand out and wiggling his fingers. Wow. So much for Lucas being afraid to push me. Consider me shoved. "Come on, Dewey," he says. "Don't be a chicken."

"Dewey?"

"Everyone needs a nickname, even the clinically insane."

Reluctantly, I uncross my arms and groan, slipping my hand into his. Our fingers lace together.

"There, that's not so hard, is it?" he asks me, pulling me to my feet.

"We haven't gone anywhere yet. Ask me again in five minutes."

The hallways are usually crazy at lunch hour, but the spring weather has drawn a lot of people outside. The pre-prom tanning fest has officially kicked off, and seniors desperate for a few rays dominate the scattered picnic tables in the courtyard. I scan the crowd through the window, expecting to see Allison, Marla and Kelly at the center of the sun worshippers, but they're not.

When Lucas and I step through the double doors leading to the front foyer, the reason for their absence outside becomes immediately clear. Of course. The talent show is a squad fundraiser, so they're in charge of ticket sales. Marla and Kelly are sitting at the sales table with a cash box in front of them. Allison and Dallyn lean against the wall nearby. My steps falter. Rather than let go of my hand, Lucas squeezes harder. I'm not sure if that reassuring squeeze says, "Stay calm, I've got you," or, "Don't worry, you've got this."

Dallyn is the first one to notice us. Kelly and Marla are too busy scanning their phones.

Dally hisses an *s*.

S for "skank." Or is it *s* for "sped?"

I cringe.

Marla looks up at us slowly, sneering.

"I'll take two tickets," Lucas says.

"Social suicide," Marla says, in a sing-songy voice.

I do my best to stab her with my eyebrows, but Lucas doesn't react, addressing Kelly instead. "Two tickets."

He gives my fingers one last squeeze, but then he has to let go.

Five minutes ago, I didn't want him to hold my hand in the halls. Now I want to cling to him like a barnacle. My arms suddenly feel like gigantic appendages dangling uselessly from my shoulders.

Lucas pulls his wallet out of his back pocket and rifles through it.

"Hey, Mar, since this is our fundraiser, do we get a say in the guest list?" Kelly blinks at me, slapping her gum around like a cud-chewing cow.

"Money is money," Marla says. "Doesn't matter where it comes from."

"True." Kelly looks up at Lucas. "Tickets are seven-fifty each. That's fifteen . . . dollars . . . all . . . together." She says this slowly, like she's talking to a four year old.

I cross my arms. I'm afraid to leave them dangling in case the urge to swing out and pop her on the nose overwhelms me.

Lucas tosses a twenty dollar bill on the table.

Kelly scoops it up and slides a clipboard forward. "Write your names on the guest list."

"Want some help with that?" Marla asks.

Lucas poises the pen above the page.

"Hannah. That's H-a-n-n-a-r-k," Marla continues, her voice sweet as honey.

She's so hilarious. Bet she's been sitting on that one for weeks, wondering when she'll get a chance to use it. Lucas writes Nancy and Declan's names on the page. He shakes his head and slides the clipboard back to Kelly.

Kelly looks at it and frowns.

Marla raises an eyebrow. "Fake names aren't allowed. Admin won't let you in."

Again, Lucas ignores Marla, holding out his hand to Kelly. "My change."

Kelly tosses a five at him. I roll my eyes at the wall behind her, catching an unfortunate glimpse of Dallyn's tongue probing Allison's mouth.

Gag.

Dallyn backhands his mouth after they kiss. The two of them probably consume at least a tube of lip gloss a day. It's become a food group. Fruits and vegetables, gloss and other slimy lip products.

"Okay, let's go," Lucas says, before I can invent another food group.

I drag my eyes away from Dallyn and Allison a second too late. Dallyn puckers his lips at me, blowing me an air-kiss.

Allison is too busy sliming Dallyn's neck to see this, and Lucas is focussed on jamming the tickets into his wallet.

Lucas reclaims my hand and smiles at Kelly. "I hope you break a leg tomorrow night," he says. "And you," he adds, bobbing his chin at Marla. "Hope you break both legs."

Somehow I don't think he's speaking metaphorically.

He tugs on my hand. "Come on, Hannah." I can't help looking back over my shoulder as we make our way out of the lobby. Marla's fiery glare is fixed on the very spot where Lucas's hand meets mine.

She doesn't just hate me because Allison told her to; she hates me because she's jealous.

I throw a little extra wiggle into my walk and toss my hair over my shoulder.

Suck on that, bitches.

Chapter 26

Four-Letter Words

IN WRITER'S CRAFT, we get our portfolios back. I got a B+. I can't remember the last time I earned anything other than an A on a portfolio. I flip through the pages and then toss my folder on the desk. I cross my arms and sulk at my computer screen.

"You okay?" Lucas asks. "Still thinking about what happened at lunch?"

I shake my head, not sure what to tell him. Complaining to Lucas about my mark won't help. He'd probably be thrilled to get a B+ on a writing assignment. I can't gripe to Mr. V. either.

My whole assignment was a fabrication based on a dog that didn't really die because it didn't even exist. Knowing I probably deserved a B+ doesn't make me any less stressed. Now there's even more pressure to make sure my next portfolio is stellar.

I try to get ahead on my interview assignment, but having the subject of the interview sitting right beside me makes me self-conscious. I end up spending most of the class helping Lucas edit the first draft of his article about his Aunt Trudy. Uncle Ken is a class-A dick, and reading about all the sacrifices Aunt Trudy has made for Nancy really makes me want to strangle him. Of course, I can't mention anything about that to Lucas. I limit my critique to his spelling and homonym issues.

As we pack up at the end of the day, Mr. Vesters watches us. He must know we're an item now. Oddly enough, I want to thank him for sort of bringing us together. I imagine myself sprawled out in my room, doing Mr. V.'s nails as I tell him all about my relationship with Lucas.

What do you prefer? Fire engine red? No, no—this metallic blue! It would go great with your sweater vest . . . .

I shake my head to clear the image. Way too weird.

In the hall, Lucas walks beside me, but we don't hold hands. I feel dismal, cut adrift. Now that we crossed the hand-holding-in-the-halls hurdle once, just strolling beside him isn't enough. I quickly slip my fingers through his. He smiles and lets out a sharp breath.

"I wasn't sure what to do," he says. "After the ticket buying thing . . . ."

"That's okay." We reach my locker and I pull it open. "I'm over it. Honestly."

He leans against the locker beside mine and crosses his arms. "So from now on I can hold your hand at school? No questions asked?"

I mirror his posture. "Yeah, I'm cool with that."

"Cool." He leans forward into my space. I can tell by the way he's looking at me that he's weighing his options, trying to decide if my conciliatory mood means I'm ready for a hallway kiss.

I'm not. Not today. One hurdle at a time.

I break the tension by stuffing textbooks into my backpack. Once I heft my bag onto my shoulder and slam my locker, the stillness of the moment is gone. I'm safe.

For now.

On the way to the parking lot, Lucas checks his phone messages and groans. "My uncle texted to tell me to come straight home. He has a bunch of appointments at the office tonight. That was one of the conditions of me using the car you know? If he needs it . . . ."

If I thought I was glum in Writer's Craft, this news makes me positively morose. "I was really looking forward to you coming over today."

"Me too."

He has no idea how much I need to spend time with him—how much I've been looking forward to escaping from everything for a couple of hours.

I'm wearing my new black bra!

Stupid Uncle Ken.

Lucas pushes the school doors open, and we emerge into the bright afternoon sun. He squints at a police cruiser parked at the curb. "Huh. That's the first time I've seen a cop car here. We used to have the cops at my old school all the time. I guess that's another reason to be glad I switched schools." He smiles at me as he says this.

"And the first reason?" I say. Sure, I'm fishing a little, but I'm depressed. I need the validation.

"The awesome Spec Ed department, of course."

"Ha. Very funny."

"You know I'm kidding." He throws his arm around my shoulder, pulling me close. I try to lose myself in this moment, like I don't have a care in the world. Sometimes it's fun to pretend.

We're almost at my place when Lucas sneaks a quick look at me.

"So I was thinking this afternoon. Everyone's talking about prom. Want to go?"

Ha! "Not even remotely."

"Wow, feel free to take a few seconds to think about it."

"I don't need to think about it. There's nothing to think about. Prom is my least favourite four-letter word. I have zero desire to go."

"Are you embarrassed to go with me?"

"Of course not." I reach for his hand and thread our fingers together. Guess I'm not the only one who needs a little reassurance today. "It's not that I don't want to go with you. I don't want to go. Period. Girls like me don't go to prom."

"Girls like you?"

I stare at my feet and tap them together. "I just don't think I'll have fun, that's all."

"Well, I definitely won't have fun if you don't go."

My head snaps up. "What do you mean? You'd go to prom without me?"

"Declan's graduating. He wants to take Nancy. Aunt Trudy might want me to go to make sure Nancy's okay. Maybe I should look for another date."

"Lucas. Don't."

"Don't what?"

"Don't mess with my head like that."

He sighs and rests our linked hands on his thigh. "There's nobody else I'd ask to prom. You know that."

"Do I?"

Again, he sighs. I'm afraid he might start running out of oxygen if he keeps breathing out like that. He's quiet for the rest of the drive.

I stare out my side window, wondering if every teenage relationship is as fraught with ups and downs as ours seems to be.

In my driveway, he cuts the engine and narrows his eyes at my garage door. "Can I come in for a bit?"

"I thought you had to get the car back."

"Ten minutes won't make a difference."

"Okay."

Lucas follows me into the house. We both kick off our shoes, and he drops his jacket over the family room armchair.

"Do you still have that book of poetry by Emily Dickinson?" he says.

"Yeah, it's in my room."

"Can you get it?"

Jesus, now what's he up to? A poetry reading?

"Please?"

I contain my exasperation and turn to head up the stairs. On the third step, I spin around. "You can come with me. If you want."

Lucas follows me.

I've never had a guy in my bedroom before. No big deal. It's just a room.

It's a room with a bed in it.

There are two condoms in my nightstand drawer.

I try to forget about the bed and the condoms and shuffle around the papers on my desk to find the Emily Dickinson book. Lucas ignores the bed and seems to have forgotten about Emily Dickinson.

He stares at my bookshelf, his head tilted as he scans the spines of the books. I didn't tell him about the condoms. Maybe if I had, he'd be rifling through my nightstand.

"Hey, do you really want to look at this?" I ask him, holding out the book of poetry.

He spins around, smiling. "Nah, that was just a ruse to get you up here," he says.

"Ruse? Nice word."

"Thanks. It's one of my favourite new four-letter words. I learned it from my girlfriend."

He draws me into a hug, immediately crushing the frosty wall that sprang up as soon as we started talking about prom. After a few minutes, he takes the book out of my hand and steps back, tilting his head toward the bed. "Is it okay if I sit . . . ?"

"Sure." I sit on the edge of the bed too. Lucas skims the book's index and then he flips to a page near the middle and hands me the book.

"Here. Can you read this to me?"

I glance at the page. It's a two-stanza poem called, "I'm Nobody! Who Are You?"

"Is this supposed to make me feel better?" I say. "A poem about what it's like to be nobody? Because that doesn't sound too uplifting to me."

He drops his head down, a quiet sigh escaping his lips. "You said girls like you don't go to prom. I don't know what that's supposed to mean. If you're a senior, you get to go. End of story. But if you think you're not important enough—if you're nobody—it doesn't matter, because I am, too. That's the whole point of the poem."

"That's a nice idea, Lucas, but a poem isn't going to change my mind about this."

He takes the book and tosses it on my nightstand. "Emily Dickinson helped me get my foot in the door with you. I figured it was worth a try."

"You're through the door now, Lucas. Hell, you're in my room. You don't have to win me over with poetry. And you can't fix me with it either."

"Fix you. What do you mean?"

"I don't know. Sometimes I feel like you're trying to change me, or make me act differently. This is me. I'm cynical, I question things, and I don't always fit in. A lot of the time, I don't want to."

"I don't want you to change. I just thought prom would be a cool thing to do together. High school is almost over. You know—"

"You're the only one at school I'd want to celebrate the end of high school with. Why don't we do something else together that night? Anything else. Just us."

Lucas stares down at the carpet for a few minutes. "So you'll let me plan something?"

I look at the carpet too. Apparently my carpet is fascinating. "As long as it's far away from prom, you can plan something. Look, do we have to talk about this right now? You have to go soon. You said you wanted to spend some time alone today. We're alone now."

I lie back on the bed and tug on his hand.

He leans over and cups my cheek with his hand, his thumb tracing a gentle line under my eye. He stares at my mouth, and then his lips meet mine, warm and soft at first, but then more demanding. His tongue dips into my mouth, and his hand moves from my cheek to my neck, across my collarbone and gradually lower.

"Let's go out tomorrow night," he whispers between kisses. "I'll get the car, and we'll drop Nancy at the talent show, then the two of us can go out alone. On a date."

"Deal," I whisper back, tugging on his hair to bring him closer.

This time when he kisses me, his teeth close gently on my bottom lip. Biting. No, not biting—tugging, teasing. I want to roll on top of him, hold him down, demand and take as much as he's prepared to give. The devil and my conscience start duelling in the back of my mind.

The Devil: Hey, there are two condoms in the nightstand.

My Conscience: Now would be a terrible time. The first time should be special, not rushed.

The Devil: But those condoms are practically begging to be used. And Lucas is amazing. It'll be special regardless.

My fingers tighten in Lucas's hair. He tenses and swears.

The four-letter words are flying today.

"Sorry." I relax my hand, and the tension leaves his body.

"It's okay."

He kisses me again, our bodies melting together with lips and tongues leading the way. A slow simmering sensation rolls through me, as if my bones are dissolving into the mattress. This feeling multiplies tenfold when Lucas slips his hand under my knee and pulls my leg around his hip. I curse the inventor of clothes and utter a number of embarrassingly encouraging sounds which Lucas responds to by retreating and resting his forehead against mine.

"This sucks. I really have to go. My uncle will be mad. I don't want to lose car privileges."

"Just a few more minutes?"

"A few more minutes," he says, rolling me on top of him. He slips his hands down my sides, bringing them to rest on the back pockets of my jeans. While kissing me, he slips his hands inside my shirt, tickling that spot just under my rib cage that makes me flinch and squirm.

I giggle against his lips. "Don't do that. It tickles."

"I like the way you move when I tickle you." As he says this, his fingers skim across my side again. Again, I wriggle against him, an

involuntary reaction, but obviously one he enjoys.
 "God, I hate my uncle right now," he whispers.
 "Me too."
 He has no idea.

Chapter 27

Karma

I LEAVE FOR school the next day with a Post-it note in my pocket, determined to resume my lunch hour routine. I also have a ham and cheese sandwich in my lunch bag. Apparently, Mom is determined to keep making me sandwiches I won't eat.

Lucas is right on time. I'm curious to know if his uncle stayed at the office again, but my mom came home right after work—alone—and that's all that matters right now. Instead of pulling away from the house when I get in the car, Lucas gives me my good morning kiss and keeps his hand on my cheek as he peers into my eyes.

"Tell me something, Dewey. Do you have a Post-it note in your pocket?"

I nod.

"What does it say?" he asks, his tone and expression equally serious.

"796.76."

He sits back and lets out a slow breath. "Can I be sorry-lost-boy for a minute?"

"I've missed sorry-lost-boy. Go for it."

"I shouldn't have made you feel bad for not wanting to leave the library at lunch yesterday. What happened when we were getting tickets was stupid. Those girls are idiots, but I get how it would wear you out having to deal with them every day. Which I guess explains why you wouldn't want to go to prom. I get it."

"You do?"

He reaches for my hand and rubs his thumb across my wrist. "I really do. Sorry I pressured you."

"I guess I'm sorry I can't be a normal, regular girl. It would make everything easier."

He smiles and kisses me again. "Hey, if I wanted things to be easy, don't you think I'd have given up by now?"

Gossip has always travelled swiftly. In the age of social media, it travels faster than a fire ravaging a forest during a drought. No longer involved in the social media circuit, I'm used to being a little out of the loop, but within five minutes of being in math class, I've caught the general gist of the current hot topic.

Dallyn was hauled to the office during fourth period the day before. The vice-principal searched his locker, found a small bag of pot and suspended him for five days. This news isn't shocking. Everyone knows Dallyn smokes up. Tons of people use drugs. The only difference is that Dallyn got caught. This isn't surprising, either. A chronic attention seeker, his actions are neither subtle nor inconspicuous.

"That explains the cop car yesterday," Lucas says, as he walks me from my math class to English class.

"Do you think he got charged?"

"Not for a small bag of weed. That's personal use. He probably got a fine. They usually bring the cops in to scare kids a little."

"How come you know so much about it?"

"Like I said, the police were always at my old school. This sort of thing happened every week."

We're just rounding the corner near my English classroom when Allison rushes past us, a sobbing blur of ponytail and lip gloss. Marla bounces along behind her, apparently too wrapped up in her bestie's meltdown to pay any attention to us.

"Someone's not happy," Lucas observes.

"Dallyn's been suspended again. That probably means no prom for him."

"Will Allison go anyway?"

"There's no way she'd miss it."

Lucas leans his shoulder on the wall outside my classroom. "I can't think of a single person you have less in common with. How did you hang out with her for three months?"

I shrug and tap the side of my head. "Temporary insanity."

Maybe it makes me a horrible person, but I can't help enjoying Allison's misery a little. Mr. V. might call this turn of events poetic justice. I prefer to call it Karma.

After enjoying 796.76 while eating a quiet lunch in the library, celebrating Allison's sorry situation and contemplating the date-night ahead, I'm about as giddy as I can get by the time Lucas drops me off after school. That leaves me a couple of hours to get ready for our date. Not that there's much to do. It's not like I need to get glammed up. The evening's activities have been narrowed down to 5-pin bowling, mini-putting or laser tag. I'm leaning towards one of the latter two choices. The thought of wearing bowling shoes a million other women have worn before me makes me want to throw up a little.

To kill time until Lucas picks me up, I do my homework and eat dinner, a tuna casserole without a single pea in sight. Mom has never before bowed to my request that she eliminate the peas from tuna casserole. She's totally buttering me up.

I could get used to being buttered up. Lucas could get used to it too. On the way to Writer's Craft, he ate the ham and cheese sandwich Mom made for me.

Once I've cleaned up the dinner dishes, freshened up my mascara and eye-liner and brushed my teeth, I perch on the top step of the porch to wait for Lucas. Screams of laughter drift over from the park across the street—a sure sign that spring has sprung. My mood lifts even more. If I'm not careful, I could be positively euphoric by the time Lucas arrives.

Finally, his car appears at the corner. I leap to my feet and drag my purse over my shoulder. The car crawls down the street and edges into the driveway.

Lucas emerges from the back passenger side door.

"Hey!" he calls out, giving me a quick wave. "You'll have to get in the back with me. Nancy's in the front with my uncle. We're dropping him at the office before taking her to the school for the talent show."

Oh. My. God.

I descend the porch steps, my legs quaking like rubber tree limbs beneath me. Maybe I should let myself fall over—fake a faint or something. But it's too late for that. Lucas is right in front of me, holding the driver side back door open. I duck my head and slide into the seat, and Lucas closes the door behind me. Uncle Ken's wide, horrified eyes meet mine in the rear view mirror.

He knows.

He must have had heart failure as he realized Lucas was directing him to pull in to a driveway he's parked on several times over the past six months for less than savoury reasons.

And now we're trapped in the cramped quarters of a car. Together.

"Hey, Hannah-banana," Nancy says. "We're playing eye-spy. Wanna play? Maybe you'll be better at eye-spy than you are at Bananagrams."

Lucas laughs. "Hey, be nice." He grabs my hand and mouths an apology in my direction.

"It's okay," I whisper. Nancy's well-intended insult is the least of my concerns.

Uncle Ken sighs. "I think I'm all spied out for one evening. You won, Nance. *I Spy* champion, as usual."

His eyes flick up to the rear view mirror again. The only thing he's spying with his little eye right now is me and every alarming thing I represent.

"So, uh, Hannah," he says. "Have you lived around here long?"

Ah, very clever. Uncle Ken is fishing for confirmation before forcing himself to acknowledge that he's well and truly busted.

"Since last August," I say, arching a brow at the mirror. "It's just me and my mom. It's a small place, but it's enough for us. We can't afford much, anyway. She's just a waitress. Her name's Leanne."

He nods and clears his throat. That seals the deal, right there. There's no more room for uncertainty—although he's probably wondering what the hell I'm going to do or say next.

That makes two of us.

Lucas sweeps his thumb across the top of my hand and gives me a baffled smile. I can't blame him. None of the stuff I just said to his uncle was important or even relevant. He probably thinks my moronic babbling is a result of awkward turtle syndrome. I clamp my mouth closed, not because I don't want Lucas to think I'm an awkward turtle, but because anything else I might want to say to Uncle Ken isn't fit for mixed company.

I stare out the window as we leave the part of town devoted to subdivisions and approach the downtown area. Like all small town main streets, it's a series of strip malls, restaurants and gas stations. I figure we're getting close to Uncle Ken's office when he starts giving Nancy a pep talk, reminding her to call him, her mother or Lucas if she gets upset or needs anything.

"She's gonna be fine, aren't you Nance?" Lucas says, reaching between the seats to lightly tousle her hair.

She slaps his hand out of the way. "Of course I'll be fine."

Uncle Ken pulls into a parking lot with a dentist's office, a convenience store and his office—an end unit with a sign above the glass storefront reading, "Kenneth Gordon Chartered Accountant." He parks in front of the convenience store and then turns to Nancy.

"Have a good time, pipsqueak. Remember to count to ten and breathe if you need to, right?"

"Dad," Nancy whines. "I'm not a baby."

Uncle Ken nods. He leans over and kisses her on the forehead.

My heart slides sideways in my chest. How could he screw around on his wife? How could he do that to Nancy? Uncle Ken opens his car door and starts to climb out.

Before I've had a chance to weigh the implications of my words, I say, "Lucas, I have to go to the bathroom. I don't think I can wait. Would it be okay . . . ?" I dart my eyes at his uncle.

"Oh, sure," Lucas says. "Hey, Uncle Ken, can Hannah use the washroom in the office?"

Uncle Ken pops his head back into the car. "Definitely. Of course." He looks a little grim, but what can he do? He can't exactly refuse.

I scramble out of the backseat. "I'll just be a sec."

Lucas nods. "Do you want me to come in with you?"

"No, I'll be fine." Will I be fine? I don't even know what I'm doing. I follow his uncle to the front door of his office. As he pulls the door open, a little bell jingles. He shrugs out of his coat and hangs it on a coat rack near the door, while I stand stupidly behind him, trying to formulate coherent thoughts.

When he turns around, he gives me a quick smile, all mouth and no eyes, the kind that you know is all for show. But his face changes when he smiles, and I can see why Mom likes him. He's got this boyishly handsome thing going on—thick blond hair and the kind of eyes that probably twinkle when he flirts.

Clearly, Mom never got close to his nasty shoes.

"The bathroom's back there." He waves a hand vaguely behind him.

When I don't move, he puts one hand on his hip and runs the other through his hair. "You don't have to use the washroom."

This is a statement, not a question. I shake my head and shift my weight. "You know who I am, right?"

He nods. He must know there's no use pretending. This is it. This is my chance to say my piece. I take a deep breath and pretend Lucas is coaching me on.

Don't worry, you've got this.

"So where do you tell your wife you are? When you don't come home, I mean."

His face reddens with what must be embarrassment or shame. Or maybe he's annoyed that I'm quizzing him.

"I know you probably think this is none of my business, but my mom's involved, so I think it kind of is."

He blinks at me, and then he turns to look at the battered brown couch pushed up against the back wall of the office. "Working late and sleeping here. Trudy doesn't like me driving when I'm tired."

"Like on Sunday night."

He raises his eyebrows. They seem to be saying, "How'd you know I stayed out Sunday night?"

"Lucas drives me to school every day. He was late on Monday because you didn't come home. You weren't with my mom, though, were you?"

He doesn't answer. He frowns, and his eyes flicker over to his desk. I check out what he's looking at—a collection of family photographs lined up beside his computer.

"Hannah, your mom's great," he says.

I tilt my head toward the pictures on the desk.

"So is your wife. Nancy's great, too."

He huffs out a half laugh and nods. "Touché."

"Look, you probably don't want to hear this, especially not from me, but what you're doing is wrong."

He presses his lips together tightly. "Does Lucas know?" he asks.

"I haven't told anyone. If I told Mom you're married, she'd hang you out to dry."

His expression falters. It's satisfying to see how unsettled he looks. If this were a boxing match, I'd have him on the ropes right now. He's waiting for the knock-out punch. What he doesn't realize is that I'm not going for a knock-out. Knocking him out would take down too many other people. I just want to rattle his teeth enough to scare him.

"What are you going to do?" he says.

"I don't know." I pause, wanting to make him sweat for a few more seconds. "Maybe what you're going to do is more important. Like, maybe you should stop . . . working . . . so late."

Uncle Ken blinks. Then he flushes a dark crimson. "You're probably right."

"I know I'm right."

I give him one last steadfast look, and then I back away a few steps before turning and heading for the door. Outside, I take a few breaths to steady myself, hoping I didn't just make a colossal mistake.

Chapter 28

The Landmines Left Behind

NANCY AND I wait in front of the school, while Lucas collects Declan from the car that's just pulled up to the curb. She drums her fists on her thighs. I feel antsy, too. Since we left her father's office, I've been at war with myself. One side of my brain yammers, "You should have kept your mouth shut," while the other side fist-pumps in celebration.

He got a warning. That's more than he deserved.

Suddenly, Nancy stops thumping her legs and says, "Lucas really likes you."

Like everything she's ever said to me, this random comment is directed toward my stomach.

"That's good," I say. "I like him too." And there's the understatement of the year.

"I wonder if Declan likes me as much as Lucas likes you," she says.

"I'm sure he does. He likes spending time with you, right?"

"I guess. He's never kissed me, though." She says this in a theatrical whisper.

"That takes time. You can't rush into stuff like that."

"So that's normal?"

"Totally normal," I assure her.

"I don't want to talk to my mom about this stuff. She wouldn't understand."

Should I tell her she can talk to me anytime? Do I want to become Nancy's one-stop shop for girl talk? I'm not sure I'm up to the task. "It can be awkward talking to your parents about this sort of thing, that's for sure."

Nancy looks at my shoulder. "My mom is overprotective," she says. Her eyes slowly move upwards until it appears she's making eye contact with my ear. Nancy has never allowed her eyes to move beyond my waist. Something tells me this is huge.

"She doesn't want you to get hurt, that's all," I say.

"I guess."

I study her, wondering if her eyes will keep moving and eventually meet mine, but they snap back down to the ground when Lucas appears with Declan in tow. Declan gives Nancy an awkward wave. It's actually a little like a salute. He's cute in an extremely dorky way.

"Okay, you guys. Have fun." Lucas hands them each a ticket. "Mr. Wilding from the Spec Ed department is one of the supervising teachers, so track him down if you need help. We'll be back at nine-thirty to pick you up, Nance. Your mom will be back then too, Declan. Both of you wait inside the doors until we get here, okay?"

Nancy nods, her expression solemn. She turns abruptly and heads for the doors. Declan follows, calling out for her to wait up. Once they've disappeared inside, Lucas shrugs and takes my hand.

"Guess they're fine."

We make our way back to the parking lot.

"So where are we going, anyway?" I ask him.

"I don't know, I thought we'd . . . ." Lucas doesn't finish. He squints into the parking lot. "What the . . . ?"

He starts running, tugging me along with him.

"What's going on?"

"Wade!" Lucas shouts this as he lets go of my hand and picks up his pace. "Get away from my car!"

Dallyn is crouched beside Lucas's uncle's car, right beside the door holding something. Car keys. It looks like he's about to gouge the car door. He rises as we get closer, but rather than running away, he jams his keys in his pocket and heads towards us, arms swinging purposefully. He shoves Lucas with both hands, sending him stumbling backward against the hood of a nearby car. Then he grabs Lucas by the shirt and pulls him upright.

"You couldn't keep your mouth closed, could you, sped? I thought we had a deal, but you ratted me out anyway. How much did you tell the cops? Huh?"

I grab Dallyn's arm and tug on it. "Get away from him, Dallyn."

Dallyn turns and snarls at me. "Don't touch me."

Lucas presses his hands into Dallyn's chest and shoves him away.

"Get out of here, Wade. You're suspended. If you get caught on school property, you'll make things worse."

"You think I care what the school does?" Dallyn clenches his fists at his sides and gets right up in Lucas's face. "I don't give a flying crap. Why don't you man up and fight back, retard? Or are you afraid to fight without a knife?"

Lucas clamps his mouth shut, and his jaw twitches. He tilts his head. They're almost nose to nose.

"Lucas, don't," I plead. "Leave him alone. Let's just go."

"Shut your face, slut." Dallyn says this without looking at me.

Oh God. Dallyn, leave me out of this.

Lucas leans forward. "Don't call her that, Wade."

"I'll call her whatever I want. It's true. She's a slut, just like her mother. Did you tell him about your mom, Hannah? Did you tell him she's banging my twenty-three year old brother?"

Dallyn's eyes bounce back and forth between the two of us. His nostrils flare.

I open my mouth, but I can't think of anything to say that won't sound like a lame denial or a whiny complaint.

"Wade, this is stupid. I know all about Hannah's mom," Lucas says. He takes a slow steady breath. I can actually see him trying to control his anger. He nods at his uncle's car. "Get in the car Hannah. We're leaving."

Dallyn shoves Lucas again. "You're not going anywhere, sped."

He curls his hand into a fist and draws his arm back. I cover my mouth, bracing myself for the moment of impact. Just as Dallyn's fist connects with Lucas's chin, a shriek rings out behind us.

"Dallyn!"

We all turn. It's Allison. She runs toward us from the front of the school with Marla behind her. They're both in full cheer squad get-up, hair and make-up completely over the top. They look like a couple of clowns who got lost and were pulled into a change room before a pep rally.

Allison wraps both hands around Dallyn's arm and drags him away from Lucas. "What are you doing? You're not supposed to be here!"

Dallyn yanks away from Allison, massaging his cut knuckles. "You expect me to sit around and do nothing while this loser runs around spreading lies about me?" He casts a wild-eyed look at me and then at Lucas, who still leans against the car, now rubbing his cheek and working his jaw back and forth. Dallyn advances on Lucas again, spitting accusations. "You two are made for each other. I bet you told your slut girlfriend everything, and she spilled to admin."

"I didn't tell anyone anything, and neither did she." Lucas speaks in a low, steady voice, breathing furiously through his nose.

Please don't hit him, Lucas, please, please, please. "I didn't say anything." I shake my head. "I don't even know what's going on." *Just leave us alone.*

Allison's features twist into an expression of utter disgust. She barges forward, pushing Dallyn out of the way so she can get closer to me. "How can you say that with a straight face? If he didn't snitch, you must have."

Lucas stands beside me and slips his arm around my waist. Part of me is grateful that the attention has shifted from him to me, but I don't want him to think he has to fight this battle for me.

"I didn't say anything about Dallyn, just like I didn't tell guidance what you did in January. I don't know who told them, Allison, but it wasn't me," I say.

"I saw the pictures you turned in," Allison says. "There were pictures in that folder no one else saw. I private messaged them to you."

"I'm telling you, it wasn't me. Why would I do that?"

Marla takes a few steps forward. "Because you're a nark and that's what narks do," she says, as if she's the first person in the world who's taken the time to clearly define the term for me.

"I didn't do it." I direct my words at Allison. "I just wanted the whole mess to go away. Once guidance knew what happened, everything got uglier. It would be stupid of me to do that to myself."

"It had to be you," Allison insists, jabbing the air in front of me. "The only other person who had those pictures . . . ." She turns her head slowly and looks at Marla.

Marla bites her lip and takes a step back.

Allison opens and closes her mouth. She looks back and forth between me and Marla.

If epiphanies came armed with frying pans, Allison would be getting clocked with a huge skillet right about now. To be fair, I'm only a few seconds ahead of her, but it does seem to take a few solid whacks of that pan before she fully understands what's happening.

"You," she says to Marla through gritted teeth. "You bitch! You narked? If it wasn't her, it had to be you. How could you do that to me?"

Marla blinks a few times, but then she crosses her arms.

I wish I had a bag of popcorn. This is getting interesting.

"What about what you did to me?" Marla says. "You let her ruin my whole year." She sneers at me. "When Lisa quit, Hannah got nominated for cheer captain, and you helped her. I'm supposed to be your best friend. I've been on the team since ninth grade, too. I should've been nominated for cheer captain instead of her. But that wouldn't have worked out for you. I might've won, right?"

Wow. I took Marla for a fool, but I was wrong. Allison and Dallyn may have publicly humiliated me on Twitter, but by the looks of things, Marla revealed the whole story to Mrs. Palmer, taking out both me and Allison in one bold move.

Allison leans toward Marla with a sneer. Dallyn grabs her arm, but she shakes free of his grasp and pummels his chest. "Did you know about this? Is that why you keep defending Hannah? Because you knew she didn't nark? Or do you really have the hots for her?"

"I didn't know, I swear. And I don't have the hots for Hannah, Ali. I keep telling you. It's his fault," Dallyn says, jerking his thumb at Lucas. He grasps Allison's wrists to stop her from walloping his chest. "I've been sticking up for her because Lucas threatened me. He told me to call you guys off or he'd cut me, just like he cut that guy at the mall."

Lucas isn't paying attention. He's peering over Dallyn's shoulder. I follow his gaze. Dallyn, Allison and Marla follow suit. A crowd is gathering at the front of the school and a few people head this way. Nobody wants to miss the fireworks. With a crowd forming, the supervising teachers will sniff out the action in a heartbeat.

Lucas tugs my elbow. "Get in the car," he whispers.

I round the car and hop in. Lucas jumps in as well. He jams the keys in the ignition and barely gives the engine a chance to catch before he throws the car into drive. He speeds out of the parking lot, away from the three people who made the last few months of my life complete hell.

They're finally facing the unattractive truth. Like land mines left behind after a war has ended, if they detonate now, there's no one left to blow up but each other.

Chapter 29

Made for Each Other

ONCE WE'RE A couple of blocks away from the school, Lucas pulls over to the side of the road, turns off the engine and leans forward, resting his forehead on his hands, which are still wrapped tightly around the steering wheel. He breathes deeply a few times.

"Lucas, are you okay?" I rest my hand on his shoulder. "You were great back there. It would have been so easy for you to completely lose it. I'm really proud of you. Did he hurt you?"

He leans back and turns to look at me, rubbing his cheek gingerly. "He would have hit me harder if Allison hadn't distracted him. I'll be fine. I was more scared for you. Are you okay?"

"Weird as it sounds, I'm good. I'm actually glad that happened. At least they all know I didn't do anything."

"The truth finally came out, that's for sure."

"About me not being a nark, you mean?"

"That . . . ," Lucas reaches for my hand. "And other stuff."

I question him with my eyes.

He shrugs a little. "Was it true what Dallyn said about your mom and his brother?" he asks.

"Oh. Right." I nod. There's no point trying to backpedal now. "It's partly true. Dean hooked up with Mom at the club she works at. He helped her get home one night when she had too much to drink. They didn't sleep together. He slept on our couch."

Lucas whistles.

"So you didn't know," I say. "Why did you tell Dallyn you knew?"

"Because knowledge is power, and I didn't want to give him that power. Plus, I hated the idea of him thinking he knew more about you than I did. My pride I guess." His neck turns splotchy. Even the tips of his ears are going pink.

"I'm sorry I didn't tell you. To be honest, my mom is kind of mortifying most of the time. She can be a real train wreck."

Lucas nods. He smiles a little. "I thought you didn't want me to meet your mom because you're embarrassed of me. Like maybe I wasn't smart enough or good-looking enough. But it's been her all along. You were afraid of me meeting her."

"God, Lucas, it's not you at all. It's totally her."

"What a relief." He chuckles and leans over, pressing a kiss to my forehead.

Again he's taken me by surprise with his reaction. He's relieved, not angry. I'm feeling my own fair share of relief. It feels so good to have everything out in the open. Well, almost everything. I can't spell out all the stupid things my mother does without revealing his uncle's escapades, but at least he gets the idea.

I settle back into my seat. After what Lucas has told me about his past, there's something else I want to know, and I need to put a little distance between myself and his sweet forehead kisses before I ask.

"Lucas, did you really threaten Dallyn? Is that why he's been sticking up for me?"

"Of course I didn't threaten him. At least not physically."

"What do you mean?"

He grimaces and scans the houses on the side of the road. "You know the day I had that fight with Rory at the bus stop?" he says.

"Yeah, what about it?"

"Well, the guy who was with Rory that day was Dallyn. He was the one who upset Mark in the first place by calling him a retard."

"Wait, you knew Dallyn before?"

"Not exactly. I didn't know him that day at the mall, but as soon as I saw him at school here, I recognized him. He was the one selling stuff to Rory."

"Dallyn's dealing?"

"Turns out he has quite a business going at the mall."

"What an idiot! So Dallyn knows you saw him that day?"

"After Marla told me what happened at the New Year's party, I tracked him down and told him to stay away from you, and to get his girlfriend and her dippy friends to leave you alone as well, unless he wanted me to show the police some YouTube footage I have of that little exchange of his at the bus stop."

"You have video of the deal going down?"

"Not really, but he doesn't need to know that. The unedited video doesn't show his face, just him running away."

"You didn't nark him out to the cops, though, did you?"

"Are you kidding? I wouldn't want to stir things up with the people he's hanging out with. I think he's into some bad stuff, like way more dangerous than weed."

"He'll get caught. Maybe this time it was just possession, but he's too careless. He'll get busted."

"That's why I minded my own business. I figure when it comes to people like Dallyn, you just have to give them space to screw up one too many times."

Like Uncle Ken. Maybe the same is true of him. I gave him something to think about tonight. He'll either sort out his messed up life or keep pushing his luck until he eventually gets caught. I'll keep my fingers crossed for the first option.

"So when Dallyn let you drive him home from my place that night, it was because you had something on him," I say. "I wondered how you'd made him co-operate. And that's why he's been defending me too, and telling Allison to leave me alone—which explains why she thinks he likes me."

"Well that, and the fact that he probably does." Lucas's lips tighten as he looks down at our joined hands.

"Why would you say that?"

"He told me he doesn't think I'm good enough for you. He wouldn't say something like that if he wasn't into you."

"That doesn't make sense. Why would he treat me like dirt if he liked me?"

"Because he's a coward. Going out with Allison has perks. Going out with you . . . ."

"I know," I say, thinking of Marla's words from yesterday. "It would be social suicide for him."

"Pretty much." Lucas tips my chin up, forcing me to look at him. "Hey, his loss. My gain." His voice is soft and reassuring.

I search his face and find exactly what I'm looking for. Compassion.

Affection. And something else. Something I'm almost afraid to hope for because if I'm wrong, I'll be crushed.

Once so afraid of being trapped in the liquid amber of his eyes, I now want to throw myself into them, head first. I want to roll around in the amber until his eyes touch every part of my body. This, I realize, is both a metaphorical and a literal wish.

"You shouldn't look at me like that, Dewey," he says.

"Like what?"

"Like the way you're looking at me."

"I'm just looking at you the way you're looking at me."

"Really?"

"Uh-huh."

"Well, I've changed my mind, then. You can look at me like that all night." He leans across and kisses me, his hand moving gently in my hair. We rest our foreheads together and breathe for a few moments. I want to hand him my heart. It's as fragile as a robin's egg right now, but I know it'll be safe in his hands. It would be so easy . . . .

I summon up the courage to say the words that would show him how I feel. I test them out behind my teeth before I speak. "You're kind of awesome, you know that?" Really? How did these stupid words slip out instead of the ones I'd wanted to say?

He squeezes my fingers, and then he restarts the car. "Yep. A dyslexic, knife-wielding maniac. Awesome."

I smile out at the road and then close my eyes, feeling weightless and entirely liberated.

The sun is setting. Along the sidewalks, streetlights blink on, and the neon signs of the downtown strip flicker to life. Lucas stops at a red light and scans the streets around us. "I don't even know where I'm going. Where to?"

I consider the options we had lined up for tonight. Bowling. Miniputting. Laser tag. I can't imagine doing any of those things. "Would you mind if we just went somewhere quiet?"

"Somewhere quiet. Hmm." Lucas frowns and makes a quick right turn. "I think I know the perfect place."

Lucas drives south, leaving the strip malls, restaurants and entertainment complexes behind. We continue until the road narrows and asphalt gives way to gravel. Eventually the road ends at a parking lot that runs alongside a grassy expanse of lakeside parkland. Beyond the grass, there's a beach. It's not a beautiful beach, and the lake's not glamorous, but there's a sunset and the water is sparkling. If Lucas is aiming for romance, I'm not about to burst his bubble.

He wraps his arm around my shoulders, keeping me tucked against him as we walk across the grass. When we reach the point where the grass meets the beach, we look out at the water for a long time. Lucas finally sits, and I join him, both of us stretching our legs out into the sand.

"I hope Nancy's okay," he says.

"I'm sure she's having a blast. I think it's cool for her to do stuff like this on her own. I bet it makes her feel like a regular kid. And she really likes Declan."

"She told you that?"

"We were talking when you met Declan. She even looked at my ear. It's the first time she's talked to me without looking at my stomach."

Lucas doesn't laugh when I say this. I'm glad he doesn't laugh. I wasn't trying to be funny.

"That's progress," he says. "It means she trusts you. She's working her way up to making eye contact."

"That's nice to know. I mean, I never really thought I'd . . . I don't know. It's hard to explain what I—"

Lucas squeezes my hand, cutting short my awkward explanation. "I get it. She can be a total pain in the ass, but she's got a way of sneaking her way into your heart."

"That must be a family trait." My cheeks flush as I wonder if Lucas understands what I'm trying to say.

He examines my face and tucks a few stray hairs behind my ear. "Come with me for a second?" He stands and tugs on my hand. Together, we walk down to the water's edge. "Okay, close your eyes," he says.

"Um, okay." Will he reach into his pocket and pull out a box with a piece of jewelry in it or something?

"Okay, you can open them."

I open my eyes, but he's not dangling a necklace in front of my face, or holding open a little box with a charm or earrings in it. He's just grinning. "What?" I ask him.

He leans forward, pointing at the wet sand, where he's written:

I ♥ Hannah

"You heart me?" I smile and beat back the ferocious spasms

wracking my chest.

He grins back at me. "Yeah, I'm pretty sure I do."

Before I can think, before a single second passes, I say, "I heart you, too—like, big, puffy heart you." I tell him.

"Big, puffy heart? That doesn't sound healthy. Will you be okay?"

"Don't worry about me. My left ventricle is incredibly resilient."

He laughs and then he bends down to retrace the letters with his finger, starting with the last letter of my name and working his way up to the heart. "This is how I wrote it—backwards. I'm dyslexic and your name is H-A-N-N-A-H both ways." He stands back, admiring his handiwork. "I never thought I'd say it, but Dallyn was right. We are made for each other."

"Dyslexia doesn't work like that, Lucas. You told me so yourself."

"Maybe not, but I'm taking it as a sign that we were meant to find each other. Let's call it a sign from the universe. A really organic sign from the universe. We were meant to meet and fall in love."

My whole body reacts to his words. My stomach flips, my heart soars, and I instantly get a huge lump in my throat. I'm worthy of Lucas's love. Something inside me explodes into a million pieces, and I know it's a good thing. It's nothing concrete, nothing tangible. It's something you can't see or touch, but something that's been there lurking inside me for a long time. It's the last little piece of loneliness—like a bookmark—a place holder inside me, wherever loneliness lives. Lucas has found it and ripped it to pieces.

I throw my arms around him and sigh against his neck. I squeeze him tightly enough to cut off his circulation, but I don't care. After a few minutes, he manages to untangle himself from my grasp. He takes my hand and leads me back to the grass that edges the beach. We sit and Lucas leans in, nudging my hair away from my cheek. His breath tickles my ear. I smile and tilt my head back.

He kisses me for a long time—soft, slow, time-dissolving kisses. It's a good thing we're sitting, because if we were standing, my knees might dissolve too. Finally, he rubs his nose against mine and sighs. I sigh right along with him.

"When did you get to be so sexy, Lucas?"

"I'm sure I've been sexy all along, Dewey. You didn't notice because you always have your nose stuck in a book." His lips hover near mine. "Do me a favour? Let me kiss you like that in the hall at school tomorrow? Please?"

"If you kiss me like that in the hall at school, the custodians will have to come and mop me up. That'll give the haters a crapload to talk about."

"Fuck the haters."

"Fuck the haters." I laugh, turning these words over in my mind. "Very eloquent. A new mantra, I think."

"A new mantra. Hmm. Do you still have today's Post-it with you?"

I slide my fingers into my pocket and take out the yellow slip of paper with today's call number on it. Lucas unfolds the Post-it and then digs around in his pockets and produces one of those little golf pencils. He rests the paper on his leg and writes Lucas ♥ Hannah on the back. He holds it out for me.

"What do you think of that for a new mantra? I could write that on a Post-it note for you every day. Maybe that would help you get through your morning classes. Then we could sit outside at lunch time and eat together."

"I'm not sure."

"Why don't we give it a try tomorrow? If that goes okay, we can do it again on Thursday. One day at a time. One foot in front of the other."

"The journey of a thousand miles begins with one step?"

"Exactly."

I take the Post-it. Lucas watches me refold it so his words are on the outside. I slip it carefully back into my pocket. He smiles and pulls me close.

We stare out at the water. I imagine sitting with Lucas on the low wall outside the school—every day—me eating my celery and peanut butter, Lucas eating his lunch and then chasing it with whatever sandwich Mom made for me. I picture myself reading to him, or helping him with his homework, or simply sitting like this, our hands linked—just being together.

And maybe I'd be okay with that.

After all, the universe has spoken.

Author's Note

HEARTFELT GRATITUDE to Beverley, Jennifer and Jan, whose enthusiastic reactions to my first draft gave me the courage to pursue the goal of publishing.

To the Rebelight team: thank you for taking a chance on a newbie. I am so thankful for your kind, nurturing approach. Most sincere thanks to Melinda and Deb. Your instincts and keen editorial eyes helped make *Hannah Both Ways* a better story with every revision. I appreciate the efforts of everyone involved in making the book beautiful, inside and out.

Finally, to my family, your love makes me a better person. My writing journey would have been entirely impossible without your unfailing support.

~*Rosie*

CPSIA information can be obtained
at www.ICGtesting.com
Printed in the USA
LVOW04s1559270716
498006LV00021B/1018/P